B307   Art by W. Hullidge, from the collection of Thomas L. Cathey

FROM THE LIBRARY OF

J. BRODERICK Dec '04.

KATHARINE ATHOLL
1874-1960

AUP Titles of Related Interest

THE ELGINS, 1766–1917
a tale of aristocrats, proconsuls and their wives
Sydney Checkland

PATRONAGE AND PRINCIPLE
a political history of Scotland
Michael Fry

CROMARTIE: HIGHLAND LIFE 1650–1914
Eric Richards and Monica Clough

ONWARD AND UPWARD
extracts (1891–96) from the magazine of the Onward and Upward
Association
James Drummond

LITTLE GREY PARTRIDGE
First World War diary of Ishobel Ross
Introduced by Jess Dixon

ARTHUR BERRIEDALE KEITH 1879–1944
Ridgway F Shinn

HALDANE
the life and work of J B S Haldane
Krishna R Dronamraju

KATHARINE ATHOLL
1874-1960
AGAINST THE TIDE

S J Hetherington

ABERDEEN UNIVERSITY PRESS

First published 1989
Aberdeen University Press
A member of the Maxwell Pergamon Macmillan Group

© S J Hetherington 1989

The Publisher acknowledges subsidy from the Scottish Arts Council towards publication
of this volume.

British Library Cataloguing in Publication Data
Hetherington, S J
    Katharine Atholl, 1874–1960: against the tide.
    1. Great Britain. Politics. Atholl, Katharine
    Marjory, Duchess of, 1874–1960
    I. Title
    941.082'092'4

    ISBN 0 08 036592 2

PRINTED IN GREAT BRITAIN
THE UNIVERSITY PRESS
ABERDEEN

To all my family, past and present.

SJH

Contents

List of Illustrations

Preface

I am grateful to many people for much generous help, interest and guidance during the preparation of this work.

His Grace the Duke of Atholl DL gave permission for me to write the book and allowed me to use the Charter Room at Blair Castle, where Kitty's papers are housed.

I must thank Kitty's family for allowing access to her papers and for providing personal comments and recollections: Lady Warner, Kitty's niece and literary executor; Mr and Mrs Edward Aglen; Mr and Mrs Paul Ramsay, who allowed me to visit Bamff House and gave me a great deal of help.

Kitty's friends gave time to record their memories of her and I should particularly like to thank Major Robert Campbell-Preston, OBE, MC, Miss Barbara Smythe of Methven, and Mrs Elizabeth Irvine, who provided such clear impressions of her.

Sir Graham Macmillan OBE and Mr Eric Birnie MBE both made Conservative and Unionist documents available for my inspection.

Mrs Jane Anderson, Archivist at Blair Castle, was of great assistance, as I was able to draw freely on her detailed knowledge of the Atholl family. I am grateful for a medical opinion from Dr Richard Burslem in Manchester and for further medical comment from Dr Colin Hodge in Glasgow.

Mr Donald Stewart, sometime keeper on Atholl Estate, provided recollections of his father, Peter Stewart, piper to the 8th Duke of Atholl. Mr Alec Macrae of Pitagowan (sometime Pipe Major with the Atholl Highlanders) was of great help regarding the Dunne aeroplane experiments.

Lord Home of the Hirsel KT, DL, gave an account of the period 1935-9 in an interview. Sir Patrick Donner also gave his personal view of the period, as did a retired senior civil servant who did not wish to be named.

I am grateful to a number of distinguished academics and historians who gave encouragement and provided comment and guidance. (Mistakes and errors of judgement are all my own.) Mr John Grigg provided corrections throughout the entire manuscript and gave enthusiastic support for the project. Dr Martin Pugh of the Department of History at the University of Newcastle very kindly read the manuscript and suggested necessary alterations and areas of further research. Both commented on the Indian chapter: neither agrees with Kitty's point of view.

Dr Stephen Ball of the Department of History at the University of Leicester gave initial impetus to the study of Kitty's policies. Dr Richard Griffiths of University College Cardiff gave encouragement to research on fascist tendencies in Scotland during the period 1935–9. Mr Richard Gott provided a lengthy interview on the anti-appeasers. Mr John Barnes and Professor Tom Nossiter of the London School of Economics very kindly offered, and gave, excellent advice. Dr Brian Harrison of Corpus College Oxford provided help and information on Kitty as one of the earliest 'Women in a Man's House'. Professor Brian Simon of the University of Leicester read and advised on Chapter 11—Education.

I am also much indebted to Mr Charles Rigg, senior history teacher at Stranraer Academy, who has made a particular study and written several papers and articles on the 1938 by-election in West Perthshire. He kindly read and commented on the book, provided material and suggested the title.

Dr William Harding contributed newspaper material. My brother-in-law, Scott Hetherington, read and advised on the early chapters. Lady Alexander read and discussed aspects of Kitty's character with me.

I also wish to record my thanks to Mr Colin MacLean, Managing Director of Aberdeen University Press for his valued advice and assistance.

Mrs Anna Buchanan patiently typed part of the manuscript. VICS of Perth gallantly came to my rescue on several occasions when I misused my word-processor. I am indebted to the staff of Stirling Library, Stirling University Library, the Sandeman Library in Perth, Perth City Art Gallery and the Scottish National Library.

To all those mentioned, and to many others, I give my warmest thanks; but above all I must thank my family. My husband Alastair provided reassurance, was forbearing about the constant mess of papers which littered our diningroom for two years, prodded or coaxed me into action when nerve failed and gave good counsel.

My daughters Jane and Bridget, my son Angus, my son-in-law David, my stepsons Tom and Alex, and my stepdaughters Lucy and Mary made cheerfully encouraging visits and telephone calls.

My mother was warmly supportive throughout the project and provided much help and comment drawn from personal experience.

SJH

The Duchess opposed cruelty with a consistency which bred indifference to the political colour of its perpetrators. She was thus prepared to welcome the victims of Russian tyranny, of German racialism and of fascist nationalism to the glowing hearth of her indignation, earning for herself, according to the affiliations of her critics, the alternative titles of 'Red Duchess' and 'Fascist Beast'.

Mary Stocks

Introduction

This is the life of a girl born in the middle of the Victorian era and brought up in an academic but socially privileged household in Perthshire. Her first intent was to be a musician. She made a brilliant success at the Royal College of Music in London as a composer, but more especially as a performer.

Katharine sacrificed a musical career to marry the Marquis of Tullibardine, heir to the Duke of Atholl. Intellectual, cultured and unworldly, she was perhaps as unlikely a choice of partner for the sophisticated young Marquis as Jane Eyre was for Rochester: and became as necessary to his existence. To their mutual regret they had no children.

The Marquis of Tullibardine was a soldier and at his wish Katharine followed him to Johannesburg during the Boer War and to Egypt during the First World War, helping in hospitals and organising concerts to entertain the troops. He inherited the title, the estates, and a heavy legacy of debt in 1917.

Reflecting on her marriage, Katharine commented, 'My husband and I made a success of our marriage, largely because we tried to devote ourselves to causes in which we believed. We took immense interest in each other's activities, but sometimes our paths diverged. One of us would be fighting in one cause while the other was battling in aid of another.'

The Duchess had turned increasingly to local politics and committee work and unexpectedly, in middle age, she became a Member of Parliament. Especially towards the end of her time in parliament, she was a controversial figure. She visited Spain during the Civil War with two other MPs, Eleanor Rathbone (Independent) and Ellen Wilkinson (Labour). They were in Madrid when it was bombed and besieged. Their purpose was to organise humanitarian relief work, which they did, but Kitty offended orthodox conservatives by her criticism of the government's line of non-intervention in Spain, which she observed to be working unfairly in favour of the rebels.

Unlike most conservatives in the mid 1930s the Duchess saw fascism as a far more immediate threat than communism. She had read the unexpurgated version of *Mein Kampf* in German, arranged for its translation into English as a warning of Hitler's intentions and tried to focus the attention of Britain's leaders on its most menacing passages. (Chamberlain read it only after Munich—too late.) She became an outspoken opponent of appeasement. In the spring of 1938 she resigned the party whip, having found to her cost that party discipline impaired freedom of speech. By the autumn of 1938 the Conservatives of West Perthshire had had enough. The constituency association was dominated by right-wing landowners, the aristocracy and ex-service figures. Encouraged by Conservative Central Office, it decided to adopt a new prospective candidate for the next election.

Having received a private report from the Soviet Ambassador on the build-up of the German air force, Katharine resolved to warn the country of the dangers it faced: she resigned and called a by-election, in which she stood as an Independent candidate. On a day of wild winter weather and heavy snow, she lost by a narrow margin.

1 This photograph appeared in *The Bystander*, 31 July 1940, with the caption 'Bicycling Duchess'

'Of course,' said my friend, 'I remember the Duchess of Atholl very well. When we were children during the war we visited an uncle in Dunkeld sometimes. The Duchess used to be about the village quite often, on her bicycle . . . a little woman, and she loved to argue. When she saw my uncle walking with us, she used to get off her bicycle and greet him. Then they'd begin to have an argument—or perhaps it was that they simply continued the same argument they always had. My uncle obviously disagreed with her completely, but he admired her very much too. We thought she was very old and quaint.'

To those wartime children, in 1942 or thereabouts, she probably did seem to be quite old, as everyone over thirty does to all children. She would have been in her late sixties then, still vigorous and forthright, with a clarity of vision and a determination of purpose which had characterised her whole life. The children, seeing only a small, plainly clad woman on a bicycle, were unaware that they were in the company of one of the most distinguished Scotswomen of the twentieth century: Her Grace the Duchess of Atholl, DBE, Hon DCL, FRCM, former Member of Parliament for Kinross and West Perthshire. She had been Scotland's first woman MP, the second woman in Britain to hold ministerial office; author and politician with an outstanding ability to foresee events; musician of great distinction; hostess, with her husband, the 8th Duke of Atholl, to kings and queens, statesmen and the most eminent people of her day; a woman of formidable intellect and relentless zeal; above all, a woman of integrity, courage and compassion.

Chapter 1

Bamff and Wimbledon, 1874–95

She was born Katharine Marjory Ramsay at 8.25 a.m. on 6 November 1874, in Edinburgh, though her parents' home was Bamff House, near Alyth in Perthshire. The lands of Bamff had been a present to his doctor from a grateful patient: Neis de Ramsay, Katharine's ancestor, was physician to King Alexander II of Scotland and saved the King's life by performing on him the first successful abdominal operation ever recorded. The King's malady is a matter for conjecture, but the efficacy of the surgery is not: Alexander lived for a further seventeen years. The charter of the lands of Bamff was Neis de Ramsay's reward in 1232 and Bamff has been the family home of his descendants since that date. Over six hundred years and perhaps twenty generations separated Neis and Katharine, but something of the firmness, courage and decisiveness with which he wielded that knife may have been handed on in her genes: those at any rate, are the qualities which which she tackled her life.

The name Bamff is Gaelic (*Banba*) in origin. It meant 'place of piglets' and was also one of the terms of endearment for the land of Ireland itself, called after an Irish swine goddess. It was probably named by a homesick Scottish-Irish tribe pushing east from Dalriada into Pictish territory.

Bamff House is large and elegantly proportioned, originally dating from the sixteenth century, but eighteenth- and nineteenth-century additions have added to its elegance and comfort. It is surrounded by gardens, parkland and acres of farmland, set in isolation amidst rolling hills at the point where the great congregations of deciduous trees for which Perthshire is famous give way to a wilder, moorland landscape.

Katharine's father was Sir James Ramsay, tenth baronet. The first baronet was Sir Gilbert Ramsay, honoured by Charles II for his contribution to victory in the Battle of Pentland Hills in 1666. This was an unsuccessful insurrection by Presbyterians against the imposition of Episcopalianism: generations later the Ramsays were still staunch Episcopalians.

Sir James was born in Versailles in 1832 and spent his childhood in France before going to Rugby and Oxford, where he gained a double first. He came from a line of distinguished scholars: his uncle, Sir James Ramsay, had been a classical scholar. Sir James died in 1869 and was succeeded by his brother George, a philosopher and writer. Sir George died only two years later, in 1871. Sir James, his son, now combined the existence of highland laird with that of historian. The walls of the library at Bamff were lined from floor to ceiling with bookcases filled with rare books and works of reference. Amidst the hills of Perthshire he researched and wrote major works, including a history of England of the Lancaster/York period—*The Scholar's History of England to 1485.*

Sir James was also a fearless mountaineer and one of the early members of the Alpine Club. Until quite late in life he kept fit by jumping over a tennis net several times each day before breakfast. In 1925, when Sir James was ninety-two, King George V asked him how he remained so healthy; Sir James responded that it was due to 'temperate living, and plenty of work both indoors and out-of-doors'. Only two days before he died, in that same year of 1925, he was doing both—working out-of-doors cutting wood and indoors reading proofs.

He had celebrated his eightieth birthday in 1912 by setting out with two of his daughters on an expedition from the Angus border near his home to walk to Braemar, climbing Lochnagar on the way. They carried no map but, as on another occasion many years before, Sir James expected to be given directions at a cottage known as Bachnagairn. This proved to be an empty ruin, so they simply climbed from the south-west along a ridge until they could see the top of the mountain beyond. By the time they reached the summit daylight was already fading and they took a shortcut off the track, following the line of a stream which they knew must lead to the River Dee and Braemar. They reached the road as darkness fell, but had several further hours of walking towards Braemar—the sisters holding hands and singing hymns—until, at midnight, they arrived at their destination, though there was some difficulty in waking the hotel staff. They had walked for twenty-five miles, climbed some 5,000 feet and crossed some very rough moorland. After a day's rest at Braemar they set out again, to walk down Glen Tilt—a wild mountain pass—to visit Katharine and her husband at Blair Castle, a further distance of twenty-five miles and at least 1,000 feet of climbing: no mean feat at any age.

Sir James was still a young man when his wife died, leaving him with three small daughters to bring up. He had moved to Bamff on his father's death in 1871, and at the age of forty in 1872 had stood as a Conservative candidate in a by-election in Forfarshire. This was a temporary aberration, as he was a Liberal by conviction. Having lost by a narrow margin he accepted his defeat philosophically, attributing it to his dislike of the Earl of Dalhousie (a distant relation whose lands fell within the constituency), to his dislike of landlords generally, and to the fact that his opponent was the farmers' choice.

2 Bamff House

His dislike of landlordism may have stemmed from his Irish mother's influence. Her maiden name was Emily Lennon: although not Catholic herself, she may possibly have been of Catholic descent. She had always spoken strongly against evictions on the part of Anglo-Irish landlords and in favour of Catholic emancipation. Sir James must have been aware of a certain inconsistency in his own attitude, however, since he now found himself landlord of 18,000 acres of Scottish countryside.

Many years later one of his sons commented that following the election 'he consoled himself by hurrying off to London to propose to Mother, having apparently had his eye on her for some time'.

'Mother' was a pretty eighteen-year old orphan, Charlotte Stewart. Charlotte (who disliked that name and was known in the family as Sharlie) was one of the Stewarts of Ardvorlich in West Perthshire. Ardvorlich House, the family home, lies on the southern shore of Loch Earn and its lands extend along the lower slopes of Ben Vorlich. The Stewarts were descended from King Robert II: this was not unusual, since Robert II fathered twenty-one children, and by the nineteenth century there were 1,500 of his descendants living in Perthshire alone. Robert himself was the grandson of Scotland's hero, King Robert the Bruce. No Scot could claim finer lineage than that.

Charlotte's father, William Stewart, was a major in the Bengal Artillery, serving in Gwalior at the time of the Indian Mutiny in 1857. Because of anticipated trouble it had been suggested that all British women and children should be sent to safety in Delhi, but the commanding officer had refused permission, saying that it would create a bad impression on the Indian population. Major Stewart, then aged thirty, and his young Irish wife Jane were both killed in separate incidents on 14 June 1857. Jane was murdered with her baby son in her arms, but Charlotte, their daughter, was hidden and protected by her Indian ayah until the trouble was over. She was carried to safety in Agra, eighty miles to the north, by a faithful family servant and was eventually restored to her parents' people at home. She grew up to become, in her daughter's words, 'a beautiful woman of rare charm, with a voice of exceptional range and expressiveness'.

Charlotte became the second wife of Sir James in August 1873. The new Lady Ramsay was not very much older than her two older stepdaughters and as they had been motherless and independent for some years it is not surprising that the atmosphere at Bamff was strained at times. Katharine, born the following year, was the eldest child of the second marriage. Charlotte went on to produce two boys, Nigel and Douglas, and two more girls, Ferelith (known as Fairy) and Imogen (known as Baba). The older sisters were Emily (Dolly), Lilias (Lily) and Agnata. Dolly and Lily never married and remained at Bamff until Sir

3   Kitty aged about thirteen

James's death, at the age of ninety-two, in 1925, when they moved to Edinburgh. In later life, when Dolly was blind and Lily deaf, they were still to be seen striding vigorously up Glen Clova.

Kitty, as Katharine was always called, was quite a lonely child. The youngest of her half-sisters, Agnata, was seven years older and was at boarding school in St Andrews. Nigel and Douglas were particularly close friends: Ferelith and Imogen were also a 'pair'. Kitty was not particularly robust: she was prone to bouts of throat infection throughout her childhood, for which the state of the drains at Bamff was blamed. Certainly there were outbreaks of scarlet fever among the servants from time to time, which might tend to confirm that faulty drainage was a problem. This was a fairly common hazard at the time: typhoid and scarlet fever took their toll of family and staff alike, but as the servants at Bamff were accommodated in cramped quarters in the attics, the illness tended to spread quickly and easily among them, causing severe symptoms and occasional deaths.

With few companions and frequently confined to the house by illness, Kitty read a great deal. Her father helped to choose her books and as his choice tended towards the classics and history (though some adventure stories were included) she became rather bookish and perhaps intellectually precocious. Sir James was essentially a kind man, but he was exacting and a stern disciplinarian. Like many Victorian fathers his attitude was authoritarian and repressive and he could be short-tempered. The children's surroundings were gloomy: Sir James directed that the nursery quarters should be decorated in dark brown paint in order to save money on constant redecoration. In accordance with the Victorian outlook on morals and chastity, the children were taught that the sisters and brothers must not touch each other, even accidentally in play. Despite the freedom and beauty of their surroundings at Bamff, life may have seemed constrained and restrictive: though having known nothing else from infancy, they were probably unaware of their emotional deprivation.

Lady Ramsay was a much warmer, more demonstrative parent, but she too was in awe of her husband. Sir James set great store by a first-class education and—unusually for his time—saw to it that his daughters, as well as his sons, were highly educated. Dolly, Lily and Agnata all went to St Leonards. Two of them went on to Cambridge University. Lady Ramsay was determined that her own children should be no less successful than her step-daughters and from early childhood there was pressure for academic achievement from both parents.

In such an academic household it would have been virtually impossible to escape being of an academic turn of mind. As Kitty outgrew the nursery and joined the family she was greatly influenced by her father and older sisters, whose conversation and discussions were purposeful, never trivial. Dolly and Lily, serious and dedicated scholars, were responsible for Kitty's schooling in the early years. Perhaps it was unfortunate for Kitty that she, like her father and sisters, would take life seriously, with little time for frivolous pursuits. Not that she despised such things: she simply did not recognise them.

Kitty's position in the family also affected her emotional development. As the eldest of the second family she was constantly reminded of her obligations. She was expected to set the pattern of behaviour, to be responsible for her younger brothers and sisters and to be concerned for their welfare; consequently a certain rigidity, a quality of uprightness, began to develop. She suffered from an inability to express herself emotionally: she could never show sympathy or affection in the form of a warm hug or a squeeze of the hand. Natural warmth and spontaneity had been lost. Her younger sister Ferelith, free from responsibility for the others and less subject to her father's scrutiny and authority, developed a much more lively, outgoing personality.

Sir James was not a wealthy man. Kitty learnt to practise thrift from her earliest days and would never be able to enjoy spending money: which, as it happens, was just as well. Nonetheless, she had been born into a world of privilege, comfort and certainty. For the mid Victorian upper and upper-middle classes, Imperial Britain relaxed in a sunlit serenity born of the certain knowledge of its own benevolent superiority over the rest of the world. Not that Kitty felt a personal sense of superiority, but an acceptance of her position in life was inevitable. Few at that time questioned the entitlement of birth which stationed 'the rich man in his castle, the poor man at the gate'. The poor men at the gate of Bamff—or, rather, six miles away in Alyth—were, in any case, country people living simply but relatively well on the edge of the prosperous farming Vale of Strathmore. The Ramsay children could have known nothing of the abject, dehumanising poverty of the slum-dwelling masses in Britain's cities.

The young Ramsays were brought up without an emphatic sense of Scottishness. Although they were proud of their origins and traditions (Kitty particularly loved dancing reels and strathspeys, her brothers learnt piping) Sir James, who had practised at Lincoln's Inn in his younger days, was Oxford- and London-orientated. Charlotte, too, had spent part of her childhood in London, which she frequently visited. Letters to Bamff were addressed to Alyth, Perthshire, North Britain: common usage in those days, but a more fervid nationalist might have insisted on the use of the Scottish title. It was, after all, the time of a pinnacle in nationalist feeling, when many Scottish people were contributing to the building of the Wallace Monument in Stirling in tribute to their heroic martyr—in part at least a gesture of independence towards their southern neighbour.

4 Kitty before marriage, about 1895

If her father laid the foundations of her literary education, it was her mother who stimulated Kitty's love and knowledge of music. Although piano lessons did not begin until she was eleven, she was musically aware from infancy. She listened at first with childish pleasure, later with appreciation and understanding, as her mother played and sang. Her older step-sisters later acknowledged that even in those early, difficult days of household acrimony when they and Charlotte understood each other little and liked each other less, Charlotte's voice provided a solace and a bridge between them. Although untrained, her singing voice had a uniquely beautiful quality which enchanted everyone who heard it and she composed songs for herself, some of which were later published.

When she was thirteen, Kitty's parents decided to take the younger members of the family to London to be educated, whilst Dolly and Lily remained at Bamff: it was convenient for Sir James's historical research, Charlotte would enjoy London life, Kitty's health might improve and both she and the boys were in need of more formal education. For the next seven years Bamff became a delectable holiday retreat and for some years the Ramsay parents made a home for their children in a large and pleasant Wimbledon house with a lawn tennis court. Due to Lady Ramsay's sociable personality, it was a home constantly filled with friends and music.

Kitty was enrolled at Wimbledon High School for girls: a new and exhilarating environment. Wimbledon was an enlightened school with a very good teaching staff, and she was an eager student. More importantly, as it happened, she was taught music by a particularly inspiring teacher, Miss Emma Mundella. Over the next four years, between Emma's dedicated tuition and Kitty's own capacity for hard work, her natural gift developed into real musicianship.

During that summer of 1887 Agnata, who had won a scholarship to Girton three years earlier, surprised the family by heading the Classical Honours list at Cambridge—an outstanding achievement for a woman at that time. She went on to do something even more unexpected: having returned to Girton for one more year she became engaged to the Reverend Dr Montagu Butler, Master of Trinity, a tall, portly and awe-inspiring widower with a large white beard, thirty-four years her senior. Although this may have seemed a somewhat unlikely attachment, they had interests in common, as Dr Butler, a former headmaster of Harrow, had been Senior Classic of 1855.

For Sir James, Montagu Butler must have been an ideal son-in-law: only a year younger than himself, Montagu had a mind and an intellect equal to his own and a similar dedication to work for the illumination and edification of mankind. Although greatly respected, he was not universally popular; but Agnata was apparently happy and the marriage produced its own crop of gifted sons. But Dr Butler already had a family: two sons and a daughter—Ted, Hugh and Queenie, all a year or two older than Kitty. Over the years many family visits were exchanged between Trinity and Wimbledon. Both sons enjoyed music-making and Kitty often accompanied them on the piano as one sang and the other played the violin. As time passed Charlotte, who also joined in the music recitals, must have noticed a dawning affection between her slightly prim young daughter and the studious, almost equally musical Ted Butler.

Prim she may have been, but Kitty was developing into a very pretty young woman: tiny—about five feet tall—with a pale, clear complexion, a mass of long, dark hair, a full mouth and a well-defined nose. (In later years her husband would refer to her nose, teasingly, as a 'hebraic snout': she attributed it to her mother's grandmother, Charlotte Debnam, who was of Armenian descent.) Her eyes were beautiful and compelling. A relation of the Atholl family, Miss Barbara Smythe, has said 'Kitty had the most beautiful eyes I think I ever saw. They were navy blue, and they sparkled.'

When she was seventeen Kitty took the examination for the Associateship of the Royal College of Music, which she found terrifying, as she had to play to an audience of eminent musicians, including Hubert Parry and Franklin Taylor—who, she was convinced, sat glowering at her 'weak' left hand as she played. Her younger brother Douglas wrote to her from Harrow.

Dearest Kitty . . . Thankyou for the penwiper. It is a very useful thing. I thought of your dreadful ordeal on Thursday afternoon, though I could not get the boy with the telescope to lend it to me to look for the dome of the Albert Hall. I hope you got through it all right.

She did. She now hoped to follow a musical career and had already refused the offer of a scholarship by Miss Maitland, Principal of Somerville Hall, Oxford, as Somerville College was called at the time. She entered the Royal College of Music in May 1892. It had been founded only nine years earlier. The number of pupils accepted was small (about fifty and mostly male) and the teaching staff was outstanding. The Principal was its founder, Sir George Grove, who looked on his students as his 'children' and the college as a large family. Other staff members included Hubert Parry (who succeeded as Principal in 1894) and the hot-tempered, red-haired Irishman Charles Stanford. Kitty's piano teacher was the ageing Ernst Pauer; organ and counterpoint lessons were from the great Bach scholar Walter Parratt. Her greatest delight were her

5 Kitty, about 1896

lessons in composition from Parry himself: a great privilege, as he normally chose to teach only pupils taking composition as their first subject—for example, her near-contemporaries Vaughan Williams and Gustav Holst.

Kitty blossomed and gained confidence under Parry's tuition. She came away from her lessons—held at his home—bursting with new ideas. He was pleased with her early compositions and commented that she should certainly do extremely well. This was high praise coming from him, as he was known to be an exacting teacher who did not suffer fools gladly. Kitty liked him very much: he was a man of enormous vitality, with a boyish sense of fun. Despite his outspoken radical views, with which she could not agree, Parry and his wife remained among her closest friends until his death in 1918.

For the next two and a half years Kitty devoted herself almost entirely to music. Life at the college was demanding and left little or no time for the social activities enjoyed by other young women of her age and class. That presented no problem, as she was dedicated and determined. She persevered with her piano technique and her reports were excellent. In 1893 she won a piano scholarship. Parry lamented that he had not been able to hear her play, but warmly congratulated her on her 'first'. Later, however, she returned the money involved on hearing that the young violin student whom she had narrowly beaten into second place would otherwise have to leave due to lack of funds. Admirers of the music of Samuel Coleridge Taylor must be grateful to her.

Although almost totally preoccupied with her music, there were pleasant diversions. Still solitary by nature, she spent a good deal of time reading and visits to theatre and opera were fitted in whenever possible. Lady Ramsay was in the habit of going to watch the debates in the House of Commons from the Ladies' Gallery, perhaps more for social than for political reasons. Curiously, perhaps, for a young girl, Kitty enjoyed going with her occasionally, absorbing the sense of occasion and admiring sparkling performances by some of the great statesmen of the day—unaware that a quarter of a century later she herself would stand and address that same House as a junior minister.

For the moment her sights were set on a musical career. Until that time there had been few outstanding female musicians—a number of amateur ballad writers; a few notable exponents such as Clara Schumann. A contemporary of Kitty's at the Royal College was the singer Clara Butt. In the ranks of composers, Mahler had selfishly cut short his wife's promising career so that she might devote her attention to him. There was the splendid and formidable feminist composer Ethel Smythe, sixteen years older than Kitty and already well launched into her career as a composer: and a few others. But for the most part the field of female musicians remained empty. It was Kitty's ambition to be one of the successful few, either as a pianist or as a composer—she was as yet uncertain which.

When Kitty was within one term of finishing her studies at the College, Lady Ramsay and her Irish Aunt Mary combined to persuade Kitty to leave and come home to Bamff. The family was returning north. Charlotte was concerned about her daughter's health, her tendency to overwork and to ignore social pleasures. She pointed out that Kitty could just as well compose music at home, and great-aunt Mary suggested that it was time for her to have a little fun out of life.

Unaccountably, Kitty agreed to abandon her studies with only one further term to complete; and she apparently did so without great protest. It seems strangely out of character for someone so eager, so dedicated, so determined to succeed. It is possible, but perhaps not likely given her determination and previous successes, that she was over-anxious and nervous at the prospect of her final examinations; this might have made Charlotte apprehensive for Kitty's well-being.

Kitty had been brought up to act unquestioningly on the advice of her parents. She would have been aware, of course, that a career in music would have required several further years of study abroad, in Leipzig, Paris or Rome: her decision may have been made out of consideration for her father, knowing that with two sons and two more daughters to educate, this would have been difficult for Sir James to finance.

From Charlotte's point of view the security of a socially advantageous marriage would be infinitely preferable for her daughter in comparison to a lonely struggle against the odds to achieve recognition and a career as a musician. The trauma of her childhood experience in India (as a result of which she suffered nightmares all her life) and her upbringing as an orphan—which, despite family members and legal guardians, must have been an isolated existence—influenced Charlotte's own outlook. For her, marriage had brought stability, security and the warmth of a large family of her own. Stability and security were what she sought in turn for her daughters.

There is one other possible reason for Kitty's sudden decision to return north: her developing attachment to Ted Butler, which will be discussed in Chapter 12.

Whatever the reason, the return to Scotland would, for better or worse, affect the course of her life fundamentally and irrevocably.

Chapter 2

Bardie at Blair, 1895-7

Now re-established at home in Perthshire, the family settled down to a mixture of entertainment and historical research. The disparity in the ages of Kitty's parents was matched by a disparity in their dispositions. Sir James was not a gregarious man and he preferred to stay at Bamff writing, reading, 'wooding' and walking in the company of his two eldest daughters, to visiting country houses for sociable houseparties. However he had no objection to his wife's accepting invitations. Despite his affection for her, he was probably too preoccupied to notice her absence.

Lady Ramsay was a popular guest. She often visited Taymouth Castle, home of the Earl and Countess of Breadalbane, where King Oscar of Sweden was also a frequent visitor. The King had an excellent singing voice himself and he and Charlotte sang duets together: a cordial friendship developed and Sir James and Lady Ramsay paid a visit to Sweden as guests of the royal family. Charlotte also often attended houseparties given by the Airlies at Cortachy Castle, the Duke and Duchess of Montrose at Buchanan Castle, and the Earl and Countess of Strathmore at Glamis. Once, whilst staying at Moy Hall in Inverness-shire with the Mackintosh of Mackintosh, Lady Ramsay met John Stewart-Murray, Seventh Duke of Atholl. He was in some ways quite similar in character to her own husband: only a few years younger, an amateur historian and artist, inclined to irascibility when crossed. The encounter resulted in an invitation for Charlotte and her eldest daughter Kitty to stay at Blair Castle in north Perthshire for the annual Atholl Gathering in August 1896, for which there was always a large houseparty.

Lady Ramsay was naturally delighted to accept the invitation. Kitty was not, and went under protest. She did not know the family, but she had heard that they were very 'stuck up' and she guessed that they were probably rather boring. However she had never seen Blair or the countryside surrounding it. It was only twenty-two miles as the crow flies from Bamff, but the crow would have to fly over some of Scotland's finest and highest mountains to reach it. She grudgingly decided to make the best of it and took with her the things she felt might help to make the visit at least bearable—her bicycle to explore the countryside, a novel to read and a volume of scores of Beethoven quartets to work on.

On the appointed day guests arrived in small batches by various trains and the Atholl 'bus' was sent to meet them. Lady Ramsay, the Duchess of Buccleuch and her two daughters, were sedately transported to the Castle, but Kitty had to ride her bicycle and went spinning up the long avenue of lime trees leading to the Castle forecourt. The twenty-six year old Marquis of Tullibardine, eldest son of the Duke and Duchess, a cavalry officer on leave from his regiment, came down the steps to meet her and was surprised and rather amused to see the small figure flying along in a blue coat and hat with a dashing red ribbon round it. Although it was of no consequence to either of them, they were distantly related: sixth cousins once removed by one line of descent and fifth cousins once removed by another.

As it happened the Marquis (who had abbreviated his title of Tullibardine as a child and was known as Bardie) was feeling as annoyed as Kitty over her invitation, about which he had not been consulted. Her inclusion had meant that one of the girls he had particularly wanted to invite had been excluded and he was used to getting his own way. He was also accustomed to rather more conventional young women than the slightly offhand girl who now dismounted from her bicycle—women who smiled, flirted and set their caps at him. After all, as he was only too well aware, he was one of the most eligible bachelors in the country. He flirted back with enthusiasm, but was apt to be caustic and rather lofty in speaking of them. Writing to his mother about the composition of this particular houseparty, he had said:

> Lovat might be able to come, but I doubt it. His brother Hugh would do well and one of the girls—Maymie for choice. Lady Bates's girl is nice too, though her mother is an ass; the same remark applies to the Buccleuchs and the eldest girl; there are the Abercorns too—and dear Gwen! and that horrid girl Marie! You need not be afraid of my falling in love with any of the above list!

Lady Ramsay and Kitty were warmly greeted by the Duchess of Atholl. On being conducted to her room Kitty was amazed and delighted to find that the Duchess (having apparently been well briefed) had arranged to have a piano installed there, for her to practise on—a thoughtful gesture which must have required some organisation. Kitty began to revise her view of the prospects for the next few days.

Kitty was not the only young woman to arrive by bicycle that day. Dertha, the Duke's eldest daughter, gave an account of another arrival in a letter to her younger brother George:

6   Kitty about the time of the meeting with Bardie, 1896

The Gathering went off rather well. As far as I can remember the party were the Duchess of Buccleuch and two girls, Lady Ramsay and daughter, Ethel Fraser and Hugh Dunmore, Fincastle and Muriel Gore Brown, darling Elspeth Campbell (Papa's latest) and her horrible brother and the usual lot. Elspeth was to arrive on Monday at the same time as the Smalls and Bill. Hamish and I came back to the Castle about 6.30 pm and found father 'accidentally' walking up and down in front of the House—nearly had our noses bitten off, so went in and peeped from a window. First out got Mr Small (His Grace cut him); then Mrs Small (his Grace turned his back); then Bill (His Grace looks anxiously at the bus); then at last another female . . . it was Mrs Small's maid! His Grace rushed up to Jackson 'with enquiries—there was no other lady, Jackson swore. His Grace cut everybody dead, rushed into his room and banged the door—and no sooner had he got there then the young lady arrived on a bicycle!

If the old Duke's lack of courtesy disconcerted his guests, his general behaviour was a constant source of irreverent amusement to his sons and daughters. Dertha in particular was in the habit of giving accounts to other members of the family about 'Father's latest'. Young women, married and unmarried (the married ones often the wives of friends), moved in and out of his life with what must have been, to him, satisfying frequency. His clumsy attempts to cover his tracks were observed and recounted with cynical delight by his offspring. The relationship between the Duke and his wife Louisa was one of cool, slightly detached friendship. Nor were the Atholls a particularly close or affectionate family: they co-existed in a state of mutual tolerance.

Bardie was heir to estates running from the Inverness-shire border at Dalwhinnie almost to the county town of Perth some sixty miles to the south and to the Aberdeenshire border in the east. With the exception of a few small estates which had earlier been carved out of Atholl territory, almost every hill and glen, every tenant farm, every shooting lodge in this wild countryside belonged to Atholl. The Duke was a grandee of grandees; he had more titles than any other peer, including his dukedom, two marquisates, five earldoms, three viscountcies, seven baronies.

Blair Castle looks like an illustation from *Grimms Fairytales*. It is a vast, white-harled, castellated building set in wide parkland beneath the hills. It dates from 1269, but was extensively rebuilt in the mid eighteenth century. Its history is as romantic as its appearance—visited by King James V and by Mary Queen of Scots; stormed by Cromwell's troops; haven for Prince Charles on his journey south; besieged by the Jacobites the following year on their way north to Culloden, when it lay in Hanoverian hands. Queen Victoria and Prince Albert were 'enchanted' by it when they stayed there for three weeks in 1844. By royal decree the Dukes of Atholl enjoy the unique privilege of maintaining a private army—which, in practice, consists of estate workers, tenants and local inhabitants, the officers mainly relatives and friends of the Duke: its existence reinforced a sense of comradeship in the district. In short, a semi-royal principality existed in Atholl whose like existed nowhere else in Britain.

Kitty was completely unimpressed by all the grandeur, and it certainly did not occur to her to gush over Bardie, whom she had seen once before at a Perth Ball. She had noted a face which seemed curious, rather enigmatic—a very white skin with quiet grey eyes, well-cut features, but with sandy eyebrows and moustache. She had not admired him on that occasion, and on that first evening, at dinner, seated at one of the smaller tables in the diningroom, she caught a glimpse of him as he sat at the main table and felt extremely thankful that as one of the junior guests she had been spared the 'honour' of sitting beside him. After dinner,

7   *Left to right:* George, Evelyn, Helen, Dertha, Bardie and Louisa

however, he politely came to invite her to play for the assembled guests—he too had been well briefed—and later still, at a tenants' ball at the local hotel, they danced several reels together. Much ice apparently melted beneath the chandeliers during the course of the evening.

On the following afternoon, however, Kitty was displeased. He had invited her to walk round the castle grounds with him, but on discovering that she was expected to follow meekly in the wake of Bardie and another girl she turned back abruptly. When he re-appeared to enquire what had happened she did not hesitate to make her feelings clear. He had a lively sense of humour and took the rebuke well, but he must have been surprised and intrigued: Kitty was spirited and independent and, unusually for a girl of twenty-one in his experience, was not afraid to say what she thought. She represented a challenge.

The weather was hot and sunny throughout the visit. Bardie, having apparently abandoned attempts to entertain the other young women in the party, rowed her around in a small boat on the loch in the grounds. One afternoon they climbed Craig Urrard, a sizeable hill behind the

Castle. As they climbed the Marquis spoke of his view of life and of his sense of duty towards other people. It was Kitty's turn to be surprised—she had not expected a philosophical discourse from him. It was no doubt his intention to impress, and he had the advantage of her, as she could only listen as she struggled up the hill on that hot August afternoon in the unsuitable, uncomfortable clothing of the day—a long, fawn-coloured woollen skirt and coat, a high-necked, whalebone-stayed blouse and a hat.

When she left Blair she made up her mind never to pre-judge people again. She admitted to one of her sisters that she had gone expecting to find arrogance and had found humility; had expected stand-offishness and had been overwhelmed with kindness; had expected to be bored and had been greatly entertained. The novels and scores had not been opened, the bicycle had not been used.

Bardie returned to his regiment in the south, and wrote to her at Bamff, making two fundamental errors in doing so. Firstly, he addressed the letter to 'Miss Ramsay' with the result that it was opened by Dolly. Secondly, he had been misinformed and was under the impression that Kitty had gained first class honours at Girton—Agnata's reputation as a blue-stocking had rubbed off on Kitty. His own letter was a leg-pull.

> . . . X (an ordinary girl) Hulloa—look at that scorcher there on a bike! Y (who has been educated at Girton College) 'My dear, you should not say scorcher, it is vulgar; but use the word 'asterlator' from the Latin word astalar, to burn or scorch.' . . .
> Best wishes to Lady Ramsay and hoping you will leave off scorching.
> Yours sincerely . . . Tullibardine.

He was unabashed to learn of his mistakes and wrote again cheerfully:

> Dear Miss Ramsay . . .
> . . . I am very sorry I was ass enough to address your letter wrong. I hope your sister was not scandalised at being called an asterlater by me—or did she think me a lunatic? . . .
> Yours sincerely Tullibardine.

> Dear Miss Ramsay
> . . . Enclosed you will find the pipe tune you wanted. It is a nice tune on the pipes but I fear it will not be mistaken for our old friend Chopin on the piano. I am just off for a course at Chatham, where I shall become so learned that I hope to be able to talk to people educated even at Girton. A certain officer corroborated your opinion of me—I heard him tell a friend that I was a swaggering young cad and not a gentleman. I must say I gave him provocation, as we were making a bridge and I pushed him over the edge! . . .
> Yours sincerely Tullibardine.

A further meeting took place at a Perth Hunt Ball in September. Bardie kept the correspondence going, sent her one of his drawings for Christmas, and early in 1897, now stationed in Cheshire, he intercepted Kitty and her mother for a fifteen minute meeting as they passed through Crewe railway junction on their way to London. No doubt Kitty was only one of many young women with whom he was corresponding, but he was evidently fascinated by this unusual, rather remote girl. For her part Kitty was probably attracted by his self-confidence and by his impish sense of humour, which she had not encountered among her own serious-minded family or friends. He wasted no time in making arrangements to meet Kitty and Lady Ramsay when he came to London in February.

> Eaton Place 18/2/97
> Dear Miss Ramsay
>   . . . I see you are right about Arthur Roberts—so I have wired for seats at the Geisha—dinner at the Coburg Hotel. . . . I have given up the 'Old Hundredth' and taken to 'O God Our help in Ages Past.' There is a grandeur and depth in it that suits my voice.
>   Yours . . . Tullibardine.

There were one or two further chaperoned meetings in London before Kitty and her mother returned to Scotland at the end of February. Bardie was apparently by now deeply in love. It is not difficult to understand why he had been initially attracted by Kitty's cool, detached manner at their first few meetings; it is more difficult to analyse his reasons for falling in love with her, surrounded as he was by the attractive, husband-hunting daughters of wealthy aristocrats. But Kitty had unintentionally bewitched him: in his own way and for the rest of his life he would be dependent on her.

Kitty was less sure. She was almost certainly aware by now that he had 'intentions'. She recognised that a powerful and arresting personality had entered her life and that he seemed likely to ask her to marry him, but she had many reservations. Although attracted, she was not in love. Perhaps she was 'in love', so far as she could judge, with Ted. She longed above all to devote herself to music and she realised that commitment to Bardie and his way of life would prevent that. She was as yet very uncertain of her feelings.

Lady Ramsay had arranged to take a house for the entire family in Egerton Gardens in June. She and Kitty left Scotland in advance of the others in order to go to Westmorland so that she could perform some of the Song Flowers which Kitty had set—from Stevenson's *A Child's Garden of Verses*—at Kendal Musical Festival. Kitty loved these poems of

8 The Atholl family about 1882. *Left to right:* Louisa, Evelyn, Bardie, Hamish, Dertha, Helen, George and the seventh Duke

Stevenson's, though perhaps the idea of setting them had originated with Parry himself. The songs, though perhaps failing to explore the nuances and undercurrents of Stevenson's poems, greatly pleased the audiences at Kendal and generous reviews appeared in the local newspapers. Kitty was a very young composer. She was unsophisticated for her age, and, due to her upbringing, emotionally repressed. It could not be expected that she would produce complex or stylish music at this stage.

The year 1897 was Diamond Jubilee year and all over the country Queen Victoria's loyal subjects were preparing to celebrate and to watch the festivities. London, of course, was at the centre of pomp and procession. Bardie, now stationed at Windsor, was taking part in it with the Blues, though he modestly suspected that the reason why he had been chosen for this honour was because he had recently bought (at his father's expense) a beautiful charger called Juniper.

Kitty's letters, all from 97 Egerton Gardens, indicate the course of events:

> Dear Lord Tullibardine   I have only just come in and got your letter. I fear it is too late for a play, as we should like to have done one very much. Also I am sorry to have missed you if you came this p.m., as I think you did. We are so sorry we can't come to lunch on Sunday—I had just written to ask you to lunch here. Do if you can—shall we do the Zoo afterwards? I am sorry about the lozenges—I bought them and sent them off directly I got back from Ascot on Saturday. I am so cross you didn't get them—I hope you are all right now. Yours very sincerely 'G K'

G K was an abbreviation for Grey Kitten, a name invented by Bardie. On 19 June she sends more lozenges and hopes he will get them in time for the Jubilee, adding: 'Mind you see that Juniper behaves himself on Tuesday. I shall be at Gwyder House, Whitehall, in a blue hat, but however I don't suppose even your all-seeing eye will be able to make me out!'

On 21 June she informs him that the blue hat has been cut down to a blue toque in consideration for others and wishes him Good Luck for the Jubilee.

24th June 97
Dear Lord Tullibardine   How much of you is there left after the Jubilee? It must have been very trying, riding all those hours in the blazing sun. I hope you got back to Windsor all right and that Juniper was not too flighty. I tried to make you out as you passed our stand, but couldn't. These crowds and heat are very exhausting. There is hardly anything of me left but my nose, which is bright cherry coloured from sitting for hours without shade in the sun. If you are not too busy with functions and duties,

could you lunch here on Sunday? It would be nice if you could and we might perhaps do the Zoo afterwards? I won't ask you to the Albert Hall—it would be too hot, I think—I might not be able to keep off musical talk, which I know is tabooed! Yours very sincerely, G K.

After lunch on Sunday, in the unlikely setting of the Zoo, Kitty hesitantly agreed to a secret engagement.

Sunday, June 27th 97.
My dearest one,   I said I wouldn't write, but I can't resist the wish to do so—I do so want you to understand how frightfully happy you have made me today. It seems so wonderful and beautiful that you should care for me as you do. I can't understand how it has all come about and feel quite dazed with happiness. I don't know if it is very forward of me to write to you like this—it may be—but I cannot bear to think that you may have meant what you said this afternoon—that I didn't care as much as you did. How can I tell what I feel? Anyway, I couldn't this afternoon, so write this to try to fill up the gaps. How I wish this afternoon could have gone on for ever—at least some parts of it. It all seems too perfectly happy. This is all very incoherent and scrappy and I am afraid, terribly forward, but if we have to keep up appearances before other people, I suppose we may drop them when writing to each other. I hope you have written to me tonight . . . Yours G K.

The reason for the need for secrecy was because of Bardie's ambition to join the Nile expedition. Since January 1885, when General Gordon had been murdered in Khartoum by the Dervish army of the Mahdi during a Holy War to sweep the Christian infidels from the Sudan, British patriots had been pressing for revenge.

Britain was anxious to preserve Egyptian independence because of the importance, strategically and commercially, of the Suez Canal. There was also a desire in some quarters to see a Trans–African Railway stretching through British controlled territory throughout its length from Capetown to Cairo. Gladstone's Liberal administration was not sympathetic to such ambitions, but it alternated with a Tory administration which was. Sir Herbert Kitchener, a tall, haughty, aloof soldier who had had a somewhat meteoric career from young subaltern to Commander of the Egyptian Army at the age of thirty-two, longed for the opportunity to rescue the Sudan from the fanatical Dervish regime, which terrorised the population and actively encouraged the slave trade. His chance came when the Italians in Ethiopia requested assistance from Britain and he made a partially successful foray into Sudanese territory in 1896.

Preparations were made to consolidate and attack again, but Kitchener was in no hurry and he quietly built up his army, training the Egyptians and hand-picking his officers from the British Army when home on leave. Bardie had encountered him at a gathering in London in 1896 and as a very junior subaltern he was delighted that the great man should there and then have invited him to be part of the expeditionary force when the time came. Nothing could have been better calculated to further Bardie's career.

But Kitchener refused to take on officers who were married, or even engaged. He himself was unmarried and was likely to remain so. He was truly a solitary, uncommunicative man with scant sympathy for human emotion. His officers must be like himself—dedicated to soldiering, single-minded, ruthless to the point of cruelty. Any hint of an 'attachment' on the part of one of his officers would be enough to disqualify him for inclusion in the Expedition, and Bardie, who was determined that nothing should spoil his chances, explained all this to Kitty on the Sunday afternoon of their engagement. She wrote:

30th June 97
Dearest
    I am beginning to feel rather overwhelmed at the bravery of the step we have taken (don't misread this into thinking I repent it) and I think it is too good of you to have done it, with every reason for not wishing to do anything yet. I do thank you from the depth of my heart for having made me feel at peace about ourselves—and don't think for a minute that I don't understand all the reasons you have given me for keeping things dark for the present. As to waiting, I am proud to be able to give you proof that I care for you. It is all so difficult to realise as yet; I felt very weird this afternoon and was afraid your mother was unhappy about it. Perhaps she may get happier, though—I do hope she will—as I so thoroughly understand and sympathise with what she is probably feeling. Anyhow God Bless you for the happiness and love you give me. Yours G K.

Whatever Louisa's reservations, Charlotte must have been elated. It is impossible to estimate her own role in the matter. Perhaps it all came as a pleasant surprise. On the other hand the possibility may have been in her mind when she and Kitty paid their visit to Blair Castle. Whatever the truth, she must have been gratified by the outcome: with no personal wealth and, as the daughter of a baronet, a fairly modest position in the social order, her daughter was about to make a brilliant marriage: a little self-congratulation was surely permissible. Sir James may well have been less enthusiastic. Given his disapproval of landlordism (he did not place himself in that category) and his own intellectual élitism, it would not be surprising if he regarded Agnata's as by far the better match. Kitty, however, was now genuinely and demurely in love:

3rd July.

. . . On the surface we seem to come from opposite poles of everything—
it does show me what a powerful force love is, and how it can sweep away
everything. I have not a doubt as to the happiness and rightness of the step
we have taken and the more I see of you the more certain I feel. I wish I
weren't so shy of you sometimes. It seems odd to be so shy of anyone, but I
am, in this case! That is how I managed to give you the impression that I
didn't like what you did on Sunday. That isn't true. I like every proof you
can give me that you care for me—it was only that it was a shock at first. I
think it is only right to show you a bit of what I feel—as I am afraid there is
a good deal of me that you don't know. You have taken a very brave step. I
hope you may never repent of it . . . your G K.

12th July.

. . . This was one of our happiest afternoons, I think, though it came to an
abrupt conclusion! I am too proud for words that you should have told me
you would give up anything for me. I was, as usual, sticky and couldn't tell
you what is perfectly true: that if I knew from the moment I married you I
should never hear another note of music, I should do it, and be happy all the
same. This is quite true, in spite of all the nonsense I have talked about
marrying a musical person. You come before everything. I hope, dearest,
that this letter will stop you saying silly things such as that I don't half
care—O I feel such a brute when you do and would not have you think it
for the world as it is absolutely untrue. Yrs. Kitty.

Kitty was to suffer from her inability to show her feelings all her life.
She would be shy, reticent, apparently withdrawn and at times
formidable, even with those closest to her. She was acutely aware of this
and it distressed her. She commented to Bardie 'Most people find me
difficult to know, but I don't think you will, very, as you are so
sympathetic.' Her shyness was not accompanied by physical frigidity.
Initially timid, she became eager and responsive and looked forward to
marriage with growing enthusiasm. If her feelings towards Ted were of
youthful tenderness, those for Bardie were fast becoming passionate.

In mid July she and her mother set out for Bayreuth, the picturesque
town set in the hills of South Germany where Wagner had built his great
concert theatre only twenty years previously. They were to attend
performances of *The Ring* and *Parsifal* conducted by Hans Richter—
described by Kitty as 'the greatest conductor there is of Wagner'. Kitty
was not a ramping Wagnerian by any means, but she expected to be
impressed, and she was not disappointed. It was a magnificent experience:
the staging was lavish, still based on Hoffman's original and sumptuous
designs for the first productions. Wagner had stipulated that the orchestra

be invisible, so that the music seemed to come from a 'mystic gulf' and the audience almost felt transported, part of the spectacular sound and scene. Kitty wrote to Bardie 'Just fancy! The first scene is supposed to take place at the bottom of the Rhine, with slippery rocks and Rhine-maidens swimming and diving about in the water! It sounds too hideously absurd and impossible, but they do it marvellously!' The powerful music with its great outbursts of overwhelming passion and poignancy reflected her own emotions; she was young, newly in love and filled with *sehnsucht*; she told Bardie that it seemed rather silly to have gone all that way and then cared most about getting a letter from him at the end of it all.

Kitty and her mother returned home and joined the family at Bamff for the rest of the summer and autumn, fending off rumours of an engagement. The situation was embarrassing for Kitty and her family. They were truthful and frank by nature and it distressed them—annoyed Sir James—to have to be evasive. Her great aunts and the Countess of Airlie, who were curious, shrewd and observant, were apt to ask questions and to comment. Bardie was not particularly discreet himself and the rumour gathered momentum. Eventually the *Pall Mall Gazette* printed the story and the item was copied by the local newspaper, the *Dundee Courier*. Emphatic denials came from Bamff. Bardie suggested that the best method of defence was attack: they must start a rumour of their own, to the effect that the Countess of Airlie and the Earl of Mansfield were to become engaged as soon as the Earl had saved up enough money to buy the ring.

Kitty and her mother were invited to Blair for a few days in the autumn while Bardie was on leave. The old Duke received Kitty with cool courtesy, probably sharing his wife's view that the attachment was unlikely to last. He must have been hoping desperately that Bardie would marry an heiress. Kitty was not the wealthy daughter-in-law he had been hoping for.

From the days of the first Duke the estate had been impoverished, despite its extent and importance. It was said of the first duke (created in 1703) that he had to borrow the money from his neighbour, Robertson of Lude, to go to London to receive the title from Queen Anne. On Atholl there were 144,000 acres of deer forest and 136,500 acres of moorland—high, mountainous land, unsuitable for any other use. There were 4,000 acres of arable and pasture land on tenanted crofts and farms, and 3,500 acres of woodland and forest. But despite these vast landholdings the saga of financial profligacy which afflicted succeeding generations of Atholls was lengthy and cumulative. By the time of the seventh Duke the estate was in debt to the tune of £400,000—perhaps £17 million by today's standards. He must have been extremely worried, but apparently saw no reason to trim his sails and was at that moment planning to build a house at Dunkeld at a cost of £14,500 and to spend £6,000 on improvements to the Castle.

It would have been a godsend if Bardie had decided to marry someone with a bit of money—a wealthy American if necessary; but the family's close friendship with the Royal Family would have made a marriage to a royal princess acceptable all round. The Princess Victoria was about the right age and unattached. Queen Victoria had been particularly fond of Bardie's grandmother, the Duchess Anne, one of her ladies-in-waiting. Anne had recently died and the Queen had been grief-stricken. A marriage between her granddaughter and the Duchess Anne's grandson would have had royal approval.

The old Duke had not married for money himself. His wife Louisa had been one of the 'beautiful Moncrieffe sisters'—of impeccable Scottish ancestry, but of relatively modest means. The marriage had produced seven children—three daughters and four sons—sufficient, one would have imagined to ensure the continuation of the line in direct descent for generations to come.

The eldest daugher, Dorothea (Dertha) had recently married and gone to live in Henley with her husband, Harry Ruggles-Brise, who was in the army. As it happened, they would not have any children. Helen, the second daughter, was as yet unmarried and would remain so until she was almost fifty. The third and most beautiful of the daughters, Evelyn, developed psychological symptoms in her late teens. The problem followed a bout of badly treated diphtheria and an occasion during which she was lost in the snow on the hills. The family blamed either or both events for her condition, but it may have been a form of schizophrenia. Antagonism towards her mother in particular caused the parents to decide to send the young girl abroad—first to Switzerland and then to Belgium, in rooms with a companion/housekeeper. She did not see either parent again and felt all her life that she had been cruelly treated. Her brothers and sisters visited her from time to time, though she usually hid under the piano or shut herself in another room and conducted conversation through the locked door. She wrote long, perfectly rational letters to them throughout her life. A gifted needlewoman, some of her magnificent lacework is on view at the Castle.

None of the daughters, then, would provide the Duke and Duchess with grandchildren. Of the four sons, all younger than the girls, the eldest died in infancy. When Bardie arrived he was welcomed as the heir with relief and joy and quickly learnt the secret of male charm, climbing on to his mother's knee, gazing into her eyes and saying sweetly 'Bardie's a dear little boy, isn't he?' The two younger sons, George and James (Hamish), would remain unmarried. George was engaged to be married

9   Lady Evelyn Stewart-Murray aged about eighteen

when he died. Although it was not yet realised, the provision of grandchildren for the Duke and of direct heirs to the estate and title would be entirely a matter for Bardie and his future wife.

After producing her brood, Louisa may have considered—with some justification—that she had done her duty well and truly by Atholl. Still a beautiful woman, she felt free to begin her own pursuit of happiness, spending much time abroad and, rumour had it, gambling at the tables in Monte Carlo—though never remotely on the scale of her friend the Countess of Breadalbane, who was said to have been the first person to lose £1 million in one night at the gaming tables. Louisa suffered from bronchial troubles and it suited her health to spend the winters in Switzerland or the south of France. She and the Duke tended to play box and cox at the Castle and it often happened that one arrived at Blair as the other departed. Both were at the Castle, however, as were a number of other guests, during the visit of Lady Ramsay and her daughter.

Bardie was always Louisa's favourite child and she was inclined to be possessive and protective. Although he tried to reassure Kitty that she had come round and was now on their side over the engagement, Kitty must have been conscious of a disapproving, less than welcoming air at the Castle in those autumn days of 1897. A less self-composed, independent young woman might have found the Duke's attitude daunting, but Kitty sensibly ignored the problem and treated him with polite respect. She and Bardie made the most of their time together, escaping from the inquisitive scrutiny of fellow guests as often as possible to walk in the gardens or into the hills.

To be fair to Louisa, she was to be a sympathetic and benevolent mother-in-law: she and Kitty developed a mutual affection.

Chapter 3

Kitchener and Khartoum, a DSO—and Marriage At Last 1897–9

Bardie returned to his regiment: Kitty remained at Bamff. At New Year she and her mother went to visit the Gerald Balfours in Dublin. The Balfours, who were close friends, were both exceedingly musical. They had arranged a musical 'event' in which both Lady Ramsay and Kitty would take part. They were accustomed to joining the Balfours for similar occasions at Archerfield in East Lothian, but since 1895 Gerald Balfour—brother of Arthur—had been Chief Secretary to Ireland and the concert would take place at Chief Secretary's Lodge. Such events were renowned in musical circles for setting extremely high standards: there was nothing remotely amateurish about a Balfour private concert.

Bardie was staying with friends for a hunting expedition in Cheshire, in his view a much more interesting and amusing activity. He wrote to Kitty adjuring her not to 'talk bosh about Bach and Wagner to your Irish friends'. This was accompanied by a brilliant, unflattering, cartoon of his bucolic-looking host on horseback.

Suddenly he was notified that he had been accepted for the Nile expedition and was due to sail from Folkestone on 2 January. Lady Ramsay and Kitty immediately cut short their visit to Ireland and hurried to Folkestone to see him off. Kitty's feelings were mixed: taking an optimistic view, his departure meant that plans were well ahead in Egypt and the expedition would be over in the foreseeable future. On the other hand she found it unbearable to think that Bardie was off into a world of unknown dangers for an indefinite period.

After seeing him off Kitty went to stay with his sister Dertha and her husband at Henley. She found Dertha 'very nice . . . one can see that she is a much more docile person than Helen, for instance. There is something touching about the way she absolutely accepts Harry's word on everything. One feels she has really found the right hole in the world into which to fit.'

Kitty wrote almost daily with whatever news and comment she could think of to cheer him up. Bardie replied, though less frequently, having other preoccupations. Lady Ramsay also wrote to him, for her own reasons. Due, it is thought, to a German governness who had been employed for Ferelith and Imogen, Charlotte had been introduced to Christian Science, founded in 1879 by Mrs Baker Eddy, an American who was among the first to find financial reward from the spiritual needs of the wealthy. Her message was that sickness of spirit, mind or body comes from within: catching a cold is the result of having entertained 'the wrong thought'; an acute appendix likewise; doctors and medicines are useless and indeed harmful in the process of healing and as such are forbidden.

Lady Ramsay, Dolly, Lily, Agnata and Imogen (who was still a child) became converts. Sir James, Nigel, Douglas and Ferelith did not, and remained devout members of the Scottish Episcopal Church. The old rift between Charlotte and her stepdaughters was healed, but at the expense of alienating her own family to some extent. It was difficult for each side in the argument to be dispassionate, to step outside their own entrenched viewpoint..

Kitty's attitude was ambivalent; whilst admitting the wisdom of much of the teaching of the Christian Scientists, she could not accept it totally. She was sympathetic to her mother's need to embrace this new-found faith, whilst herself remaining an interested but uncommitted observer. In her enthusiasm, Lady Ramsay felt the need to proselytise and hoped to convert Kitty and Bardie to the movement. She and Dolly had become 'teachers' and it was in this capacity that she wrote to her future son-in-law. In sickness or in danger, she was his self-appointed healer, the medium through whom he would be aided.

Bardie had not asked for this favour. He thought it was 'a lot of bosh and blasphemous rubbish'—but was too polite to refuse and agreed to try it out tentatively. Kitty teased him, enquiring how it worked with regard to sea-sickness, though adding that she was glad to hear that an injury to his hand had healed after a week of Christian Science. In March she wrote, with a hint of reproach:

> Bardie, now that you are taking medicines for a chill Mother has had to stop treating you, but she will continue to help by thinking the Right Thought for Danger. It is a very serious matter to her . . .

As the years went by Kitty's attitude against the movement hardened as she witnessed the premature deaths of members of her family, due, she believed, to lack of medical help.

Some of Kitty's Stevenson songs had just been published and were being well received and selling better than she had hoped for: the publishers had sold 975 copies up until January and the proceeds were

£8. 8s. 9d. She began to set a further group, which she composed during that early spring, curled up in a favourite hollow in the firwoods above her home.

Meantime, far from Kitty's cool green hillside, Bardie had arrived in Cairo and travelled on to Wadi Halfa to report to Kitchener. He was appointed Staff Officer to Lieutenant Colonel Broadwood of the 12th Lancers, who was in command of Egyptian Cavalry, and he travelled southwards up the Nile to join him at Berber. The Mahdi's successor, the Khalifa, and the main body of the Dervish army were some 200 miles further south at Khartoum, but there were strongholds of Dervishes all along the Nile valley.

Bardie was in time to take part in a cavalry reconnaissance on 4 April, in which the entire unit narrowly escaped being wiped out, and in the horrifying battle for Atbara on 8 April. It was his introduction to warfare and was particularly atrocious—600 British and 3,000 Dervishes lay hacked to pieces or mortally wounded in the searing heat of the day.

Kitchener showed neither pity nor mercy towards his enemies, nor indeed particular concern about his own casualties. The Army settled down in encampments to await a further march southwards. Skirmishes would take place at intervals, but the great assault on Khartoum was still several months off. Bardie's artistic skill and his ability to recall details of a landscape led him to be used to reconnoitre and to draw maps of the territory for the commanders.

The desert was baking hot and teemed with flies. Enteric fever and dysentery were rife. But in spite of the primitive conditions and privations, Bardie enjoyed the excitement of it. His attitude to war was rather like that of a boy scout having adventures; he liked being able to use his own initiative and was brave and resourceful, riding out from the camp on watch for pockets of Dervish warriors. On one outing he found and rescued a Dervish woman who had been abandoned, on another a small lost native boy whom he brought back to camp and looked after until they miraculously encountered his mother. He was also able to save the life of a fellow officer found dying of amoebic dysentery and dehydration. In the midst of it all he wrote home to Kitty asking her to order a large chocolate cake to be sent out to him from Buzzard's in London, to which she replied, with seeming lack of sympathy: 'You poor thing! It is like a schoolboy asking for a hamper! Mama will see that it is sent to her little boy and will not order too rich a one!' But she was far from unfeeling and she found his letters describing the fighting in the bush extremely disturbing. She could not bear to contemplate what he had to do and commented '. . . It must be awful to have to kill someone—or else ! You didn't like it, did you? . . . It makes one realize what narrow threads people's lives hang on . . .'

Lady Ramsay had suggested to Kitty that she should return to the Royal College of Music for the summer months, to complete her final year. Conscientious she would always be, but now that Kitty's eyes were set on wider horizons there was no danger of her overworking. Kitty had willingly agreed and looked forward to it eagerly, though she found the idea of returning rather strange at first. The College was in a fine large red building in one of the roads off Exhibition Road in South Kensington. Its policy was to produce good all-round musicians, not simply concentrating on one particular subject. To her satisfaction Kitty now had piano lessons twice a week from Dannreuther, considered to be the finest piano master in the country at that time, and in composition for orchestra once again from the great Hubert Parry himself. Her own technical approach to composition leapt forward at this time. Perhaps her new insights were due to sheer hard work, but it may also have been due in part to emotional development since her engagement to Bardie. Parry himself did not believe that long hours of study would in themselves produce greatness.

Kitty's final term also underlined the fact that she had the potential to become an excellent pianist. Her abilities were extended and improved to a remarkable degree. Dannreuther (himself a composer of note) was a wonderful teacher. He had been Parry's own teacher of piano and Parry still deferred to him over his own compositions. Dannreuther concentrated in particular on Kitty's phrasing to make her music consecutive and intelligible. He was strongly of the opinion that she should continue her studies with him, as she had the makings of a fine concert pianist. She was eventually forced to confide in him, to his profound disappointment, that her future lay elsewhere. When she had completed her summer term she left the college very much better equipped as a musician—in technique, style and substance.

The Ramsays had understood that the engagement was to be announced in mid May. Charlotte felt that she did not wish to have to go through the season having to tell 'tarradiddles'. But Louisa visited Colonel Brocklehurst, Bardie's colonel, who absolutely forbade it, pointing out that it would be regarded as grossly unfair to other officers that Bardie had gone out under slightly false pretences. His further advice was that it might be too expensive for Bardie to remain with the regiment if he married. It was estimated that it might cost him £1,000 a year, and this was beyond the means of the Duke. Louisa told Kitty discouragingly that it might be necessary for them to wait some time before marrying.

London 6th July.
    . . . so strange to look back on what was happening a year ago—it seems so very young, our love of a year ago compared with what we have been

through since, doesn't it? I remember wondering sometimes a little if a year would prove our love to be real and enduring or if it would show it the reverse and if we should have the constancy to stick to each other . . . I sometimes thought it might be only a passing affair and from what you had once or twice said about yourself I thought perhaps you were a person who wanted a thing very much at one time but might not want it for very long! Now those ideas have vanished into thin air long ago. I think your Mother and perhaps others rather doubted we should stick to each other for a year—I remember her saying once or twice 'If you both wish it at the end of a year'—doesn't it make you happy to think we have belonged to each other for over a year now!

Staying at Blair in July, Kitty reported to Bardie that she thought she and his father were quite good friends now—she found the Duke in very good spirits and thought he had been very nice to her. She began to think optimisically of Bardie's return: 'Dearest what fools we shall be then . . . all this year will vanish like a dream. . . .'

But a great deal had to happen before anyone was able to return from Egypt. Gradually the force made its way up the Nile, reaching Omdurman towards the end of August. Kitchener demanded that the Khalifa's forces should surrender. No reply was received and British/Egyptian gunboats began firing. A fearful battle followed. Bardie was in the forefront, riding across the desert, constantly under attack from Dervish horsemen, to deliver messages between Colonel Broadwood, General Macdonald and Kitchener. Having informed Kitchener that the cavalry were falling back, he was able to size up the situation and guide them into a position from which they could draw the enemy down-river, riding back through enemy lines to inform Kitchener of the change of tactics. His Arab horse was shot from under him, but he escaped. His courage and initiative were later acknowledged when he became the first officer in the Household Cavalry to be awarded the DSO. The slaughter was appalling. Thousands of Dervishes lay dead or dying in the gruelling heat of the day as Kitchener's forces entered Omdurman and went on to capture Khartoum.

On the following day Bardie and a young officer in the 21st Lancers named Winston Churchill—who was also acting as war correspondent for the *Morning Post*—were moved by compassion and returned to the Kerreri plain to give water to wounded and dying Dervishes. Kitchener was wholly unmoved and later instigated the looting of the holy places of the warriers. Bardie, having had such an example set by his lofty superior, was not to be outdone. When he returned to Blair months later, trunks full of Dervish weaponry and loot arrived, including a finial from the tomb of the Mahdi. (Possession of these objects always worried Kitty and after Bardie's death many of them were returned to Khartoum out of respect for the beliefs and traditions of the Mahdi's people. They are now in the museum at Khartoum.)

Kitty waited anxiously at Bamff, knowing that every day the Army were getting seven or eight miles nearer the enemy. While playing a set of tennis, she received a telegram with the tidings of the capture of Omdurman and of Bardie's safety. She found the news overwhelming and could hardly believe that the campaign was almost over at last: 'I can't take in what it means to us . . .'

Bardie returned to London in early October in an extremely weak state. He was suffering from a bad bout of enteric fever and for some days his life was in danger. Louisa kept a close eye on him in hospital: not until he was well enough to make it clear that he very much wanted to see Kitty did she permit Kitty and her mother to come down from Bamff to visit him. Kitty was amused to be given a dose of sal volatile by the nurse before entering the sickroom, in case she felt faint with emotion at the re-union—and was further amused and rather pleased to find that Bardie was sufficiently well for a little of 'the old Adam' in him to be evident during their meeting.

By November Bardie was well enough to leave hospital to convalesce at Eaton Place, while Kitty returned to Bamff. At last, in mid November, the announcement of their engagement appeared in the *Morning Post* and the *Scotsman*. Bardie absent-mindedly forgot the *Times* and *Telegraph*. News of his award of the DSO and of his having been mentioned in despatches also appeared in the newspapers. He chided Kitty with omitting his decoration from his envelope and received a quick retort reminding him not to leave ARCM off his letters to her in future.

Bardie went to Windsor to receive his decoration. He arrived in time for lunch and was promptly invited to stay for dinner, and so had to wire to Eaton Place to have his dress uniform brought down. According to his own light-hearted account he 'flirted madly with various middle-aged princesses and ladies-in-waiting' before receiving his award from the old Queen, who congratulated him on his forthcoming marriage but remarked that Lord Kitchener would not be at all pleased to hear of it. Bardie replied that that was just sour grapes on his part . . . 'Anyway we both agreed that we were nice people and departed with many congratulations to each other. . . . After the Queen had left I went and made myself agreeable to your friend Parry who was conducting a band so placed that no-one could hear. He said you were no good at music and had better take up book-making.'

Early in the New Year Kitty's second group of Stevenson's songs was published and acclaimed. The popular singer Kennerly Rumford frequently chose to include the songs in his performances and persuaded Kitty to arrange them for orchestra. Rumford, described by Sir Henry

Wood as 'a typical English gentlemen whose birthright shone through every bar he sang', was the husband of Kitty's contemporary at the Royal College, Clara Butt. His enthusiasm boosted Kitty's morale, as his concerts were always well attended.

Bardie's health was still poor, as were his finances. No date could be set for the wedding. He suggested that they might manage to marry sooner if they lived at Blair with the family to begin with. Having by now made several visits to Blair Castle and his family, Kitty was not enthusiastic, though she agreed that if by doing so they would save £300 a year it was something they ought to consider.

Bardie returned to army duties in the New Year, but was sent to Harrogate to 'take the waters' for three weeks in April, whence he was pursued by an old friend, Miss Enid Wilson. He delighted in teasing Kitty:

> She is a nice girl and so pretty. . . . I am rapidly falling victim to Enid. We drink water together at 8–12. I always go for tea and usually for dinner. In fact everything except bath together as that is not allowed. I am teaching her housekeeping about which she knows nothing and we go out and buy the fish. There! I feel sorry for Tittums! I can see what's coming. You had better anticipate events I think. It will be more dignified to break it off. . . . Why did I ever get engaged—especially when there are Enids in the world! I wish there were a few Tittums here however as well . . . Dear old Tittums, wasn't I horrid . . . I am so longing for you again . . .

If Enid had any hopes, they were dashed when arrangements were made for a wedding in July. The old Duke had hoped for a Presbyterian wedding. Dertha had been married by this form in the ballroom at the Castle, and to the Duke's mind anything other than a Presbyterian wedding would be unthinkable. Sir James Ramsay, however, announced that if it was to be a Presbyterian wedding he would be unable to give his daughter away. (The Ramsays had been staunch Episcopalians for many generations.) For some time there was an impasse until Lady Ramsay, with her usual tact, and presumably swallowing her own Christian Science principles, managed to arrive at a solution to which the Duke reluctantly agreed: Montagu Butler, Agnata's husband, would officiate at an Anglican ceremony in St Margaret's, Westminster, assisted by Archdeacon Aglen, the Ramsays' friend and Rector of their church in Alyth.

Financial arrangements also had to be made. Bardie expressed the wish to Kitty that he might be a fly on the wall when the two fathers discussed finance: but if the interview was at all acrimonious neither of them mentioned it. Sir James sold a family Romney to finance his side of the marriage contract, and had a copy made to replace it. One of the terms of the agreement was that sufficient property was entailed in order that Kitty, if widowed, would receive an annuity of £2,000 from Atholl and a further £2,000 from Bamff.

Kitty was interested in fashion and enjoyed choosing her trousseau. She was very thankful, having previously been a sartorial rebel, that the 'intolerable' tight-fitting bodices, stiffened with whalebone, which she had particularly loathed had gone out of style and had now been replaced by soft, loose dresses and blouses which were much more comfortable.

The wedding took place on 20 July 1899. Eight bridesmaids and two pages—Agnata's sons—were in attendance. Six NCOs of the Atholl Highlanders were posted on each side of the chancel, and a guard of honour was provided from Bardie's troop of the Blues. Kitty wore the famous Atholl emerald tiara, which was presented to her on her wedding morning. The bridal party left the Church to the strains of Parry's Wedding March from *Aristophanes*.

The honeymoon was spent in Holland and Belgium, where Kitty met Evelyn for the first time. They also went to Medemblick, to visit the tomb of Lord George Murray, Bardie's ancestor, the great Jacobite general. From Belgium, Bardie wrote to his father:

> You have been more than good to me through all this job, so thank you, and to Kitty too. You may I feel sure be always certain of her loyalty and she certainly has got a useful and practical head. I am quite satisfied and after all it is better than wealth alone, though the latter is not to be despised. Please do what you can to have as little fuss as possible when I arrive! I do hate it so—that kind of fuss!

Kitty was twenty-four, Bardie twenty-nine. It was just three years since their first meeting, two years since their secret engagement. At last it seemed that they could look forward to the future with eagerness: to a shared life, a home of their own, a family, and to all the pleasures of being the young Marquis and Marchioness of Tullibardine.

Chapter 4

With the Scottish Horse in South Africa, 1899–1902

The Marquis and Marchioness of Tullibardine returned from their honeymoon in late August 1899. Bardie had asked that there might be as little fuss as possible, but tradition demanded that they should be welcomed home as generations of family brides and grooms had been welcomed by Atholl estate tenants and workers. They left the train at Perth and proceeded north by carriage, passing through small towns, villages and clachans on their twenty-six mile journey. At each, the carriage was halted, the assembled crowds cheered, Kitty was given bouquets of flowers and Bardie was given a glass of Atholl Brose—a delicious but potent whisky-based drink which was made from a secret recipe. His ability to make a speech, as required, at each stopping place was evidently unimpaired, though he must have been relieved when they finally arrived at the entrance gates to the Castle. Half way up the long front drive the horses were taken out and relays of men dragged the carriage to the Castle, Pipe Major Aeneas Rose playing, seated on the box. On arrival at the Castle, according to custom, the bride was carried in by the two oldest tenants on the estate, James Robertson of Strathgroy and Donald Stewart of Clachan Farm, Struan, who luckily also represented the two main clans in the district.

Kitty was now part of a family which rejoiced in its Scottishness and firmly maintained its traditions, albeit traditions partly at least inspired by Sir Walter Scott and encouraged by Queen Victoria. Despite having been educated at Eton—which inevitably reduced their ability to identify with their own people—the Duke and his sons were careful to retain and foster the aura and mystique of the highland chieftain in his native stronghold, surrounded by his loyal and devoted clan.

The Duke and Duchess and their daughter Helen, were, of course, living at the Castle and a great many events were held in celebration, including the Atholl Gathering and the annual ball; there were balls for people on the estate and also at Bamff and Alyth for Kitty's family and friends.

Bamff is large and elegant and was run with style—with Charlotte as chatelaine it could not be otherwise—but its elegance paled into insignificance in comparison with the grandeur of Blair, with its magnificent rooms, sumptuous furnishings and retinues of kilted servants. Butler, footmen and male servants had four sets of regulation wear: walking out dress for times other than meals; undress livery for lunch and tea; dress livery for dinner. Full dress livery was reserved for formal occasions, when they appeared resplendent in a hard tartan kilt, white sporran, pink and white hose, rosettes, tunic and plaid, brooch, waist belt and buckle, brogue shoes with toe and ankle buckles.

After dinner each evening the pipe-major would enter and pipe round the table, playing requests by members of the family and guests before being rewarded with a quaich of whisky. Every morning at eight o'clock precisely he would pipe up and down the narrow, antler-festooned 'Long Corridor' of the bedroom wing, to awaken and salute its inhabitants. In later years one of the Duke's pipers recalled encountering Kitty hurrying to catch an early morning train as he was making his way along the corridor; in order not to impede his stately progress she—then aged fifty-five—climbed onto the window-ledge to allow him to pass.

Those early weeks of marriage to Bardie during that late summer and early autumn of 1899 were probably the happiest weeks of Kitty's life—certainly the most romantic and carefree. Even for a young woman of such personal modesty, the combination of marriage, of being with Bardie, to which she had looked forward for so long, her new position as Marchioness, the elegance of life at Blair, the social round and above all the knowledge that she was loved by Bardie, admired by many and envied by others, brought delight.

But by early October Britain had again involved itself in a colonial war, this time at the other end of the African continent: the Boer War.

Its origins were complex, but a major cause was the desire of the descendants of the early Dutch settlers in the republics of the Transvaal and the Orange Free State to free themselves from the vestiges of British authority. Gold had been discovered in the Transvaal and the Boers were finding their country swamped with foreigners of all sorts.. They sought to protect themselves by introducing strict new laws regarding naturalisation and franchise. Britain reacted sharply on behalf of the disfranchised 'Uitlanders'; negotiations were entered into without goodwill on either side and when they inevitably failed war followed. Britain expected the war to be over by Christmas, although the Boers were in a strong position. They had 100,000 fighting men on the spot. Britain had 14,500. But men and materials were poured into South Africa and by the end of the war two and a half years later there were 400,000 British and colonial troops in the field.

10 'Soldier Brothers Three'

One of the most eager volunteers was the young Marquis of Tullibardine. Kitty and Bardie had been married for three months when he sailed for Capetown with the 1st Royal Dragoons. Indeed it seemed that all Kitty's young relations were off to the war all of a sudden. Bardie's younger brother George, who had been serving in India, left for South Africa in October. Dertha's husband Harry left on 25 October and Kitty's own young brother Nigel went out with the Black Watch in November.

Kitty was understanding, though privately dismayed. For Bardie there was the glamour of embarkation, the company of his fellow officers and the excitement of what lay ahead: for Kitty, the wrench of separation and the unknown stretch of months or even years to come.

Eaton Place, 6th November 1899.
My own darling husband
  How very strange it is to think that this is the first time I have written those words! I don't realise yet that you are gone, and I have been so very

busy since you left that I haven't had time yet to sit down and mope, though I long for my own darling at every minute. There is a great deal to tell you, dearest, and it has been a very eventful week, both as regards the war and us personally. To begin with, I went on Tuesday morning to barracks, to see all your things and what was to be done with them, and while there asked for Lord Binning and saw him. I told him all that you told me to say but as he is not going out he was afraid he could do nothing for you and he told me to tell you that there was lots of useful and necessary work to be done at the base, about which no-one ever heard and for which there was little kudos to be gained, but which was most valuable work all the same—I know how trying it must be to think that you may not see the most exciting part of it all, but dearest, I do feel a good man can do good work and work on which other people depend, wherever he is.

London has been full of bad news and worse rumours since you left. I wonder if you have heard of the Column that was captured on Monday. It was dreadful in London on Tuesday, people talking and thinking of nothing else and people all reading papers in the streets . . . Hamish was so pleased and excited at his getting his commission, but think of my feelings when I went with him to the War Office next day and he found that there were only vacancies in regiments at or going to the Cape, and that the commissions had only been given to fill up those vacancies. I really felt as if it would be the last straw, if Hamish had to go as well as you and George, but of course he was frightfully excited about it.

Bards, dearest, your father wrote me such a sweet letter after you had gone, saying he felt so much for me and that he would look after me and try to make me happy while you were away. I wonder if you are having a good voyage. I do hope it isn't dreadfully rough. It is strange to think of you in that tiny little cabin with Mr Guest, instead of being cosy in No 7 with Tittums.

Darling, darling, how I do wish you were here, but you know I have been and am wonderfully happy and calm about you—I feel that all must be well and that everything is happy really, and that we have such a lot to be thankful for, in having these happy happy months. How I wish that when I went upstairs I could find Bardie's head on the pillow, swearing at me for being late! Goodbye for the present, my own dear husband. God bless and keep you, and may you never feel far from your own little wife Kitty.

Kitty went home to Blair, but very soon returned to Bamff to be with her grief-stricken parents on learning that Nigel had been killed. The Highland Brigade, newly arrived from home, had been lured into a Boer trap—a 'drawing-room general's mistake'. Nigel and his comrades were mown down below the kopje at Majersfontein in the darkness before dawn on 11 December.

The battle at Majersfontein was only one of many battles which the British lost in those last months of 1899. British garrisons and civilians

11   Bardie, South Africa

were by now under siege in the towns of Kimberley, Ladysmith and
Mafeking. The litany of reverses and appallingly long lists of casualties
were received at home in Britain at first with incredulity and then with a
patriotic fervour which amounted to hysteria. That Christmas—by
which time it had been expected that the war would be over—was
recognised rather than celebrated. Yet, had the public but known it, the
tide was already on the turn.

Bardie need not have worried about having to remain at base. He was
soon in the forefront of activity as usual, and kept his father fully
informed of all that was happening, with maps and diagrams of the
situation.

28th January 1900.
Pretorius Farm near Springfield.
    . . . Here I am again—a very short letter, as I'm going to bed very sleepy.
At present we are like this (diagram of Tugela River). The Boers seems to
be of every nationality. I'm sorry to say a tremendous lot of renegade

Britishers are among them, who are 'wanted' or 'done time' at home. Aren't the Ladysmith lot doing gallantly? As you will see by my diagram our weakness lies in our long line undefended between Frere and Springfield, as till the fight comes off we shall have Hart's Brigade at Springfield entrusted with 19 days' provisions for us and nothing between that and Frere. However we are too strong to be cut off, I think . . .

On 27 February Bardie took part in the Battle of Pieters Hill, which culminated in the historic Relief of Ladysmith. His brother George, serving with the Gordons, was one of those under siege. Dundonald's Horse, an irregular corps, had been first in, in the evening, but Bardie was determined to be the first regular to enter Ladysmith. He asked permission from the Brigadier General and, as he wrote to Kitty, was off with his groom at first light next morning:

> I believed the road to be clear, but I went over the hills direct and did not spare the spur. Dundonald had arrived the evening before at about 5.30 and the people had been in a great state of excitement. Next morning they were all on the watch and they were delighted and did yell—men, women and children. The first person I met was Goulburn of the Gunners. Next Geordie, whose regiment was quartered just over the bridge. They were on parade, and I simply rode at them oblivious of everything. He did the same on foot out of a centre company and we met! Neither could speak for a minute or two, or we should have howled. Then I said 'Hulloa' and so did he. Then I had to say something, or I should have burst, so what of all things do you think I said? I said 'The gardener's dead!'

In February 1990 Hamish had left for Scotland for the Cape with the Cameron Highlanders. Now all Louisa's sons, and her son-in-law, were at the war in South Africa. She would not live to see them return.

Reinforcements kept pouring in and the British moved inexorably northwards through Boer territory. By June 1900 they had entered and taken Johannesburg, the Boers' main stronghold, and it was clear that although the Boers would continue to fight on meantime, ultimate victory for Britain was now assured.

It was at this point that Bardie had an idea. He had been pining to see Kitty. 'Bardie is lonely', he wrote. After the fall of Johannesburg, in June, he wired home suggesting that she should come out to South Africa. The war, it seemed, was almost over; they could meet and travel home to Britain together. The Duke and Duchess and Sir James were appalled and begged Kitty not to go: if the war was nearly over it would be much more sensible to stay at Blair with the family and wait for Bardie's return.

Lady Ramsay understood, though losing Kitty would be more of a wrench for her than for anyone. In any case Kitty's mind had been made up from the moment the wire had arrived. She had packed and set sail within a fortnight and landed at Durban a month later. Bardie was on the quayside, waiting to take her up to Pietermaritzburg to stay with the Governor of Natal—Sir Walter Hely-Hutchinson—and his wife, where she could wait until they were free to go home. As it happened, Kitty's 'little trip out' was to last for two years.

After staying in Pietermaritzburg for two months (Sir Walter had been forbearing but sorely tried over the constant piano practice which assailed his ears) Kitty moved up to Newcastle, much farther north and about halfway between Durban and Johannesburg, where Bardie had found her rooms—with a piano—in a convent. This meant that she and Bardie were able to see each other more frequently. But the war, which had seemed to be ending, dragged on. Bloemfontein and Pretoria had fallen to the British; all the railways were now in British hands; yet the Boers continued to fight a strong guerilla war with extraordinary tenacity.

Lord Roberts, Commander-in-Chief of the British forces, returned home and Lord Kitchener took charge, determined to finish the matter off as quickly as possible. With his customary lack of pity he adopted a 'scorched earth' policy. Boer farms and homesteads were burnt, while their occupants—men, women and children—were herded into camps and held under such atrocious conditions that 4,000 women and 16,000 children died.

Kitchener recognised that further reinforcements, particularly mounted infantry, were required. In December 1900 Bardie was ordered to raise a colonial regiment to be known as The Scottish Horse, to be drawn mainly from the Scottish communities in Johannesburg, the Cape and Natal. Kitchener's command to Captain and Brevet-Major the Marquis of Tullibardine was to 'send out the Fiery Cross'. On 15 December Bardie was gazetted Major-Commandant. He nominated Captain Arthur Blair as second-in-command and Captain Sir William Dick-Cunyngham as adjutant, and the three set off to recruit in Johannesburg, Cape Town and Natal.

Bardie went to Maritzburg, where Kitty was very ill with enteric fever, from which she took several weeks to recover. While she was recuperating he began recruiting: within six weeks the Scottish Horse was four squadrons strong and growing. Pleased with this success, he applied for permission from Kitchener to ask for recruits from home and from Australia. The Fiery Cross went out to the Highland Society in London and to the Caledonian Society in Melbourne. In response, a contingent of 250 first rate horsemen arrived from Australia. Many years later, in 1938, a Scottish trooper in the regiment, John Basil McCaw, wrote a *Book of Reminiscences* whilst living in Singapore and recalled the arrival of the Australian troopers:

> . . . When we arrived at the camp (Jo-burg) or very soon after, the Marquis had given orders to his camp Adjutant, Captain Mummery, to muster all the horses available, as he wanted to test his new troopers' horsemanship. The Aussies were just as keen to show what they could do. There were only about thirty horses available at that time, and each man grabbed the nearest, some without even the formality of saddling up. There was a long stretch of open ground leading from the camp and about half a mile away there was a clump of trees: the men had to make for these trees, turn round and come back. The adjutant was to give the word 'Go!'. At the signal they started off and such a yelling, howling mob of apparent maniacs it would be hard to meet—one had to remember that they were not long off the Troopship, they were bursting for something to do and this test was just to their liking and they were letting off steam. As they turned at the trees to come back it was evident that the Diggers were making a race of it, with their cobbers at the starting point urging them on and making bets on the winner. Back they tore, heels digging in, the horses' mouths flecked with foam—poor beasts, they had not been ridden like that for months, and as they flashed past the finishing point the Marquis was heard to say 'For God's sake Mummery, take them off or we'll have no horses left!'

Apart from the Australian contingent, 397 men and four officers came out from Britain on a six-month enlistment and together these formed the second regiment. Bardie was ordered to establish headquarters in Johannesburg and to remain there in charge of recruiting; by the end of the war 3,500 men had been recruited. The Scottish Horse were renowned for gallantry and made a considerable contribution to victory.

Kitty composed a pipe tune which became the regimental march of the Scottish Horse, and another dedicated to Bardie, George and Hamish, 'Soldier Brothers Three' though her brother Douglas wrote critically from home that in writing these airs she had not understood the limitations of the piping scale, adding that the Duke agreed with him.

She had spent months travelling round Natal, staying in hotels or with friends. In March 1901 her sister Ferelith came out to join her for a time. Ferelith had been suffering from painful rheumatism in the joints of her legs and had also been depressed about bickering in the family on the matter of Christian Science. A spell in the sunshine and warmth of South Africa was what she needed to restore her health and spirits. Kitty, Ferelith and Hamish—who was convalescing after an illness—stayed with friends and went off on sight-seeing trips into the hills, rode across the infinite, green-brown expanses of the veldt; played tennis; enjoyed themselves; and were joined by Bardie as frequently as possible. By autumn—spring in South Africa—it was time for Ferelith to return home and there was a great deal of pressure from Blair for Kitty to return as well. The Duke wrote persuasively:

> . . . You don't know how I miss you, dear—and this time last year I could hardly bring myself to be civil to you. Familiarity has bred contempt, has not it? . . .

Kitty had no intention of returning, though she was too tactful to say so directly. She replied politely:

> October 27th, Cape Town.
> I should like to come home very much, in some ways, if I could not see Bardie by remaining out here, but I am sure you will admit I have the best of reasons for staying out when I tell you that I heard two day ago from Bardie that he had got a permit for me to be with him at Joburg! I nearly went off my head with joy when I got the news . . . I do feel lucky to have got Lord K's permission. I expect to start up about the end of the week. Having done the journey to Kimberley so easily, I don't feel afraid of this other, though it will be longer; but unless it is very hot it ought to be all right and most intensely interesting. Now when you next write, do tell me that I have been justified in not coming home with Fairy . . .

Getting permission for Kitty to join him in Johannesburg represented something of a triumph for Bardie, but he knew how to handle Kitchener. One or two fellow-officers' wives had already received permission to join their husbands. When Bardie made his request Kitchener simply looked away and grunted. Bardie seized the opportunity and thanked him profusely. Kitty wasted no time and arrived in Johannesburg on her birthday—6 November.

To her parents' consolation Kitty had been able to arrange for a memorial stone to be erected over Nigel's grave at Kimberley before going to Johannesburg. Lady Ramsay wrote long, affectionate letters to her daughter and it gave her pleasure to have clothes made and sent out: usually skirts made of pastel muslin or white piqué, which were easy to wear and suitable for the climate. Once she sent a photograph of everyone: Papa, Dolly, Lily, Ferelith, Imogen, Douglas, but excluding herself, adding 'I don't seem to take a very good photograph these days, so you must just try to remember the original'—an indication, perhaps, that Nigel's death had affected her health as well as her spirit. But at Christmas she wrote to tell Kitty that the family had had a happy day together . . . Papa had been so kind and this year had actually given presents—a 'tip' for the younger ones, a tortoiseshell penknife each for herself, Dolly and Lily. He had also received his own presents graciously—unlike former years, as she reminded Kitty, when they had gone to give their presents to him in a state of trepidation. She added:

Fuller Maitland thinks you could revolutionise the whole status of music in England if you liked. I have no doubt you could, by bringing in a sense of the reality and dignity of it and releasing it from its present hollow society basis. You know what I mean—and don't you laugh, you naughty girl.

(J A Fuller Maitland was a music scholar and performer, music critic of the *Manchester Guardian* and editor of *Music and Musicians*.)

12   Kitty in South Africa

Ferelith also wrote to confide in Kitty about an 'appalling evening' when a hapless Christian Science lecturer and his wife had been invited to dinner. Sir James had enquired why they should decline to drink wine when it was one of nature's abundant gifts and mentioned in the Bible. His guest had murmured uncomfortably that he had not realised that it was mentioned in the Bible. Sir James pounced, reminding him of the Marriage at Cana and of the Last Supper. Mrs Ewing, the lecturer's wife, explained timorously that she and her husband really disapproved of anything that made people befuddled, whereupon Sir James had thundered that he supposed that she was implying that Christ had been befuddled. It had been left to Lady Ramsay to restore polite conversation.

If the earlier period in Africa had been one of personal pleasure, the second half of Kitty's stay was dedicated to helping other people. They had taken a furnished house in Johannesburg and Bardie was able to spend time there, though he was frequently absent on duty. It also became a haven for the other members of the family: George and Hamish came on several occasions and in March her younger brother Douglas arrived from home to take up a post with a mining company. He arrived on 8 March, while Kitty was in the midst of preparing for a great concert for convalescent soldiers to be held on 15 March.

On the morning of the concert Kitty went to supervise the arrangements for flowers, flags and chairs. The Governor of Cape Colony, High Commissioner for Southern Africa, Lord Milner, attended and a Guard of Honour was provided for him. Kitty had found talented performers from both civilian and military personnel and she took part herself, playing a number of Schumann pieces. To her relief and satisfaction everyone seemed to enjoy it.

The Scottish Horse wounded were sent to hospitals in Johannesburg and Bardie put Kitty in charge of their comfort. It was her first experience of suffering and affliction. Many men had been so severely wounded that they wished they had been killed: some had lost legs, arms, eyes, others had desperate internal injuries. She was able to help them personally, visiting them, talking to them, writing home for them and trying to generate an optimistic attitude among men who no longer had cause for optimism. In addition, the entertainments and concerts which she was able to arrange were genuinely appreciated. Trooper John McCaw recalled:

> A couple of nights before we were due to strike camp an open-air concert was arranged, and the Marquis provided a piano for the occasion. A huge bonfire was lit in the centre of the camp, and all the Scottish Horse (2nd Australian contingent) was there, officers included. The Marchioness was there also and she, by request, played something for us. The candles in their

holders were not shedding a very clear light on the music, so I, sitting on a saddle quite near the piano, was called upon by our sergeant to act as candlebearer for her Ladyship, a thing I flatter myself I did very efficiently. She found, on striking the keys, that her bangles interfered with her playing, so she took them off and laid them on the piano, but they jangled a bit here, so she asked me very nicely to keep them for her. When she had played her selection, and an encore, she went back to her seat by the Marquis, forgetting her bangles, and I had just screwed up my courage to the point of stepping forward to the group when a very officious young officer strode forward and said 'Give them to me'. But the Marquis, who had noticed this bit of by-play, quietly remarked 'The soldier who took care of them may return them', which I did and received her very gracious thanks.

On 20 March Hamish arrived from Charlestown, where he had been in hospital. On the 22nd Douglas arrived from the mine suffering from an attack of dysentery and asked to spend a day or two. He then became so ill with rheumatic fever that he remained with her until mid June, his life in danger: Kitty arranged to have a nurse living in. In mid April George arrived in great pain from an eye ulcer and remained with her for a week or two. Her house had become a home and refuge for them all. She herself was also unwell from time to time and suffered a recurrence of the old problem of sore throats and headaches.

By May 1902 the long war seemed to be coming to an end and there was talk of peace at last. A Treaty was signed in Pretoria on 31 May. Its terms included the annexation by Britain of the Boer Republics and the surrender of all Boers in arms. Those swearing allegiance to the King (Queen Victoria had died in January 1901) were to be allowed to go free. Britain undertook to grant a civil administration. The Afrikaans language was to be permitted in schools and courts. £3 million was to be given to the Boers in compensation for the destruction of their homes and farms. During the course of the war 6,000 British and colonials were killed; 22,000 were wounded; 16,000 died from disease. It had cost Britain £220 million. On the Boer side over 7,000 men were killed and perhaps as many as 25,000 civilians died. No-one has established the number of black Africans killed, though historians estimate that it was probably more than 15,000.

A Service of Thanksgiving was arranged in Pretoria on 8 June. Kitty had been ill, but despite doctor's orders to remain in bed she insisted on attending with Bardie. This entailed driving by carriage from Johannesburg, starting at 5 a.m. On the way they saw Boers riding in to surrender. Kitty found the sight very impressive. During the service, which was held in the Market Square, she found herself vividly recalling the tragic losses of the war. Kipling's 'Recessional' was sung—the plea written at the time of the Diamond Jubilee for magnanimity in victory 'lest we forget' and a reminder of the ephemeral nature of existence. Afterwards they lunched with Kitchener in the room in which the peace treaty had been signed. Kitty's view of Kitchener was mixed: she was thankful that he had been able to bring the war to an end, but she found his formidable personality extremely daunting.

A month later everyone, officers, men, and civilians, had begun to pack up and set off homewards—'the Captains and the Kings depart.' Kitty and Hamish were to leave from Cape Town on 16 July, Bardie was to sail with part of his regiment on 2 August and George would sail shortly afterwards with the Gordons. At the very moment when Kitty and Hamish were setting off for Cape Town came news that Louisa had been taken seriously ill in Italy. News of her death followed soon afterwards. Her funeral took place on 17 July at Blair. She had requested that she should not be buried in the old family vault at Old Blair— understandably, for it is a dismal, dank spot. A new little family graveyard was opened nearby and has been used for family burials ever since.

Kitty and Hamish arrived in England on 2 August. London was in a fever of excitment, welcoming home its victorious army and celebrating the coronation. Kitty waited in London to see the procession: '. . .Went with the Fitzgeralds to Guard Room at Horse Guard. Cold day but fine; saw the procession very well. The Queen looked lovely but very pale . . .'

And so, after a long absence, home to Blair. During the years in South Africa Kitty had matured. She had learnt to be independent, to organise, to take responsibility for herself and for others. There had been nothing patronising in her attitude to those in pain or despair: she had seen war at first hand and had learnt to loathe it. Those memories and that loathing influenced her outlook for the remainder of her life. Many years later she would be accused of warmongering. Her accusers misunderstood: it was her hatred of war which led her to seek to prevent its recurrence at all costs.

Chapter 5

The Inheritance, 1902 and after

Within a few days of returning home to Blair, Kitty went south to Edinburgh, having arranged an appointment with Sir Halliday Croom, one of Scotland's leading physicians. Although generally fit apart from the recurrent problem with her throat, she had been suffering from acute pelvic pain. The lack of any sign of an heir was also a disappointment. She was determined to have matters attended to before Bardie's return.

Sir Halliday diagnosed internal inflammation and gave her three alternatives: to lie up at Blair for three months, with a nurse, remaining apart from Bardie during that time; to go to Woodhall Spa for a month; or to take the waters and treatment baths at Ems, in Germany, for a month. Kitty wrote to Bardie that she hated leaving him so soon, but felt strongly that she should go to Ems, where few British people went, as she could go incognito. At Woodhall Spa there would certainly be people who knew her and she dreaded gossip. She felt that lying up at Blair would also cause gossip, especially as she was looking so well and though she could pretend to sprain her knee she thought it would be trying for them both in more ways than one.

The season at Ems ended in October, so there was no time to lose and arrangements were made immediately. She stayed on in Scotland long enough to watch Bardie marching into Edinburgh at the head of the Scottish Horse, and to return with him to Blair briefly.

Together with the Duke, they went down to Dunkeld to visit the new house, now completed and ready for occupation. They had been consulted about colour schemes for their own rooms and were very pleased with the result. The new house was simple, well-designed and much more comfortable than Blair Castle, which at that time was still cold and draughty with inadequate plumbing. Dunkeld House was set in quiet, peaceful grounds overlooking the River Tay—at this point a wide, gently gliding sweep of water. A sum of £6,000 had been set aside for landscaping and Bardie was anxious to prevent the Duke from planting too many forest trees in the grounds. It was a pleasant prospect that before long it might be their home.

Kitty set off for Ems almost at once. Leaving home so soon after her return was a wrench, but Sir Halliday had been encouraging and confident that the treatments she would receive would clear up all the problems. On her return he would perform a small operation and he predicted the safe arrival of a family very shortly thereafter. Kitty wrote to Bardie as she left London for Germany '. . . any sacrfice is worth it, dearest!'

She found the regime of baths and treatments extremely exhausting, but typically did not waste her time and began having German lessons in the mornings. Whenever possible she went off for long walks in the hills and woods and in the evenings she attended concerts. Had it not been for the treatments and the separation from Bardie, the whole visit would have been very enjoyable. Bardie remained at Blair with his father and sister, but was invited for a short stay as a guest at Balmoral, where he received his MVO from the King for his efforts in South Africa.

At the end of the month Kitty returned to London. Bardie had not travelled down to meet her, but there were a number of letters waiting for her, one of which was from him. Its contents (undisclosed) caused her considerable anguish. She tore it up and recorded her distress in her diary. Two hours later, however, an apologetic telegram arrived and she made up her mind to forget all about it: fortunately Kitty had a remarkably forgiving nature.

Having travelled to Edinburgh, Kitty entered a nursing home for the small gynaecological operation recommended by Sir Halliday Croom. Bardie came to visit her a day or two later and Sir Halliday took the opportunity of reassuring them both that in his view there was no reason why they should not become parents shortly—certainly Kitty was well able to have a family.

Kitty recuperated at North Berwick, where Lady Ramsay was staying: its dry, bracing climate was recommended for those in poor health. Kitty had been appalled to see how her mother had changed in the two years of their separation. Although Lady Ramsay was only fifty, she suddenly seemed old, depressed, frail and almost unable to walk. Bardie came down to see them and Kitty begged him to persuade her to consult a doctor. Charlotte would not be moved; her faith in Christian Science remained absolute until her death the following year.

The Duke had not made Dunkeld House available to them and, as they soon discovered, had no intention of doing so. Kitty and Bardie returned to their old room—No 7 on the Long Corridor at Blair Castle, where the Duke and Helen were living. Helen had taken her mother's place, and was now in charge of the household, acting as her father's hostess, though she occasionally went abroad. This led, on one occasion, to the Duke's anger on discovering that neither she nor Kitty would be at the Castle during a visit which Miss Elspeth Campbell was about to make. Kitty

13   Blair Castle

wrote to him diplomatically, apologising for her absence, but adding, either innocently or tongue in cheek, that she was sure he need not worry, as Miss Campbell was a woman of the world who would not be unduly distressed to find that she had no chaperone on this occasion.

As it became clear that the Duke would never permit them to have a home of their own—even the suggestion of a private sitting room of their own was refused—Kitty was denied the pleasures of home-making. Though outwardly cheerful, she grieved over her childlessness and the sense of failure remained with her always. It also affected the development of her character. A child of her own would have had the effect of making her more outgoing and demonstrative. She loved children always, but she remained emotionally unresponsive. She could never pick up a niece to hug or embrace her, though she would hold out her hand to help them cross a burn or climb a fence and was always delighted to play the piano for dancing or games. Out of shyness and because she could not think of anything else to say, she would enquire of her nieces or nephews rather sternly 'And what are you reading now? What are you studying?'—and no-one was more amused than herself when a small great-nephew politely replied and then asked cheerfully 'And now, Aunt Kitty, what are *you* reading?'

Bardie also loved children and was much more at ease with them. He knew instinctively what would amuse and interest them, and as Kitty's nieces grew up and came to stay at Blair from time to time he delighted in their company, taking them with him about the estate and involving them in all that he was doing. He is remembered by all of them with warm and loyal affection.

But the arrival of nieces and nephews was in any case far into the future. Meantime Kitty and Bardie gradually lost hope of having a family of their own. The lack of children may not have been due to Kitty herself. Whatever the reason, it was an undoubted tragedy and both Kitty and Bardie shared equally in the sorrow.

From the outset Kitty had been denied the security of a normal marriage with a home of her own. Now losing hope of a family, she became increasingly aware that Bardie sought other consolations. He could always be certain of her constancy: Kitty regarded marriage as an exclusive contract. Fidelity on Bardie's part was probably never intended. His position in life, his appearance, humour and charm, made him an easy target for other women. Infidelity became a recurrent habit. In this, of course, he was far from unusual. Such behaviour was condoned within the legal system and approved of by society: a husband could divorce his wife on the grounds of infidelity alone, whereas a wife had to prove cruelty or desertion in addition to adultery.

Of Bardie's fondness for Kitty, in spite of his other relationships, there can be no doubt. His infidelities were no doubt, to him, entirely trivial and unimportant, though two at least apparently resulted in the accidental arrival of a child. Although it may be thought that he had a strange way of demonstrating it, Kitty was fundamental to his existence. Indeed it is probably true, as he had guessed during their courtship, that he depended on Kitty very much more than she depended on him. His nieces have commented: 'He was charming, and he loved pretty things, pretty objects, pretty women. But our aunt and uncle never allowed it to make any difference to them and they remained devoted to each other throughout their lives.'

Kitty adored Bardie and she could forgive him anything. Though his affairs must have been hurtful she apparently resigned herself to the inevitable. When a relative complained of some misdemeanour Kitty would smile indulgently and reply 'But you know, dear child, men are always difficult!' This did not mean that she condoned his behaviour, merely that she overlooked it. Kitty maintained her own principles, kept her own counsel and sheered away from discussing the peccadilloes of friends and acquaintances.

Louisa, Kitty and to some extent Charlotte each sought—and found—an escape route from an unsatisfactory aspect of marriage. Louisa found compensation in worldly pursuits and travel abroad. Charlotte escaped spiritually, into commitment to Christian Science and to the obligations and self-discipline which her faith required. Kitty's escape route was intellectual. For her, Bardie's infidelities had the paradoxical effect of self-liberation. Consciously or subconsciously, she became more and more absorbed in other matters—serious, weighty matters to which she brought the triple gifts of a first-class brain, boundless energy and abiding conscientiousness. As the years went by Bardie might complain of her long absences and of her absorption in other matters. She would reply politely and with concern, but perhaps not without a hint of irony 'Yes, dearie, I am so sorry not to be with you just now, but do remember it was you who first taught me about duty in the early days of our marriage.'

Thirty years later, writing on marriage in her book *Women and Politics* Kitty stated her view. She noted that Bertrand Russell and his wife (by then the Earl and Countess Russell) and others had called for a change in the marriage law because 'marriage is proving a failure in so large a proportion of cases'. They had advocated 'companionate' marriage for those not intending to have children and they wanted this form of marriage to be dissoluble by mutual consent. Lady Russell wanted any marriage which did not result in children to be dissoluble at the wish of either party, while 'Lord Russell tells us that not many people marrying in modern times are happy after the first few years'.

With all these propositions Kitty disagreed. Her impressions of marriage, she wrote, were quite different. Lifelong marriage ought not to depend on whether or not there were children.

> What sort of creed is this to offer to women in the 20th century? To the sorrow of childlessness is to be added the terror of divorce, and of divorce in a new guise. For whereas under the present law divorce may often appear to a woman as a release from a husband whose infidelity has destroyed his relations with her, divorce as proposed by Lord and Lady Russell may well be the casting off by a husband who desires children of a wife who loves him and who has yearned to be a mother, or even of a wife whose child has died and from whom no more children can be expected. Or a wife might be cast off when the lack of children was due to the husband.
>
> To allow such a proposal to become law would be to shatter the very foundations on which has been built the improved status which the Christian era has brought to women that marriage should be not only a physical union but a union of mind and character; best of all, a partnership in service.
>
> In some cases perhaps, in which the marriage has been childless, it has been an even more complete spiritual union in that husband and wife have been obliged to depend on themselves alone to perfect their partnership. Sorrow can unite as well as joy.

We may draw our own conclusions from this vigorous, if poignant, commentary. Kitty remained devoted to Bardie and wholly committed to her marriage.

For Atholl, the estate and the inheritance, the significance of Kitty's and Bardie's failure to produce children was that after the death of the youngest of John and Louisa's sons the Dukedom would pass from the Highland tradition. The heir would be a descendant of the fourth Duke of Atholl, Sir Evelyn Murray, an eminent civil servant who had spent most of his life in England. It would later pass to his son, Anthony.

The family name of the Dukes of Atholl was Stewart-Murray. The Stewarts of Atholl, though originally of Norman stock, were directly descended from the Highland, Gaelic-speaking tradition of Scotland. The Murrays were a Lowland family, descended from Sir Malcolm de Marovia, Sheriff of Perthshire, who died in 1289. Bardie had inherited a strong sense of pride and kinship with his people and he was to state his position with regard to the estate in later life:

> I look upon a landlord as a life trustee for the benefit of the estate and not as a proprietor for his own benefit. It will be an evil day when the hereditary landlord is elbowed out to make room for millionaires who buy the property for the sake of two months' sport during the year and leave it for ten months to the management of Edinburgh lawyers.

Kitty quickly became absorbed into his way of life. She gave herself no airs and was warmly welcomed by the people of Atholl. Bardie, like his father, knew everyone on the estate: having grown up among them, he knew their homes, their children and their problems and he had an easy relationship with them. Kitty, more diffident and shy, was perhaps viewed as slightly staid and solemn, but she became very well liked.

The Atholls had their own musical tradition: like almost everyone else in Atholl at the time, they all, as a family, spoke Gaelic fluently and with enjoyment—it had been Bardie's first language. Highland music played a great part in their lives. Dertha's collection of Gaelic airs and songs is held by the Sandeman Library in Perth. Evelyn and Hamish both made a profound study of Gaelic poetry and the music of Gaeldom. Evelyn's collection, amassed and collated before her banishment abroad, is held by the School of Scottish Studies. But none of them had any great love or understanding of classical music and there was no opportunity and no encouragement for the single-minded devotion which Kitty longed to give to it.

Bardie, who was genuinely proud of her, would often invite her to play to guests after dinner and she would reply 'Yes, Bardie, of course—but not if you are going to indulge in noisy card games!' He would sit dutifully for a time, but soon he would be whispering to the younger guests that they might move away and have a little game, very quietly. As the excitement increased few would notice that Kitty had stopped playing. Her gift would have developed had it met with encouragement, enthusiasm, response; but within the family only Lady Ramsay had provided that inspiration. Perhaps too there was now a lack of determination and initiative on the part of Kitty herself. She no longer sought to further her professionalism, though she would ensure by constant practice that her proficiency as an exponent was maintained throughout her life. Whatever else was happening, she made sure that she managed to practise for an hour or two each day and would use the time while her maid was brushing her hair in the morning and at night playing on a small silent keyboard to keep her fingers supple.

Kitty's temperament would not permit her to vegetate or to seek enjoyment from self-indulgent pleasures. This may be viewed as revealing a priggish side to her nature, but in reality it was due to an inner dynamism and asceticism from which she could find no escape. Lacking domestic fulfilment and deprived of the chance of developing her artistic capability, it is not surprising, given her energy and intellect, that before long she looked for other outlets. Her political career, however, was still many years ahead.

Chapter 6

Home Life, Landowning and Politics, 1902–14

Kitty and Bardie had returned to Scotland in 1902 with the intention of settling down and helping the Duke with the running of the estate. Bardie had been offered, and had refused, the Governorship of Matabeleland. Although Bardie was a pioneer by instinct, he and Kitty now preferred life in Perthshire to the status of governor in a relatively unknown part of Southern Africa. He had also retired from the regular army, though he remained in command of the Scottish Horse. Their hope had been to live in a house of their own, to begin a family and to gradually take over the management of the estate, allowing the old Duke to retire as time went on; and as Charlotte had pointed out, Fuller Maitland's hope was that Kitty would revolutionise attitudes to music.

None of these hopes was to be fulfilled. The Duke refused to allow them to live in one of his many properties, though there were many suitable possibilities, not least the lovely Dunkeld House. He may have had a number of reasons for rejecting their request. Finance was probably at the heart of it. A second family establishment would certainly be an additional drain on the Atholl purse and it was certain that he needed the income from letting as many of his properties as possible in order to service his enormous debts. Perhaps too there was an element of resentment towards his eldest son, whom he mistakenly believed to be preparing to step into his shoes somewhat prematurely. He may have convinced himself that given encouragement Bardie would, from his own quarters on the estate, begin to usurp his own position: better to have him close at hand, to keep an eye on his activities. These considerations may have been combined with a more personal, undisclosed motive—loneliness. His daughter Helen, whose stewardship of arrangements at the Castle could not be faulted, was not a particularly lively companion. In spite of his earlier resentment, he had grown very fond of Kitty and, although he would never have admitted it, he found the company of his son and daughter-in-law congenial.

As to running the estate, the Duke was adamant: while he was able to do so himself he saw no reason for Bardie to interfere. His agent and secretary were assistants enough. As it happened, his agent was not trained in management or in factoring, and it was evident to Bardie and his brothers that the secretary, Mackay, was not a man to be trusted. Bardie was convinced that if he could take over the management of the estate he would be able to save money and recoup losses. It is difficult to know what can have given him that impression: Bardie was as hopeless with money as his father and the fathers that begat them. The Atholls had invented deficit financing generations before the idea occurred to Keynes.

Had she been allowed to, Kitty could have managed the estate's finances better than anyone. Whereas Bardie was prodigal with money, Kitty was inclined towards frugality. Throughout her life with Bardie her constant plea would be 'Oh Bards dearest, we mustn't spend so much!' But Bardie had been surrounded by grandeur from infancy and he found economy irksome. One of his earliest extravagances on their return in 1903 was an Arrol Johnston motor car. Robertson, their driver, had apparently had too short a period of training, which was provided free for one week with the purchase of the car. Shortly after its arrival the limousine met its end in a ditch, though Robertson survived unscathed.

As Kitty was denied the pleasure of a home, she was insulated from the running of an establishment. She was not a practical person, ate little and cared nothing about food. Her lack of culinary knowledge quickly became a family joke. On the other hand Bardie was rather a good cook: a healthy interest in the subject, and his time in the army, had made him adept at improvising dishes which were simple but delicious. Occasionally they would go up to one of the remote shooting lodges in the hills, where Bardie would cook. Hunter's Stew was one of his own inventions. He later published a book of recipes from the Castle.

As to music, it would have been natural if at this time Kitty had begun serious composition. It would have been a fulfilling way of spending some of her time each day. Possibly, however, she felt that the conditions for creative work did not exist. She was inwardly miserable over her childlessness and deeply concerned about her mother's health. She had felt private, sheltered and happy in her hideaway in the trees at Bamff, but perhaps she felt insecure and conscious of a lack of privacy in her new environment at Blair, surrounded by servants and members of the family—though had she been determined she could have arranged to be transported to peace and solitude at nearby Marble Lodge in Glen Tilt from time to time. Abandoning composition was a tragic error.

Surprisingly, Kitty was persuaded instead to take on the task of becoming editorial director of a Muster Roll of Perthshire: a book which would list every Perthshire man who had served in the South African

War, together with a photograph and biographical details, which would be presented in bound volumes. The work would be time-consuming and demanding.

The idea of the Muster Roll of Perthshire had arisen from the publication during the war of a Muster Roll of Angus. The promoters of that book had begun on a similar work for Perthshire towards the end of the war, but it had been decided to await the return of the officers and men before tackling it properly. Kitty, having been approached to co-ordinate the work, was initially disconcerted to be asked, but on reflection it seemed to her a worthwhile return for all that she had seen of the suffering of many who had volunteered for service. She was encouraged to undertake the work by her own father and by the old Duke, who were both particularly interested in the project. Perhaps neither of them guessed how completely Kitty would immerse herself in the work and what demands she would impose upon herself. Lady Ramsay, however, felt that it was too great a commitment. She understood her daughter's character and constitution better than anyone else did, and she wished profoundly that Kitty could relax, enjoy herself, and not tire herself out over the 'wretched Roll'.

Sir Halliday Croom also had his doubts. He was still hoping that Kitty would have a child. 'Is the Muster Roll more important than an heir?' he enquired, expressing the opinion that if Kitty wished to have a child she must concentrate on the matter. Kitty politely made up her own mind— as she always did—feeling that she could cope with both if she were fortunate enough. She did, however, act on Sir Halliday's advice to the extent of spending a month apart from Bardie. She took the opportunity of spending a few weeks with her mother in Hornsea and was, in retrospect, profoundly thankful that she had been able to do so, for these were almost the last weeks of Charlotte's life.

Kitty returned to work on the Muster Roll with renewed dedication, almost to the exclusion of other matters. This was one of her particular characteristics: whatever the current cause or campaign, it tended to dominate and monopolise her life and thoughts. She worried away at a topic with the tenacity of a bulldog.

When the research was under way it was suggested that the Roll should include the names of the Perthshire men who had served in the Sudan and in the campaigns on the Indian Frontier during the previous ten years. This led to further enthusiastic delving into the archives and Kitty and her team of assistants soon discovered that such a quantity of important historical detail was being amassed that, in addition to the Muster Roll, material existed for a Military History of Perthshire, dating from the period since the inauguration of the Standing Army in the year 1660.

The compilation of the two volumes involved Kitty in four solid years of work. Many historians, including Sir James, supplied sections on particular battles, military men or forces; but a great number of the chapters were researched and written by the editor herself. Among Kitty's own contributions—forty-four in all—were definitive chapters on the battles of Killiecrankie and Sheriffmuir, with detailed maps of the engagements. It was no mean achievement for a young woman who had had no formal instruction in historical research. The two volumes were published in 1908.

Meantime life at Blair proceeded pleasantly enough. Despite their lack of a home, despite her over-concentration on work on the book, despite Bardie's restricted role with regard to the estate, above all despite difficulties with the Duke—all or any of which might have caused disharmony—Kitty and Bardie enjoyed their life together. If Bardie strayed, Kitty was absorbed; he no doubt found her detachment convenient at times, but he had no wish to be apart from her for long, for he found her presence increasingly necessary to his existence.

In the summer of 1909 he went to Canada, taking his young sister-in-law Imogen with him, as she wanted to go to Boston, headquarters of the Christian Science movement. On his arrival he immediately began to pine for Kitty and greatly regretted that she had not come too, as he knew at once how much she would have loved the country. During his travels he went to Toronto, where Douglas and his wife Hope were living. Bardie reported that he feared that Douglas was not the sort to get on in 'the Colonies'. '. . . he hates the Canadians so and has taught Hope to be rather exclusive also.' Bardie and Kitty were not class-conscious and it pained him to find his brother-in-law being so stand-offish. He told Kitty that they were 'too stuck up to mingle' and that he found the upper classes 'vile and stuck up' . . . 'I have several pals . . . the nicest people are the old Canadians. I found an old Strathardle man living about ten doors from here and Douglas had not discovered him. There's a Blair man, McPherson, working as a gardener and I investigate him tomorrow. Today I go to lunch with a Stornoway man.'

On his return from Canada Bardie thought of an interesting way of restoring the family fortunes and at the same time helping to increase the nation's defences.

John William Dunne, a rather impractical aircraft designer—more of an enthusiastic amateur than scientist or engineer—had been making paper models of aeroplanes since 1900. He had somehow managed to get himself attached to Farnborough, where early experiments in aviation were taking place, and in 1904 had designed an aeroplane which was inspired by the winged seed of the zamonia plant, with swept back wings and no tail.

Dunne's rivals were the Wright brothers, of whose designs he was inclined to be critical. He had shown his own design to the War Office, but General Nicholson and Lord Haldane came to the conclusion that it would never fly. The whole concept of flight was novel at that time and the construction of wood, steel tubes and linen covering must have seemed slightly comical. However work on a Dunne glider and the Dunne aeroplane began at Farnborough and continued for a time. By 1907, however, it was decided to move the planes to a location where they could be tried out secretly. A friend from Boer War days, now one of the senior engineers at Farnborough, approached Bardie to enquire whether a location in one of the glens at Blair might be used. The Duke and Bardie willingly agreed, construction sheds were built on a remote plateau several miles up on the south side of Glen Tilt and the planes were dismantled, transported and re-assembled by a team from Farnborough. Elaborate precautions were set up to prevent press-men from getting wind of the project.

Bardie was particularly interested in the work and on one occasion allowed himself to be tied into one of the gliders, ready to pilot it on a trial flight. Perhaps fortunately, since he had no previous experience, the glider was blown over before the flight could take place. Less fortunately, the Dunne D3 powered plane was wrecked in the hills on a trial flight during the late summer of 1907, though the pilot was unhurt. In 1908 the War Office decided that a more scientific approach to aviation should be adopted and, although the Navy was still interested, funding was withdrawn.

Bardie and his friend Lord Fitzwilliam, however, could imagine a future war in which air power would be extremely important. Now, in 1909, together with the Duke of Westminster and Lord Rothschild, they agreed to continue the work, and the four formed a syndicate to finance the building of the Dunne D4. Camps and open-sided construction sheds were set up and for the next few years the aeroplane was developed in the wilds of Glen Tilt during the summer months: work inevitably came to a halt with the approach of winter each October. The cost to the partners in the enterprise was considerable.

The prototype was eventually constructed by Short Brothers and by 1913 the machine was ready. Bardie approached the War Office. He explained that the plane was extraordinarily stable in the air, with never an accident, even when novices were flying it, adding that it was strongly constructed and appeared to stand wind better than any other machine. He suggested that it might be useful for hydroplane work, more especially as there was no tail to break. Eventually two planes were ordered by the War Office but were sold—one to France, the other to the United States—and were used with success during the war, though both were eventually lost. Members of the syndicate failed to recoup their losses. (Dunne went on to write a number of unusual books, most notably *An Experiment with Time*, published in 1927.)

While Kitty was busy working on the Military History, Bardie had turned to politics. In 1905 the Unionist (Conservative) Association of the neighbouring constituency of East Perthshire was looking for a candidate. Bardie, at something of a loose end, offered his services and was accepted. When the election came in 1906 Kitty helped him with the canvassing and found to her surprise that she enjoyed it all very much. Having lost to the Liberal in East Perthshire, Bardie was adopted as candidate for his own constituency of West Perthshire in 1907. Kitty was invited to become President of West Perthshire Women's Unionist Association. Bardie disliked the patronising Primrose League organisation, of which both his father and Louisa had been supporters. Kitty refrained from joining for the same reason. The local chairman was the Countess of Breadalbane, and Bardie raised no objection to his sister Helen becoming vice-chairman, remarking grudgingly that it would probably do his own campaign no harm.

In 1910 Kitty took a major part in Bardie's election campaign, not only canvassing for him but also appearing on platforms as the main speaker at public meetings when he was elsewhere in the constituency. Bardie had an easy manner and a camaraderie which quickly captivated an audience. Kitty was earnest and conscientious, inclined perhaps to lecture rather than amuse; she tried to inform, he to disarm. She made a personal impact. Dr Lamont, the minister at Blair Atholl, wrote to congratulate her and say that her speech in Pitlochry had been one of the best political speeches from any party since the campaign began. Bardie won the seat. In many ways relieved to have the opportunity of escaping from the Duke, they moved to the Atholl town house at Eaton Place in London.

A Liberal administration was in power: had been since 1905 and would continue until 1915, when a wartime coalition was formed. The physical condition of a large section of the population was poor, especially in the overcrowded towns and cities, where one person in three lived in squalid conditions far below the poverty line. By contrast, life in the homes of the wealthy and of the aristocracy was lavish. Large, hedonistic country house parties took place at which patrician politicians took the opportunity to discuss the affairs of the nation; aristocrats and would-be-aristocrats mingled with women guests who vied with each other for the attention of rich, powerful men. Kitty and Bardie preferred to attend discreet smaller gatherings where there was a genuine interest in music, theatre or art, though they spent a weekend as guests of King Edward and Queen Alexandra at Sandringham, where Kitty—in an uncharacteristic departure—entertained the King by singing comic songs after dinner.

Although they had held a certain regard for King Edward, both Kitty and Bardie felt more in sympathy with King George and Queen Mary when they came to the throne in 1910. The King and Bardie held each other in mutual respect, as old friends. During the 1912 Dock Strike King George was deeply moved by the distress and suffering it was bringing to the families involved and wrote to Bardie asking him to intervene in the House—an unusual step for a monarch to take. Bardie was glad to do so and appealed for an end to the strike, quoting cases of families of ten living on 2*d.* a day. His intervention was effective and he spoke at a meeting during which the strike was declared at an end. Afterwards he demonstrated his sympathy by marching down to the docks with the lightermen.

Sympathy with striking dockers was one thing, but one of the issues of the day with which neither the King nor Bardie sympathised was that of women's franchise. The suffragette campaign was creating enormous publicity and considerable annoyance. Whilst a small minority of men nobly supported the feminists, many more were outraged by what they perceived to be their presumptuous and outrageous behaviour.

Women could not vote, but they could be very useful, particularly at election times. Their role was, however, purely supportive. It was generally accepted that women should confine themselves to a subordinate position in society, with limited legal rights. In the upper and middle classes their area of activity was social, domestic, maternal. Women of the lower classes were often required in addition, to work as drudges to help to provide for the household, since their husbands were frequently unemployed. For the most part women accepted their place, but quite early in the Victorian period there had been a women's movement aimed at improving women's rights. In Scotland there was an Independent Women's Suffrage Movement dating back to 1834 and from the mid nineteenth century onwards there had been considerable feminist activity. In the early twentieth century Mrs Emmeline Pankhurst founded her Suffragette Movement and the Women's Social and Political Union (the WSPU).

It is one of the surprising and disappointing aspects of Kitty's character that, having had the advantage of a remarkably enlightened and liberal education, she should not have sympathised and identified with the aims of the suffragettes. The movement sprang largely from the middle classes, but women of all classes were active in it, including some well-known aristocrats. Kitty's close friend Lady Betty Balfour and her sister-in-law Lady Frances Balfour, daughter of the Duke of Argyll, were both strong supporters of the suffragists.

Possibly Kitty withheld her support out of loyalty to Bardie; perhaps the militant aspect of the campaign caused her to stand aside, believing militant feminists to be gallant but misguided in their approach. She believed in reasoned argument and it would have been out of character for her to take part in such activities as raiding the Dundee Stock Exchange, dressing up as Jeanie Deans during a Princess Street protest in Edinburgh, subjecting Winston Churchill to abuse during a by-election in 1908 or chaining herself to a railing or lamp-post. Kitty was too law-abiding and perhaps too prim for such ebullient activities. But the justice of the cause was self evident and her intellectual and moral support for it would have had a significant impact in Scotland.

It was apparently Kitty's opinion that women needed to gain some first-hand experience of local government before being thrown into the complications of parliamentary procedures. Certainly women had been so oppressed over the centuries that their entire outlook would have to change before they were ready to make independent decisions. It was also Kitty's belief that a woman, at the heart of her home and family, with responsibility for the nurturing and upbringing of children, was already in the best position to influence the future.

In 1912, at a time when courageous suffragettes were being brutally forcefed in prison, Kitty spoke at a large meeting in Glasgow with Lord Curzon, an old friend of her mother's, against the concept of votes for women. She was very apprehensive and Bardie wrote encouragingly that everyone was looking forward to her address, advising her to 'sing her speech out slowly' and not to be nervous. He enclosed some suffragette pamphlets for her information, though he remarked that he had had to lock one of them away as it was so offensive and 'must have been written by a prurient-minded beast'. (The WSPU was carrying out a 'shocking' campaign over the number of unfortunate young girls having illegitimate babies of whom male relatives were the fathers, the widespread trafficking in small children for male gratification, and pointing to the depravity of men who visited brothels, with the consequent transference of disease to their innocent wives.)

The pre-war suffragette movement was not successful except insofar as it was able to arouse women's consciousness. Women had to wait until they had, as a result of their contribution towards the war effort in factories, on the land, in the women's services, proved their right to vote. Even in 1918, the vote was restricted to women over thirty, although men of nineteen who had served in the war were permitted to vote.

In 1924 Kitty would vote against the proposal to reduce the age of female suffrage to twenty-one, on the grounds of particular circumstances at the time:

It is said that this proposed extension of the franchise will mean an addition to the electorate of 3,500,000 women, or as some say 5,000,000 women. Whichever be the correct figure, no one will dispute that the proposal means that women will be in the majority on the Parliamentary register. When I reach that point I cannot forget that the preponderance, whatever the exact figure may be, will have been largely due to, or at least greatly increased by, the fact that we lost 740,000 precious lives of men in the Great War and that that war is still taking its toll of ex-servicemen. Therefore I cannot help saying that I feel that to propose a great extension of this kind looks like taking advantage of the heroic sacrifices of those men.

She also pointed to the small number of women who were willing to serve on public local bodies, where their contribution would be invaluable and was indeed necessary. 'No public body can efficiently administer poor law, education, public health or maternity and child welfare without the assistance of women. These local public bodies are not receiving the benefit of all the special service which women can render and I feel sad to think that we have not yet entered more into our kingdom.'

As late as the mid 1930s Kitty would outrage feminists by speaking against equal pay in the Civil Service on the grounds that a man supporting a wife and family had greater financial need than an unmarried woman. Although never a feminist, she became a strong supporter of women's rights, on one occasion delaying the Princess Royal for half an hour over breakfast while she delivered a lecture on the subject. She was strongly in favour of having women ministers in the Church of Scotland.

The move to London had effectively separated the warring Duke and his eldest son, but Kitty and Bardie returned to Blair frequently and sporadic hostilities resumed. Bardie still felt exasperated by his lack of influence at Blair. As early as 1905 he had written to his father:

. . . to make an honest and straightforward appeal to you to consider well before you decide not to let the forest. You know I'd be the last person in the world to ask you to curtail any of your pleasures and it is not a pleasant job for me to have to ask you to do it: but we are £2000 wrong this year and shall be the same next year and either we must economize or find new sources of income. It is no good making small economies and nothing short of letting the grouse ground on the West Hough or the forest will help—if things go on as they are it will mean either bankruptcy or 'a trust', not in my time, but in yours. I do wish you would tell me things quite straight, because I honestly think I have not been fairly dealt with, inasmuch as you told me and Lowe the other day that things would be let, but as you have systematically avoided the subject ever since and not talked it over with me,

I had every reason to believe that you were going back on what you arranged. Let's have it out and see what we can do. Things are bad and we've just got to face it and we can best do it together.

The Edinburgh lawyers had worked out the savings which would be made on the Duke's death if in the meantime at least the areas on Strathord and the Middle District—areas to the south of the estate—were conveyed to Bardie immediately. They had reckoned that after deducting debts the assessors would value the estate at £500,000 and death duties would amount to £37,500. If, however, these areas were transferred to Bardie in time, they would be valued at £200,000, saving the estate £13,500 in death duties. Bardie put the case to his father, but the old Duke suspected that Bardie's wish to have part of the estate transferred to him was because he either expected or hoped for his early departure. Bardie was indignant:

> The urgency is not because of your probable demise, which I hope is far off, but because the law is to be changed with regard to taxation. I have lived at home to help you, so think I am entitled to speak out. If I am not to be trusted and if you tell people (I know of three cases in which you have) that I do things behind your back . . . it makes it impossible for me to stay at home and I must do what I always wanted to do, start an establishment of my own, which would be fairer. I don't want you to think I am not grateful to you for all you have done but some things cannot be put on a cash basis and we have willingly given up our married life, which ought to have been spent together, to live with you.

While the Tullibardines were in London the Duke became suspicious about household expenditure and—to Kitty's embarrassment, though it was not her concern—had the accounts over a two-year period audited officially. The accountants eventually pronounced that all was in order, but recommended that Bardie's accounts for the households he occupied should be separated from the Duke's for purposes of clarification. A year or two later, however, much to Bardie's satisfaction, the Duke's secretary, Mackay, was dismissed under a cloud.

In 1912 there was trouble over a car. Bardie had bought a Maudslay, a large and expensive limousine. Finding that he could not afford to run it, he hired it out to his father for £70 a year, on the understanding that the Duke would maintain it, but when it was taken to the local garage for servicing and a bill for repairs was received, the Duke refused to meet the cost, as did Bardie. Angry letters were exchanged for some time before the patient garage proprietors in Pitlochry were paid.

In 1913 there was potentially a much more fundamental quarrel, though those concerned emerged with credit. It began when the old

Duke and Helen strongly objected to Bardie's having invited a child named Eileen Macallum to visit Blair. His brother Hamish muttered darkly about 'The Macallum mystery'. It was believed within the family that Eileen, grand-daughter of Lady Macallum of 6 Curzon Street in London, was a 'natural' child of Bardie's. Details as to the whereabouts of the mother of the child are not recorded. The combination of Bardie's love of children and his feeling of obligation towards his child had led to the invitation for Eileen to come to the Castle for a holiday.

Bardie had presumably talked the matter over with Kitty. He overruled the family's objections, pointing out that Helen was depriving Kitty of the opportunity of having Eileen to stay, as having no children of her own she would want to welcome the child. He held his ground and the child arrived. Kitty noted the fact in her diary—the only item recorded for that day—without comment. Files relating to Eileen no longer exist, but it is known that the visit was the first of many over succeeding years.

The Duke and Helen had kindly wished to spare Kitty's feelings. Although he was unable to acknowledge her publicly, Bardie displayed commendable concern for his child and was doubtless a kind, charming and amusing father. Kitty, who had in any case long been accustomed to suppressing her own feelings, was probably as shy and withdrawn with Eileen as she was with her nieces, but her generosity in accepting the existence of the child with understanding and good grace is a testament to her charitable nature.

In later years Bardie and Eileen frequently journeyed abroad on holiday together and after Eileen married—about 1925—Bardie paid her husband an allowance of £150 a year. Eileen's affection for Kitty was demonstrated by the fact that her daughter was named 'Katharine' after her. Eileen's own marriage seems to have failed about the year 1932, but her attachment to her father and to Kitty remained throughout their lives. In later years Kitty became godmother to Katharine's son—Bardie's great-grandson—and remembered him in her will. (Tradition has it that Bardie also had a son by a well-born Scotswoman. It is said that both he and Kitty were deeply saddened by the young man's death in a climbing accident.)

A further dispute between father and son occurred when the old Duke visited his London home in 1914. Kitty and Bardie were in residence and the Duke was affronted to find that Bardie's secretary, who lived there, was permitted to join them for meals. He stormed from the house, telling Kitty before leaving that she must choose between Bardie's typist and her father-in-law. Bardie subsequently exploded in a letter which defined many of the problems of the Tullibardines' lives over the years:

I should never wish to admit anyone to the family circle who had not the manners of a lady or gentleman. That is why when we got Miss McBeth we were particular in that respect. You say 'it is nothing to me what the position of Miss McBeth's mother might be; if your maid confided to you that she was the daughter of an impecunious baronet would you suggest she should feed wth the family?' Well what about Alasdair MacGregor, who married your niece and who is the son of an impecunious baronet. Should I send him to eat by himself if he calls? I know you asked a ruling from Lady Lansdowne on the subject, though what she has to do with it I do not know.

If you honestly reflect, I try to meet your views in every way. You have never allowed me to have a house of my own. In the old days when it meant so much when I was first married I asked for a house over and over again on the estate; but you always refused. Now when I have most of the essentials of a house of my own in London you do not treat it as such. True it is your house, but I run it entirely—you boss it—I never complain. You object often to people coming to lunch though I pay for it—you keep the key of my cellar; you do not give me the key of yours, though my wine is in your cellar and yours is not in mine.

If I give a dinner party you sit at the head of the table, although I would look upon it with pride to be your host. If I had a son nothing would give me greater pleasure than to feel he was entertaining me.

Helen won't come to London or Dunkeld if Kitty is there and if it is our establishment for the same idiotic reason. I may not move a stick of furniture in London without incurring your wrath. To revert to the typist, if you insist when staying with us not to have breakfast with us, well there it is—just tell us when you want it and we'll have ours at another hour. . . .

Bardie himself was apparently unperturbed by the constant arguments, being well used to them from boyhood, and viewed them with equanimity. When the question of positioning the portraits of himself and of Kitty, painted in 1903 on their return from Africa, was raised, he commented to Kitty 'I think they should be hung in the ballroom, near Father and Mother. We four have been such friends that I feel that it is right that our pictures should be hung together.'

But the constant bickering throughout these years did not make life easier for Kitty, who continually found herself trying to act as a calming influence. But family arguments were only part of the picture; they were counterbalanced by compensations. Bardie's affection for Kitty, his high spirits and his fondness for arranging agreeable entertainments ensured that life was made as enjoyable as possible.

One of Kitty's personal delights was her sister Ferelith's marriage to Colonel Paul Clerk-Rattray of Craighall, near Blairgowrie, which meant that she would be a near neighbour in Perthshire. Having her sister and her young family, as they arrived, within easy reach was a constant pleasure. Ferelith had inherited her mother's charm as well as her singing voice and had a cheerful sense of humour. Perhaps Kitty did not altogether lack a sense of humour, because she loved to laugh and had the rare gift of being able to laugh at herself; but though she could sometimes appreciate other people's jokes she could never make one.

14   Kitty and Bardie, January 1914

Laughter was, however, something of an intrusion into the serious business of life. Kitty's sense of duty towards others would always bring her, sooner rather than later, to a committee table or a conference hall in earnest discussion. In 1912 she was invited to be a member of a committee set up by the Scottish Office to investigate the medical and nursing services in the Highlands and Islands of Scotland—the remote areas of Argyll, Inverness-shire, Ross and Cromarty and Sutherland (the traditionally Gaelic-speaking areas) together with Caithness, Orkney and Shetland. These were known as the 'crofting counties', where poverty existed in a very different form from the poverty of the towns and cities.

The population here was small and scattered as a result of earlier evictions and a drift towards centres of population, with fewer than four people to each acre of land. No-one would starve, since there were crops of oats and potatoes, but life was harsh: the wild weather, barren countryside and poor housing meant that there was much deprivation and many personal tragedies. The committee moved round the Highlands making their own observations and taking hearings from local people. Kitty was amazed and appalled by what she saw and heard—amazed by the stark beauty of the scenery and by the charm of the local people, appalled by the conditions under which many of them were living.

Although there was no actual starvation, undernourishment existed widely. The diet of porridge, potatoes, herrings and bread would often be small in quantity and lacked fruit and vegetables to supply vitamins; tea and biscuits were beginning to take the place of the traditional porridge and milk. Housing conditions were often primitive—cottages constructed simply of stones without interior lining, earth floors, thatched roofs, no sanitation and little or no heating or lighting apart from a peat fire and an oil lamp. Roads were poor or non-existent, doctors and nurses were too few, overworked and underpaid.

Kitty wrote to Bardie of the privation, tuberculosis and smallpox which affected whole communities, of the outbreaks of diphtheria which took the lives of so many young children whose physical condition had been too poor to withstand their illness. The committee eventually recommended increased salaries for doctors, more nurses, local dispensaries and more cottage hospitals so that health care was brought closer to the isolated communities. These proposals were welcomed and accepted by the government, but their application was prevented by the outbreak of war.

Chapter 7

War, Gallipoli and Egypt—with the Scottish Horse, 1914–16

Throughout the early years of the twentieth century there had been a growing fear of the inevitability of war. Secret alliances and guarantees between nations had had the effect of splitting Europe into two power groups, one of which (that dominated by Germany) was strongly militaristic. But when Archduke Ferdinand of Austria–Hungary was assassinated in Bosnia at the end of June 1914 few observers recognised that this was the spark which would set Europe ablaze.

The Prime Minister, Asquith, was not greatly perturbed by the news of the assassination. Kitchener was on leave from Egypt, and was among the first to recognise its implications. In July 1914, a month before the outbreak of war, Kitty encountered him at a luncheon party in London. He was in a despondent frame of mind, and asked her where Bardie was. She replied that he was up at Blair, training territorial soldiers. 'Tell him that he ought to be here!' he responded grimly.

On 4 August war was declared. On the following day, Bardie and Kitty motored down to Dunkeld, Headquarters of the Scottish Horse. The Duke lent them Eastwood House, one of his properties by the banks of the River Tay, a mile or two downstream from Dunkeld House. Two days later Bardie was sent for and Kitchener, who had been appointed Secretary of State for War, announced his promotion to Brigadier-General. The Scottish Horse was to be expanded to form a full brigade and recruiting was to begin immediately.

All over the country young men were hurrying to enlist. Although not militaristic, British sentiment was almost innocently, unquestioningly, patriotic and profoundly anti-German. The young, like the old, approved of the war. The men of Perthshire were no exception to the general enthusiasm. Kitty described recruitment for the Scottish Horse as 'extremely popular, not to say phenomenal'. She and her two younger sisters began to hold concerts for the new recruits in Dunkeld each week. Many of the Highland regiments went to France almost at once. Both Bardie's brothers, George and Hamish, were sent out. George was killed in September 1914, uncannily echoing Nigel's death immediately on going to war in 1899. Hamish was wounded and sent home, but recovered and was sent out again. He was later taken prisoner and spent the war in a German prison camp.

The Scottish Horse trained at Scone, near Perth, but were later sent for further training at Kettering, in Northamptonshire, together with units from the Black Watch. Bardie, who never cared to be apart from Kitty for any length of time, arranged for her to come south too. Meantime he had heard from General Sir John Cowan that the Highland regiments in France, all at that time kilted, were suffering from cold knees and he set about designing what he termed a 'hosetop' of knitted wool which would cover the knees and lower thighs. Fifteen thousand were required immediately and he handed over the task of organising this to Kitty. She was quickly able to find a team of willing helpers in Northamptonshire and the hosetops were knitted and despatched to France within three weeks.

With so many of his troops across the Channel in France, Kitchener was acutely aware of the possibility of a German invasion across the North Sea—the Yorkshire or Northumbrian coastlines were, he considered, particularly vulnerable. The Scottish Horse Brigade, now three battalions strong, was sent up to Northumberland to consolidate defences. Bardie arranged for Kitty to come up and stay at Blagdon, though she was now involved in the organisation of the VAD and travelled to London frequently for meetings of the central committee.

In May King George and Kitchener paid a visit to the unit and congratulated Bardie on a 'first class show'. The Scottish Horse had an excellent reputation. In the late summer, however, Bardie and the First Line of the Scottish Horse were directed to Devonport and on 18 August 1915 they set sail for an unknown destination.

The destination proved to be the Gallipoli peninsula: Turkish territory. The Turks, who had entered the war on the German side, held both banks of the Dardanelles, a narrow strait which was Russia's only sea exit to the southern shipping lane of the Mediterranean. Russia was struggling in the war with Germany on the Eastern Front and it had been hoped to use British and French naval forces—without the need for the army—to blast through the Dardanelles, partly in order to release Russian shipping blocked in the Black Sea and partly to create a diversion to break the deadlock on the Western Front.

Kitchener had suggested the idea to Churchill, First Lord of the Admiralty, on 2 January, and forced agreement through a doubtful Cabinet. French support was secured and on 19 February an assault by eight British and four French warships began. It was an ill-conceived plan which, however, almost worked. But three British ships were sunk and

15   *Left to right:* George, the seventh Duke, Hamish and Bardie

the attack was called off. When it was resumed the element of surprise had been lost and the Turks were well prepared.

By March it had become obvious that land forces to back up the naval attack would be necessary and 70,000 men, munitions and supplies were sent from Britain and France. Australians and New Zealanders were sent across from Egypt. The landings began on 25 April. Young, almost untrained boys, many of whom had only recently left school, stepped off landingcraft into an unimaginable nightmare. Thousands were killed or died of the dysentery which soon affected them all, yet the remainder fought on magnificently, moving forward, driven back, mown down. Amidst the carnage a strange camaraderie developed between the men; an esprit de corps: so that old men would one day rejoice 'I was there!'

By August the Commander, Sir Ian Hamilton, knew that without reinforcements all was lost. Men and materials, though once again not enough, were sent out. These included Bardie and the Scottish Horse. They landed at the end of August, fresh and in high spirits to find themselves involved in the real war at last.

Sir Ian recorded in his diary of 25 September that having lunched with General Inglefield he plodded through the trenches held by Inglefield's division and the Indian Brigade, where he was met by Peyton '. . . who did pilot me through the Scottish Horse section. The Bard joined us here and was in great form, full of administrative good works as in South Africa. The Scottish Horse are as keen as schoolboys out for their first shoot. They were very proud of themselves and of the effect their rifles with telescopic sights had produced when put into the hands of ghillies and deer stalkers' (*Gallipoli Diary*, Sir Ian Hamilton).

There could surely be no possibility now, in these fearful conditions, of sending for Kitty: yet Bardie could always think of something. This time, knowing that the Brigade would be sent to Egypt when the Dardanelles campaign was over, he asked her to travel out there and wait. She and her maid set sail on the *SS Mooltan* on 26 October. The voyage to Port Said entailed constant danger to Allied shipping from German warships and submarines. In order to lessen the danger from submarine attack, a ship would adopt a zig-zag course through the Mediterranean. However the weather was glorious and she found the voyage very enjoyable. On arrival she wrote home to say how lovely it was to be on land again, among a medley of people; warm streets, warm earth and a moon rising so low and so red that she thought it must be a lantern on the Nile.

She and her maid arrived in Alexandria and installed themselves at the Carlton Hotel. Kitty found the landscape more attractive than she had imagined, with much more colour and variety in the shades of sand, the wattle trees, groves of palms. As always, she lost no time in making herself useful. 'I had been accustomed for some years to a good deal of work, but never had I found so much to be done as at Alexandria.' Many officers of the Brigade, including her brother Douglas, were in hospital. Kitty wrote home for them and shopped for their needs.

She found their neighbour Charles Butter from Pitlochry—who would figure prominently in her political life many years later—extremely ill in a hospital near the harbour and used to bicycle down to see him until staff officers noticed her being stopped and surrounded by a gang of children.

The children were probably interested in 'backsheesh': they had become used to British women as a generous source of income and would surround them cheerfully, shouting 'Backsheesh Mrs MacDonald, Backsheesh!' (it was invariably Mrs MacDonald) until rewarded with a few coins. It had happened several times before and Kitty had been unperturbed. However the officers were concerned for her safety and asked her to travel by tram in future.

Douglas, too, was very ill and in a dangerously weakened state with paratyphoid. He could eat nothing and drink little. Kitty found, however, that he was able to digest Glaxo, which helped him to recover sufficiently to be invalided home within a few weeks, though still unable to walk. It was the second occasion on which she had virtually saved the life of her young brother.

Apart from her hospital work, she was made chairman of an executive committee to arrange concerts for the troops and began work on this with her customary energy, co-ordinating and liaising with army personnel to discover men with performance skills who would be willing to become part of a concert party. It was still hot throughout November and she found that she was very glad of her pith helmet, sun umbrella and tinted glasses to cut down the glare as she went about the town on her errands of mercy.

As the year drew to a close the news from Gallipoli was bad. Unlike Egypt, where it was warm, cold weather there during November had caused the death of one man in ten from frostbite and exposure. A torrential storm flooded the trenches and as the men ran out to escape they were mown down by the Turkish army. A hurricane was followed by blizzards. In early December Kitty saw men who had been evacuated from the area being brought ashore. She described them as a pitiful sight—few had greatcoats, as they had been lost in the trenches: their clothing was mudstained and she realised it must have been soaking wet when they left a day or two earlier and had simply dried on their bodies. Many had jaundice and frostbite, their feet bandaged. She found it a sad, pathetic sight. Her concern for Bardie also increased, as she heard that he too was suffering from jaundice.

In late December the inevitable decision was taken to abandon the peninsula. The troops—those left alive—must be evacuated and the evacuation must take place silently, the men making their way to waiting rescue craft which would have arrived offshore in the dark of night. Bardie and the Scottish Horse left on the night of 20 December and although Kitty was not yet aware of it the operation went perfectly: not a single man was lost.

Kitty, waiting in Alexandria, learnt of the evacuation on the 23rd and noted in her diary that heavy casualties were to be feared. There was a shortage of hospital accommodation and she accepted the loan of a house for use as a convalescent home and sat and waited for patients with an anxious heart for the next few days. She heard no more until, on the 28th, a telephone call came: it was Bardie. The arrival of the New Year of 1916 was for them, and for all who had emerged alive from Gallipoli, a time of quiet thankfulness: the jubilant celebrations hallowed by Scottish custom would be deferred for the bringing-in of later years. Nonetheless she organised a New Year's Eve concert to cheer everyone up: a platform was constructed out of boxes of butter and shortbread and all available talent was pressed into action to make the concert a success.

A week or two later Bardie and Kitty moved into a house in Cairo. Kitty's hospital work had naturally grown in proportion to the number of wounded. She was also 'at home' to VAD nurses one day a week and on another day each week she entertained convalescents to tea. On three mornings a week she went to the entertainment committee's office to help organise concerts. There were twelve camps round Cairo and 120 hospitals and convalescent homes and camps in the provinces and up and down the Canal. Concerts were looked forward to and greatly helped the morale of the troops and Kitty's committee arranged to hold two a week. Her own participation now involved considerably more than her piano recitals: she was part of a real concert party and, having found a young lieutenant who could write comedy sketches, she found herself having to play the part of 'feed': something which did not come easily to her, though as the weeks went by she became more practised, particularly as she realised how well the sketches went down with the troops; she enjoyed their laughter and response and became more comfortable. She also departed from Schumann and Beethoven, finding herself more often accompanying ragtime dances and clog dances which grew faster and faster until they ended in chaotic frenzy.

The Suez Canal had been under intermittent attack from Turks who had made their way through Palestine and the Sinai Desert, though the number of attacks was as yet small. However it was rumoured that a large number of Germans and Turks were on their way and the Canal Zone was under guard by British, Australian and New Zealand troops. Sir Murdo MacDonald, a brilliant civil engineer, was Under-Secretary for Works in Egypt, and he made preparations to flood the section of the Canal which lay below sea level in the event of attack. The Scottish Horse were part of the defending army and Bardie called for 800 men to be sent out to Egypt to replace those who were in hospital, though he tried to impress on the authorities that the regiment was anxious to return to fighting, 'not to sit in Egypt for the rest of their lives'.

The concert party went up and down the Canal Zone, including HQ at Ismailia, so, like the soldiers she helped to entertain, Kitty was in constant danger, though she apparently suffered more from shyness than from fear. At HQ she was dismayed to find herself faced not only by the troops but 'by every general and senior officer from Sir Archibald Murray downwards—I own I felt more shy than ever before, but they seemed to enjoy our jokes.' There were concerts in Alexandria, too, at a large, newly-built rest camp, where she took part in plays and recitals. She also set up a committee to raise funds, both in Egypt and at home, to provide books and games for the troops in the desert and for the provision of 40,000 fly veils, still as necessary as they had been in Bardie's days in the Sudan.

In the small amount of free time available to them, they visited Coptic churches south of Cairo, gazed in wonder at the Pyramids and Sphinx, explored endless temples and tombs. In February they took leave together and went up to Luxor for a short visit. It was, for Kitty, unexpectedly beautiful—great cliffs rising straight from the plain with wonderful pinky opalescent lights: vivid red-ochre sunsets: and the strange, unearthly beauty of the temple. The climate was delightful and Bardie at last began to recover from the terrible cough which had been a legacy of the trenches at Gallipoli.

On their return to Cairo a pleasant piece of family news awaited them: Imogen was engaged to be married. The family had become resigned to the fact that she intended to remain a spinster, but she had been wooed for some time and finally won by Sydney Armitage-Smith, one of the principal clerks at the Treasury. Lily wrote to say that Baba and Armitage, as she called him, had gone into the garden in the afternoon, ostensibly to attend to some matters there, and had not reappeared until six o'clock—after dark—both hesitantly but obviously happy, to announce their engagement. Lily wrote approvingly that Armitage was a countryman at heart, though his work kept him in London, and that he was a scholar, a poet, and extremely musical. Kitty shared in the family's pleasure and relished every detail as members of the family wrote to tell her of it. The wedding took place at Bamff in the spring, in a shower of daffodils.

In June 1916 Lord Kitchener, on his way to Russia by sea, was drowned when the ship on which he was travelling, the *Hampshire*, struck a German mine off the coast of Orkney. For some time he and his conduct of the war had been regarded by other members of the Cabinet and by the generals with increasing disaffection and his death may not have been regarded as a tragedy. He had always appreciated the contribution of the Scottish Horse, however, and had given a personal undertaking to Bardie that he would remain in command of the regiment until the war ended. That undertaking now lay with its author six fathoms deep somewhere off Marwick Head. The new strategists had other plans. In September, despite Bardie's fierce protests, the 1st and 2nd Scottish Horse were amalgamated into one battalion and affiliated to the Black Watch. The 3rd battalion was attached to the Lovat Scouts. Bardie, as GOC, was instructed to supervise the re-organisation; thereafter he and the Staff would be sent home.

It was a great blow to Bardie personally and he was hurt and angry. However Kitty made the best of it and saw to it that they went out in style. When work on the reorganisation was complete she arranged for two huge farewell concerts to be held in Cairo for the Scottish Horse and the Lovat Scouts—moving, not-to-be-forgotten occasions at which everyone sang.

Afterwards she and Bardie travelled back by sea together and, as after the Boer War, made their way home to Blair.

Chapter 8

Bardie as Duke, Kitty as Duchess, 1917–21

On their return to Blair in December 1916 Kitty and Bardie found the old Duke in poor health and spirits. He had been fiercely opposed to his daughter Helen's announcement that she wished to marry an Edinburgh businessman, Mr David Tod, which would mean that she would no longer act as his companion and chatelaine. Besides, the Duke was of the opinion that David Tod was not socially acceptable. In correspondence Bardie and Kitty had stoutly defended Helen's right to marry as she chose. All her life Helen had been a nice, well-meaning, but rather domineering, woman. Now Bardie and Kitty felt that having devoted herself to her ageing father she should be given every encouragement to enjoy the remainder of her life as she wished. The Duke did not look forward to the prospect. Of his large family, one of his sons was dead, another in a German prison camp. Dertha was with her husband, Evelyn long forgotten (by the Duke, though not by the family). Now Helen was leaving too. The Elspeth Campbells of his world had long since ceased to visit him. He was alone; and he was dying. On 28 December Helen was married: Bardie had arrived home providentially in time to 'give her away'.

Kitty helped to care for the old Duke and often sat at his bedside reading to him during the weeks that followed. It was difficult to imagine Blair without him. He was seventy-seven and had been Duke of Atholl for fifty-three years. To most of the estate people he seemed as permanent as the Castle itself. At the turn of the year his condition deteriorated. He died on 20 January 1917 and was buried beside Louisa.

Bardie and Kitty were now Duke and Duchess of Atholl. The newspapers and journals of the day were glad to turn momentarily from news of war, referring to Kitty with gossip-column blarney laced with accuracy as one of the most accomplished women in society . . . 'not only a good speaker and organizer, but a brilliant pianist . . . composes music of considerable merit . . . moving spirit of entertainments committee for British soldiers in Egypt which gave 175 performances in six weeks. . . . Petite, graceful, dark-haired and charming . . . Before the war she delighted in leading off reels at the Royal Caledonian Balls and kept up long after the stalwarts were exhausted . . . has dark beauty . . . one of the kindest and brightest of women . . . devoted to life in the Highlands . . . sings and plays charmingly . . . before the war often seen and admired in London; dresses well . . . graceful and popular . . .' etc.

Bardie, as Duke of Atholl, was required to relinquish his position as a Member of Parliament. His place was taken by a Coalition Liberal, Mr James Gardiner, who was returned unopposed. Instead, Bardie became Lord Lieutenant of the County and was soon involved in helping the war effort by co-ordinating a committee to provide more food for the nation. Local farmers and sportsmen were encouraged to produce extra beef, lamb, fish and venison. He was interested in, and knowledgeable about, all aspects of farming. He knew and understood the difficulties of hill sheep farmers, of crofters and of the keepers who managed game and deer as well as the farmers on the soft arable lands and of foresters in the shelter of the hills. One of the bees in Lloyd George's bonnet over the years had been the idea of introducing people and farming to the 'huge, privately-owned deer forests and moors in Scotland'. He and Bardie had had many an argument on the subject both in and out of the House and Bardie had been driven on one occasion to say of Lloyd George:

> The other day, having occasion to look up the subject of 'Wales' in a book of reference, I found that the earliest inhabitants were a short dark race with big heads and no knowledge of agriculture. The human race sometimes appears, even after a lapse of hundreds of years, to revert to type.

Whilst Bardie was engaged on his drive to help to feed the nation, Kitty arranged to have the ballroom and north wing of the Castle turned into a convalescent hospital and although there was an excellent Red Cross nursing staff she undertook personal responsibility for the welfare of the men who were sent there.

But matters other than war had to be dealt with. Mr Munro, the Secretary of State for Scotland, mindful of Kitty's work on the Highlands and Islands Council before the war, invited her to serve on a committee to investigate the problems and conditions under which the 'tinker' community was living. The tinkers, or travellers, were nomads by tradition and instinct. According to legend, they were descendants of a dispossessed highland clan. They were determined to live in their own way, in small groups by the edges of rivers and fields and in the woods, in low, home-made tents or in caravans.

They were immediately recognisable, with sunbleached hair, deeply tanned skin, men in trousers tied with string below the knee, open-necked shirts and waistcoats; the women were often barefoot, shawls round their head, children carried on one hip or running at their feet, usually a small black dog of uncertain breed darting about them. Among themselves they spoke Cant, a private language unintelligible to outsiders, in which they passed on their folk tales, songs and group history from one generation to the next. The tinkers were often disliked and unfairly abused by local people, who—resenting their lack of willingness to conform to the 'normal' standards of society—objected to the litter and untidiness with which travellers often surrounded themselves and the unruly behaviour sometimes displayed by male members of the group. Tinkers lived by accepting casual work—mending pots and pans, berry-picking or potato-picking in season, selling clothes-pegs, telling fortunes or begging at doors. Some of the tinkers in Tayside were pearl fishers, adept at finding the rare pearl-bearing mussels in the bed of the river. They would come into a district in family groups of a dozen or more, settle down for a time and move on quite suddenly. There was a frequently-used tinker site almost at the gates of Blair Castle, by the banks of the River Garry. Kitty knew them well (Belle Stewart, the great ballad-singer, was born in a tent on the estate, by the banks of the River Tay. Her father-in-law was one of the old Duke's pipers.)

The Committee toured the country meeting tinker families, council officials, landowners, doctors, nurses. There were many health and medical problems among both children and adults. Bronchial diseases were rampant. Babies were born in freezing tents without medical aid, on beds of straw and rags. Doctors reported to the Committee many cases of stillbirths or even of mothers suffocating their newly born babies by 'overlaying' them accidentally in the night. Education was also a difficulty. The Children's Act required that all children should be sent to school from the age of five until the age of fourteen. It did not specify any particular school, so tinker children would arrive in a school unexpectedly, stay for a few weeks and disappear without warning.

The Committee recommended that an attempt should be made to offer housing and settle the families where possible in areas where there was continuous work, in the hope that they would eventually be absorbed into the community, though recognising that the nomadic habits of a heredity of centuries would be difficult to alter. The Committee as a whole recommended that those 'benefiting' from resettlement should be banned from access to alcohol. Kitty disagreed, feeling that, however desirable, the ban was not only unfair but unrealistic. Her own concern, as always, was for the welfare of the children, who were undereducated—and worse, often underfed and underclad, especially during the long, wild winter weather.

As with the Committee on Health in the Highlands, the Government accepted the Committee's proposals but was forced to shelve them temporarily due to the general housing shortage.

16   Honorary Degree. University of Glasgow, June 1919

Kitty's sympathy for the tinker community did not amount to admiration. She recognised their independent pride and determined exclusiveness and was prepared to live and let live, but when, as an MP in 1924, the question of granting tinkers the right to vote arose, she disagreed, pointing out that they paid neither rates nor taxes:

> If Hon Members opposite saw the tinkers . . . wandering about the roads all summer and camping during winter in the woods, I do not think that they would be so ready to entrust them with the great responsibility of the Parliamentary vote . . . I do not think that the Post Office would be ready to undertake the responsibility of tracing the addresses of these people and I do not think that there will be any overweening desire among the supporters of the Hon Members to convey these people to the poll on election day . . .

In the spring of 1918, at Lloyd George's request, Bardie went to Dublin with instructions to sound out certain prominent Irishmen, especially with regard to the possibility of introducing conscription. He wrote to Kitty:

> It's a dirty job . . . the Sinn Feiners have bagged the country and the Nationalists and Patriots unless they are in the swim will lose all power. They are out for 'peace', the others for 'revolution'. I fancy Lloyd George will not face conscription until he has passed Home Rule, which at the moment nobody wants! It may, however, save his face. He has courted two ladies, Ulster and the South, and has to decide in their presence which he's got to chuck—and in the end neither will marry him. Don't blame the RC bishops—the Times and Salisbury do not help. The further you drive the Irish the more hopeless will you make it to make them a self-respecting nation in the future. They won't fight for us and to force them won't make them any better, so why try. The Nationalists have been extraordinarily frank with me—and to have Dillon bare his soul to me in perfect trust: ditto Devlin and to a certain extent Logue has been a triumph for the views I held contrary to all the others. It is miserable the mess Lloyd George is making of this show.

On his return to Scotland Bardie was appointed Lord High Commissioner to the General Assembly of the Church of Scotland, the Established Church in Scotland. The Lord High Commissioner is appointed annually to be the representative of the Monarch at the proceedings. He (or she) is present at the opening and closing of the Assembly, he resides at the Palace of Holyroodhouse, attends the Assembly daily and holds a Garden Party on behalf of the Sovereign. The High Commissioner and his wife are accompanied by a retinue of attendants and in addition on this occasion the Atholl piper, Peter

Stewart, was taken to Edinburgh to play after dinner each evening in the gallery of the Palace.

Kitty had long since (1910) decided to join the Church of Scotland and had informed the Bishop that she was leaving the Episcopal Church, since she felt that she should be a member of her husband's church and also that the plain, simple services of that church appealed to her as a way of worship.

Bardie was created Knight of the Thistle—the Sovereign's highest Scottish honour—and much to Kitty's surprise she was simultaneously created a Dame of the British Empire. Typically, she pencilled a note at the bottom of the letter from Lloyd George notifying her of the honour: 'What for? . . . Tinkers? Egypt?? Hospital?? Holyrood?' It was probably a mixture of all four.

She happened to be in London on VAD business when the Armistice was announced on 11 November 1918. Her diary for the day reads:

> Entered office of Army Matron in Chief at 11 a.m. from a normal and orderly Embankment. Left at noon to find streets crowded with lorries full of young men and girls shouting their joy. Managed to get back to the West End in time to attend the Service of Thanksgiving at St. Margaret's, Westminster. . . . Church crammed with Members of both Houses of Parliament and wives. When all were seated, the two Prime Ministers of the war years, Lloyd George and Asquith, walked up the aisle side by side.

The war was over at last. Lloyd George, who had led the nation to victory, gave thanks. Woodrow Wilson looked forward to a brightening age. Baldwin reflected on the desperate cost in young lives and on the ruin of Europe. Churchill ruminated on the need to rebuild from the devastation of the continent, with the German nation as full partners in the enterprise. The citizens of all nations sank down in relief, thankful beyond measure that the war was over, content to leave affairs of state in the hands of the statesmen.

Like Churchill and a number of observers, Kitty and Bardie were clearly aware that—for the time being at least—the people of Germany needed help rather than punishment. The country was suffering from a desperate shortage of food and fuel and as usual in such situations the children suffered first and worst. A relief committee was formed, known as the Save the Children Fund. Bardie became, and remained for the rest of his life, its Scottish President. The first children's refugee village, Atvolo in Bulgaria, was named after him.

But the victorious Allies were intent on punishing Germany for the war which had torn the world apart. Severe financial reparations were inflicted on a Germany which had already suffered a shattering blow to its national pride. Germany's method of paying reparations in the form

17 Lloyd George's visit to Blair, 1921

of goods was to shatter the economic framework on which the western world's finances were constructed, with devastating results. Out of Germany's own economic chaos and humiliation in defeat there would arise a new, radical socialist Nazi party.

At Blair the Duke and Duchess of Atholl were busily settling down to their new responsibilities. Bardie had taken on the great task of arranging for the creation of a Scottish National War Memorial and Museum at Edinburgh Castle, to contain a Roll of Honour of all Scots who had been killed—an undertaking which was to engross and preoccupy him for several years. Kitty did not waste her time either. She stood for, and was elected to, the County Education Authority of Perthshire, as the Highland District member.

At the age of forty-three, she was exactly half-way through her life. Traits in her character which had been embryonic in her youth had developed and become more pronounced. She was serious, shy of expressing her deeper feelings, logical and extremely hard working. She set herself high standards of behaviour but disliked gossip about the behaviour of other people. She liked to lead—there was undoubtedly a streak of *noblesse oblige* in her attitude to others—and she enjoyed guiding people when she felt that they required it. There was a tendency, perhaps, to dominate and she could, on occasion, be carried away with her own enthusiasm, over-zealous in making a point, which could make her a slightly exhausting companion. There was an earnest, schoolmistressy air about her, but she was unfailingly kind in a slightly detached way, deeply concerned about the welfare of those in need or distress and completely selfless in expending her energies for the general good.

A glance at the list of committees on which she sat in 1920 makes exhausting reading. These were twenty-five in number and ranged from Chairman of the Highlands and Islands Consultative Council of the Board of Health, to President of the Perthshire Federation of District Nursing Associations, to twelve Education Committees, to membership of the National Council of Women of Great Britain and Ireland—and more.

Certainly few people can have taken on more, or worthier, tasks, but it can hardly have been congenial. Week in and week out she was travelling to and from Perth by train for meetings. Children catching the afternoon trains to the villages north of Perth after school would often be told to play about a little longer as the Duchess had been delayed at a meeting: clearly the directors of the Highland Railway Company were willing to make last minute alterations to the timetable for the benefit of important passengers. Worthy tasks, certainly: but how much was Kitty enjoying her life? There is an indication that she may have passed through a period of deep unhappiness at this period. Years later she apologised to a close friend for not having acknowledged a personal document which had been sent to her in 1918 'but it came at a time of great pressure, which continued for a year or two'. There is no explanation as to whether the pressure was of a public or private nature. It was unlike Kitty not to have replied, as even at the height of her political activity she was punctilious about replying to personal letters. A partial explanation may lie in two deaths which occured in 1918, both of which grieved her—those of Montagu Butler and Sir Hubert Parry—but the expression in her eyes in photographs taken at this period in her life suggests profound personal suffering borne with patient resignation.

But if there was inner sadness there were also pleasures. By this time Kitty's small nieces were beginning to be aware of their surroundings and are able to recall their aunt and uncle at Blair and the atmosphere of pleasure which they created. There were picnics and pony-rides in the hills in summer; Christmases when the bedrooms in the attics were occupied by numerous children and their nannies, the ballroom decorated with great boughs, holly and a large Christmas tree from the estate. Aunt Kitty would play the piano for them to dance and sing and Uncle Bardie would organise games and outings in the snow.

Bardie involved Kitty in many of the games and to her credit she never minded in the least being made to look ridiculous. If she thought something was funny she would laugh uproariously and at length. Throughout their lives together, Bardie delighted in playing practical jokes on her, which she always took in good part—spoof telegrams enquiring why she was not addressing a meeting in some remote spot; trout swimming in the ewer of water in her dressing-room; comic postcards drawn by Bardie himself.

But despite his high spirits Bardie was under considerable strain. The death of his father had left him in a desperate financial plight from which only a miracle could rescue him. He had managed to repay about £30,000 of the debt of £400,000 and to discharge £47,000 each to his sisters and surviving brother under the terms of the old Duke's will. In the early 1920s sums of £2,000 and £5,000 were repaid, but there was no possibility of finding further funds. To sell off the entire estate, which might have raised just enough to pay the debt, was not an option which either Bardie or Kitty would have been prepared to consider.

In 1921 came a sudden and surprising distraction, and an apparently splendid one at that. It came from a most unlikely source: Albania. Albania had been part of the Ottoman Empire until 1912, when she won her independence from the Turks. The Albanians claimed to be descendants of the Illyrians, totally separate and distinct from their Balkan neighbours the Greeks and Serbs. The majority of the population was of the Muslim faith and they were a fiercely proud and independent

18 Kitty, 1918

people. Their tiny country was surrounded by predatory nations. Italy, Greece and Jugoslavia each sought to absorb them, but in 1920 the Albanians achieved international recognition and were admitted to the recently-formed League of Nations.

The Conference of Ambassadors in Paris was at work delineating the borders of the fragmented Balkan States; in order to consolidate their independence the Albanians were looking for a suitable and respectable Western leader to become head of a Royal House of Albania: they were looking for a king.

Balkan politics were the subject of many intrigues and foreign agents were present in all the Balkan capitals. One of the British Friends of

Albania, Jim Barnes, who had made his home in Italy, had met Bardie when he and Kitty visited cousins in Florence, and considered him to be an admirable choice as king.

Harold Nicolson records that on 4 April 1921 he presented a memorandum advocating that the Albanians should be given a fair start and then be left to work out their future in their own way. On 27 April Aubrey Herbert—a Member of Parliament with a slightly swashbuckling air and a sense of adventure—who had 'quixotically thrown in his lot with Albania', told Nicolson that the Albanians definitely intended offering the crown to the Duke of Atholl. Nicolson cautioned Herbert that before the Duke made a step in the direction of the Albanian throne he must consult Lord Curzon, the Foreign Secretary (See *Harold Nicolson: Diaries and Letters*).

On 28 April Bardie received a letter from Jim Barnes.

> I saw Herbert yesterday, and Lord Robert (Cecil). Both of them thought it an admirable idea. Lord Robert seemed particularly enthusiastic and seemed to think that the dipolomatic difficulties should be able to be surmounted without much difficulty. We agreed that the next move ought to come from Albania (secretly of course) in the form of definite proposals, that is, defining your position, powers, salary, etc., so that you may know exactly what you are in for. Herbert is writing to you and I am in agreement with him in thinking that in your own interests you should commit yourself to nothing until a perfectly concrete proposal is made.
>
> Both Herbert and Lord Robert agreed that you are pre-eminently the man for the job because the difficulties you will encounter in Albania are chiefly psychological and there are few people who appear so fitted to understand and fire the imagination of those people as you are. That is half the battle. The rest is statesmanship, and there your experience is about as wide as anyone's.

But diplomatic negotiations over Albania were still at a delicate stage. The predators were ranged along the wall ready to swoop—indeed tracts of Albania had already been swallowed up by the Serbians. At the Supreme Council in Paris the nations pushed their own interests in the Balkans. Britain, to the acute embarrassment of Lord Curzon, was forced by Lloyd George to favour Greece. Jim Barnes, though Bardie probably failed to realise it, was pushing Italian interests.

Aubrey Herbert wrote to Bardie in May, suggesting that he should talk the situation over with Lord Lothian and Harold Nicolson. Miss Denham, Secretary of the Balkan Committee in Britain, warned him . . . 'both the Serbs and Greeks will fight and lie in Paris and we can't expect to get nearly all we should for Albania.' Herbert had himself twice been offered the crown of Albania, once in 1913 and again shortly before the offer was made to Bardie. He had refused for financial and family reasons.

Kitty was sceptical and unable to share her husband's enthusiasm at the prospect of reigning in a wild Balkan land as King John and Queen Katharine of Albania: it all seemed faintly ludicrous to her. Lord Curzon agreed to see Bardie in July. He was, of course, aware of the subtleties of the game that was being played in Paris and must have recognised that Bardie was being used as a tool to promote Italian interests. Certainly at their meeting he can have given no encouragement for the suggestion, which would have caused embarrassment to the Foreign Office. Following their meeting Bardie wrote to him, backtracking:

> 26th July 1921
> Dear Lord Curzon
> First of all, allow me to thank you for the very patient and courteous interview you gave me and my friend the other day in regard to Albania. My own position is clear. It is as follows: I have recently met a few prominent natives of that country and also several people who are deeply interested in it. The result is that I also have fallen under the strange attraction of its problems and have a deep sympathy for a race that from time immemorial has put up such an extraordinarily plucky fight for its independence and nationality. Further than that I would have you understand that I do not pretend to be an expert on Balkan matters nor have I any interest direct or indirect in that country, as has apparently been put about, possibly for political reasons by certain people . . .

There, fortunately, the dream of monarchy ended—it was a merciful escape. The heads of Balkan Royal Houses tended not to live happily ever after. Albania was invaded by Italy in 1939. The former Prime Minister— who had become King Zog—and Queen Geraldine were fortunately able to escape to safety.

Chapter 9

Towards Parliament, 1922–3

A few weeks after Bardie's visit to Lord Curzon at the Foreign Office the Atholls played host, at the request of the Foreign Office, to the Crown Prince of Japan and his entourage at Blair Castle. This was regarded as a most important diplomatic visit and it was a sign of trust in the Duke and Duchess that they should have been invited to 'do the honours'.

Careful preparations had been made. Bardie always dealt with such matters with military precision, making sure that everything was timed to perfection and rehearsed in advance. The Atholl Highlanders came together to practise their parade drill—keepers, ghillies and farmworkers struggled into their uniforms amidst laughter. One of the ghillies was found to have such large feet that none of the regulation buckled brogues would fit him. Bardie thought that it would be a pity to leave him out on that account, so the toes were cut off the largest pair available, leaving his stockinged feet protruding. It was considered that the Crown Prince would be too pleased by the entire spectacle to notice: the Atholl Highlanders on parade are an impressive body of men.

Bardie decided that at the moment the Prince's carriage turned into the drive a twenty-one gun salute should be fired and a firing party was convened for this purpose. In the event, due to a mishap, the firing party actually managed only a one-gun salute. His Imperial Highness, being happily unaware of the intention to provide a further twenty, was delighted by this triumphant welcome.

The Crown Prince (the late Emperor Hirohito) was enchanted by the beauty of Blair, by the Castle, the gardens, the mountains, the rivers. Kitty's sister Ferelith and her husband were among the guests invited for the visit. Their recollections of the Prince at that time were of a shy, quiet and charming young man. Kitty played for them each evening— Beethoven, Chopin, Schumann. In their honour she had made a special arrangement of the Japanese Natioanl Anthem. A member of the Prince's suite was sufficiently moved by this compliment to walk across and join her at the piano in order to supply his own vocal accompaniment. Clearly the visit was going well.

Other excitements were in store for the Crown Prince. Bardie and his

Head Keeper, Peter Stewart, had planned a particular treat for him: he was to catch his first salmon in one of the deep, dark pools of the fast-flowing River Tilt. Catching a fish is problematical enough for the most experienced angler and the Crown Prince had never fished before. Much thought and careful preparation on Stewart's part was essential. He caught a fish of splendid proportions, stunned it, and left it tied to his line under a rock at the edge of the pool. When the royal party arrived the Crown Prince was given a lesson in the art of landing his fly gently and accurately on the water, during the course of which Stewart in his anxiety accidentally swore loudly in Gaelic. Several of the onlooking ghillies and stalkers were forced to disappear over the hill, where they lay down in the heather to explode with laughter at Peter Stewart's antics.

But now a serious point in the proceedings had arrived. Stewart artfully substituted the second rod, which had been carefully laid to one side on a protruding rock, for the first, so that the Prince now had the line with the stunned fish in play. A little more manoeuvering on Stewart's part and a final tug on the part of the Prince resulted in the appearance of a splendid fish, which was duly stuffed and taken home to Japan.

State visits can rarely have been more successful. Everyone had enjoyed it. Afterwards Lord Curzon wrote to Kitty to thank her on behalf of the Government, assuring her that the visit to Blair had been the high point of the Crown Prince's state visit. It remained in the young Prince's mind so vividly and with such pleasure that at his request it was repeated in 1938 with equal success.

Hard on the heels of the Japanese state visit came an informal visit by the Prime Minister and his wife. The Lloyd Georges were passing through Atholl on their way to the north-west of Scotland. The old sparring partners, Bardie and Lloyd George, had continued to come into contact with each other fairly frequently and on hearing of their plans for a holiday in Ross-shire Bardie had issued an invitation of his own: this would be an ideal opportunity to show Lloyd George just what a deer forest looked like. Lloyd George accepted the invitation willingly and was convinced. Bardie took him on a hill pony up over the lower grazing ground to a desolate moorland plateau covered in ciob grass. The little Prime Minister was heard to murmur 'Impossible . . . impossible . . .' again and again. Bardie had proved his point at last.

During the visit Lloyd George was able to talk to Kitty as he had not done before: previous meetings had been formal occasions with many others present. Now, in her own home, he recognised in her a formidable political mind combined with limitless energy. Towards the end of the visit he suggested to her that she should stand for Parliament. Under the circumstances it was a very fair suggestion—the Prime Minister could not have expected political advantage for himself, for Kitty was certainly not likely to stand as a Liberal. But he was not thinking in narrow party terms and in any case the wartime coalition between Liberals and Conservatives had continued into this post-war period.

The Prime Minister pursued his point: Kitty was of the right calibre and had much experience of local government and of committee work. So far, apart from a Sinn Feinner who had refused to take her seat in 1918, only Nancy Astor (since 1918) and Mrs Wintringham (since that year of 1921) had been elected. Lloyd George said that he felt that now that women had their chance they must come forward and take it.

It was a new and startling idea to Kitty. As she considered it, she must have felt that it was an odd notion. Given her own opposition to militant campaigning for 'votes for women' before the war, she must have hesitated to seem to take advantage of the situation, particularly as none of the suffragettes themselves had succeeded in being elected. (Christabel Pankhurst had been narrowly beaten at Smethwick in 1918.) Kitty's standing for Parliament could well cause resentment.

She promised Lloyd George to think about it and after his departure for the north she discussed the suggestion with Bardie. In some ways she was attracted to it. Politics had always interested her and she had certainly achieved the standard she had set for women by getting first-hand experience of local government: if the door was now ajar perhaps it needed a bit of a shove to open it wide enough to encourage other women to go through it. Bardie too was impressed by the idea; he was in no doubt as to Kitty's capabilities. The question of Albania had just been dropped and there was nothing to prevent Kitty from doing it if she wanted to. Together they sought the advice of the Conservative Party Chairman, Sir George Younger, a Scottish businessman and owner of a small estate near Stirling. He reacted positively and advised that Kitty should begin to look round for a city constituency, which he thought would be much more suitable for her than a rural one. Distances involved in a rural constituency meant a great deal of travelling and very many more meetings: a rural seat could mean addressing thirty-six meetings as far apart as forty miles during a campaign, whereas a compact city constituency could be crossed on foot in an hour and two or three large meetings could be sufficient.

Kitty decided to keep the idea in mind, but other matters intervened. The success of the Japanese visit had impressed the Establishment. The office of Lord Chamberlain was about to become vacant and Bardie was approached to take it on. It was a political appointment and apart from duties in connection with the Royal Household it involved representing the Government on the Front Bench of the House of Lords. Bardie took up his duties in November 1921 and Kitty accompanied him to London, where they became immersed in political, social and royal duties. They were already on friendly terms with the King and Queen. The King regarded Bardie as an old friend; Queen Mary was a woman after the Duchess's own heart—a kindly but somewhat distant personality with a pronounced sense of duty.

Kitty ran a salon and was responsible for a new atmosphere in which foreign legations met each other socially, whereas previously they had had little opportunity for social contact. She became friendly with many distinguished foreign representatives with whom she would correspond in later, more anxious, times. She also came to know the important national political figures of all parties—among them the Baldwins, whom she grew to like and admire. Baldwin was President of the Board of Trade and a cabinet minister, but was not yet thought of as a likely future Prime Minister. Kitty remarked, 'He impressed me by his frank, unassuming manner and breadth of view and common sense.'

Bardie was in his element. The appointment was exactly suited to his powers of organisation, his flair for coping with important people, his love of ceremony. One of his first duties was to organise a Royal Wedding at the end of February 1922, when the King and Queen's daughter Mary was married to Lord Lascelles. Bardie was also pleased to be personally involved, as Lord Chamberlain, in making improvements to the Palace of Holyroodhouse, the King's official residence in Edinburgh. After his experience of living there as Lord High Commissioner he knew only too well how necessary improvements were: the ancient palace had been greatly neglected and there were stories of rats running round the principal chambers. Queen Mary was interested in this enterprise and she and Bardie discussed alterations, redecoration and re-arrangement of furniture and pictures. Kitty and a number of other 'noble ladies' were prevailed on by the Queen each to embroider the seat of one chair from a historically important set.

Unfortunately Bardie's tenure in office was to be short-lived. After an uncertain and difficult period the Coalition Government under Lloyd George's premiership fell in October 1922. It had dealt bravely with a series of crises: a terrible outbreak of influenza in which more than 150,000 people died; shortage of coal and food; rising inflation (the pound stood at one-third of its pre-war value); a leap in the number of unemployed and a series of major strikes. It had decided to deal with the running sore of Ireland by amputation; and Lloyd George, with a team of advisers, had taken part on behalf of Britain in the Paris Peace Talks.

But many Conservatives had become disenchanted with Lloyd George personally and had lost confidence in the policies of the Government. They felt that the time had come for the Party to withdraw support for coalition politics and to follow its own line. A vote in the Carlton Club to this effect was carried by a large majority. Lloyd George was notified

19   Bardie in the 1920s

and as his majority in the House depended on Conservative support he had no alternative but to tender his resignation to the King. Bonar Law, who became Prime Minister, immediately called an election, which took place on 13 November 1922.

Because Bardie's appointment as Lord Chamberlain was a political appointment, he automatically demitted office at the beginning of the election campaign, but he believed, as he had every reason to do, that he would be reinstated immediately after polling by an incoming Conservative administration. He was wrong: Lord Cromer was appointed in his place. It is not clear why this happened. It is possible that his disputes with the Lord Steward of the Household, Lord Farquhar, had caused embarrassment. The Lord Steward's responsibility was for domestic routine of the royal palaces, whereas the Lord Chamberlain was responsible for all official occasions such as courts, levees, garden parties, receptions, investitures and state visits. He was also the intermediary between the Sovereign, the House of Lords and the Diplomatic Corps. Lord Farquhar, however, insisted that his position as Lord Steward entitled him to take precedence over the Lord Chamberlain at all times and this had led to a number of fairly public arguments between them.

Whatever the reason, King George and Bardie were both disappointed that his appointment had not been renewed. Within eighteen months King George was to negotiate an arrangement whereby the post of Lord Chamberlain and a few other appointments were to be filled at the King's discretion in return for an undertaking that those peers chosen would take no part in parliamentary matters.

Bardie and Kitty returned to Scotland. During the year it had been discovered that Bardie was suffering from diabetes. The recent discovery of insulin meant that the disease could be controlled, but it was an anxiety for them both.

The Prime Minister, Bonar Law, was also ill, and much more seriously ill than Bardie: he had developed cancer of the throat and, although it was not generally known, he could not be expected to survive for long.

The 1922 election had brought into Parliament a large number of Labour members for the first time. Their numbers had risen from sixty-three in the post-war Parliament to 142 in 1922. Many of these were from Scottish constituencies, particularly from Clydeside, and because of the radical nature of their outlook they were known as Red Clydesiders. Bonar Law, himself a Scot, though born in Canada, acknowledged their presence, commenting that although he disagreed with their policies it was splendid to hear their Scottish voices in the House. The leader of the Labour Party was also a Scot, though not a Clydesider: Ramsay MacDonald was a fine-looking, soft-spoken man from the north-east of Scotland, of much less radical outlook than his Lowland compatriots.

They had seen and experienced poverty at first hand and were convinced that only extreme socialist measures could change the quality of life for their constituents.

After only seven months as Prime Minister, Bonar Law was forced to resign because of ill health. There was some indecision as to whether to send for the patrician Lord Curzon or the relatively inexperienced Stanley Baldwin. The King was advised to choose the latter. Baldwin, little known and as yet untried, became Prime Minister in May 1923.

The first major problem facing Baldwin was unemployment, which stood at 1.5 million. In order to boost jobs at home, he and the Government advocated the introduction of tariffs and protection against foreign imports, a policy to which both opposition parties were opposed. Baldwin decided to put the matter to the country and called another election in November 1923. This was to be the election which brought Kitty into Parliament.

Chapter 10

MP for West Perthshire, the Campaigns of 1923 and 24

The boundaries of the West Perthshire constituency represented by Bardie from 1910 to 1917 had recently been extended to include the neighbouring small county of Kinross, making a new constituency of Kinross and West Perthshire. Since 1918 it had been represented by a Liberal who supported the coalition, Mr James Gardiner.

In the spring of 1923 the Chairman of the Unionist Association in the constituency, Sir James Wilson—no doubt having been briefed by Sir George Younger—approached Kitty to enquire whether she would be prepared to consider nomination as their parliamentary candidate for the next election, whenever it might be. Kitty was gratified, but as an election had taken place so recently she did not feel that an immediate answer was required and she postponed making a decision. However in the late summer she was visited by Lord Haldane, former Liberal Secretary of State for War and former Lord Chancellor.

Lord Haldane's home was in the constituency and his sister Elizabeth Haldane, a leading social reformer, was a close friend of Kitty's. They served together on many of the county education committees and Elizabeth had spoken highly of Kitty to her brother. He urged her to come forward and suggested that it was possible that many Liberals and even Labour Party supporters would vote for her if she chose to stand. Kitty privately doubted this, knowing the unpopularity with other parties of the government's stance on tariffs. She supported the view that tariffs would help to alleviate unemployment, but the Labour and Liberal parties believed that it would mean an increase in the price of food.

Mr Gardiner also came to see her to tell her that he intended to retire at the next election and to persuade her to stand. It certainly seemed that the decks were being cleared for her: but it would mean a major alteration in their way of life and she found it difficult to make a decision. King George, on a visit to Blair, disapproved and solemnly reminded her that she would be less able to perform her duties as Bardie's hostess at Blair if she was at Westminster. Bardie, though, felt otherwise. Having accepted women's suffrage, he now thought Kitty would make a first class MP and fully supported her. The Unionists eagerly pressed for a reply. It would certainly be an excellent *coup* for them to have the Duchess of Atholl as candidate. From her point of view it was flattering to be pursued with such eagerness. It was not in her nature to shirk a challenge and she finally agreed, expecting to have a bit of time in which to play herself in with the electorate. However the election was upon her and she was swept up in the campaign before she had regained her breath. The constituency did not include the big county town of Perth, but there were 2,000 miles of road and a large number of widely scattered towns and villages to be covered. A speech and visit must be made in each of them.

The Liberal Party decided to field a candidate, and Kitty's opponent was Mr P A Molteno, a landowner from Glenlyon, near Aberfeldy. She began her round of the constituency which she had in the past covered as the candidate's wife. In her speeches she supported the government on tariff controls and made a point of giving an undertaking to give careful attention to the welfare of women, children and ex-servicemen. Whereas she had rather enjoyed campaigning on behalf of her husband, she found the first campaign on her own account a considerable strain and was thankful when election day was over.

In those days the votes were counted in the County Buildings in Perth, simultaneously with those of the East Perthshire constituency, on the day following the election. Tay Street in Perth was packed with waiting electors. It was the custom for the winners to be cheered and to make a speech before being marched in triumph to the committee rooms.

East Perthshire, being a more compact constituency, declared first. Noel Skelton, the Conservative, was safely returned. A tense period of waiting followed until Kinross and West Perthshire declared. When it was announced that Kitty had won by the narrowest of margins—150 votes—there was pandemonium and she was unable to make herself heard above the uproar. Her speech over, she was escorted back to the Conservative Rooms by hundreds of cheering supporters. There the window on first floor had been taken out and she and Noel Skelton leant out together to wave to a vast crowd which gathered to salute Scotland's first woman MP. Celebrations continued untill well into the night. In its tribute, the local newspaper commented that her success—against the national tide—had been due to her own personal popularity.

Congratulations poured in from all over the country, including messages from Stanley Baldwin, Lords Curzon, Balfour and Younger and Dame Maude Royden. One of the kindest tributes came from a fellow Scot, former Chancellor of the Exchequer Robert Horne: 'I know of nobody who has given more intense and unremitting study to the

20 Silver Wedding

problems of our time in all their aspects—social and economic—than you
have done and there is no-one better equipped for social service. I regard
your presence in Parliament as a benefit to the Scottish Nation and an
ornament to the House of Commons.'

Kitty was now forty-nine. Perhaps, when she entered Parliament as it
assembled on 15 January 1924, she remembered that she was following in
the footsteps of her great-great-grandfather, James Willson of
Purdeysburn in County Antrim. She must certainly have been aware that
her life was about to change completely. For the first half of her life she
had played a supporting, traditionally feminine role: now she was to play
a significant part in the affairs of the nation. Bardie and Blair would
always be there to come home to, but now there was work to be done
which would gradually encompass her mind and spirit.

In the country as a whole the election had gone badly for the
Conservatives, though they were still the largest single party with 258

seats. The Socialists had won 191 and the Liberals 158. A coalition between Liberals and Socialists would put the Conservatives out of office. Many Liberals hesitated to give their backing to what would be the first Socialist government in Britain's history. Yet the alternative of allowing the Conservatives, who had so recently broken up the coalition, to continue in office was no less undesirable in Liberal eyes. The dilemma was made no easier by the fact that Stanley Baldwin refused to surrender the Premiership unless the Labour and Liberal parties made their position clear to the country by uniting against the Conservatives in the House.

Listening to the King's Speech, Kitty made up her mind to seek permission to comment on it and it was agreed that she might make her maiden speech on the morning of the 18th. She was extremely nervous, having stayed up rehearsing for most of the previous night, but once on her feet she found confidence and made what was judged to be a brilliant speech, ranging over a great many topics—the evil of youth unemployment, a plea that English children born out of wedlock should, like their Scottish counterparts, be legitimised in the event of their parents' marriage, an assertion that French shipbuilding firms were receiving special financial help which was enabling them to undercut Britain in this industry, and ending with a warning to the Liberals against bringing in a Labour Government 'which with all due respect to the Hon Members who compose it, I think the country has shown in the election that it does not want'.

As she sat down the House adjourned for luncheon and she found herself surrounded by a throng of admirers. Lloyd George himself and two other leading Liberals, J E B Seeley and H A L Fisher, came across to offer their congratulations, generously, since they cannot have enjoyed her final remarks.

Outside the House, too, her speech was widely acclaimed and next day several newspapers praised it, describing it as 'the sensation of the debate', 'undoubtedly a very able speaker', 'delivery and voice attractive', 'the ordered sequence of her arguments and practical commonsense show her to be a debater who will probably make her mark in the House' etc. She had made a very satisfactory beginning. A deluge of telegrams and letters of congratulation from old friends and new acquaintances arrived by every post. Gerald Balfour exclaimed to his wife 'To think it was Kitty!', his thoughts returning to the old days at Archerfield and Dublin, when as a shy young girl she had delighted them all with her music.

On 21 January Labour and Liberal votes combined to force the Conservatives to give way to a Labour Government under the premiership of Ramsay MacDonald. The Liberals had forced the Conservatives out of office, but there was no agreement between the Liberals and the Labour Party.

21   Kitty and Bardie accept the good wishes of local children, Silver Wedding 1924

22   Family, Silver Wedding party, 1924

There were now eight women in Parliament: three Labour, three Conservative and two Liberal. For them the House presented certain problems which did not affect their male counterparts: the women were not permitted in the Smoking Room, where much of the business was arranged between the parties, and so were often insufficiently prepared for what they would face in the House. Their offices and retiring rooms were small, inadequate and awkwardly situated, but they made the best of it and co-operated willingly when party loyalties did not prevent it.

Kitty was invited by the editor of *The Spectator* to respond to Christabel Pankhurst's suggestion of forming a Women's Party in Parliament. She thought it would be a grave mistake, as it would antagonise men and create a gulf far wider than class or party: class or party could be changed, sex could not. However she made it clear that fellow women MPs could count on her full co-operation whenever possible.

Of all the women in Parliament at the time Nancy Astor had by far the greatest flair. Kitty greatly admired her quick wit and brilliant repartee; Nancy could always deliver a *bon mot* or 'the perfect squelch' as required. She was also a stylish dresser and had the benefit of wealth and of splendid homes in London and at Cliveden, not far from London, where she and her husband Lord Astor entertained the influential and important people of the day. She also had a healthy disrespect for stuffy men, which often made her a somewhat unruly member of the House. Kitty, however, had a better brain. Both were capable women, but whereas Nancy was quicksilver, inclined to be flippant and superficial, Kitty was deep-thinking and dedicated. Nancy's life was that of a wealthy socialite: Kitty's was restrained and somewhat impoverished. Cliveden and Blair were on different planets.

Throughout 1924 the Conservatives were critical spectators of the Labour Government. Kitty found that there were many opportunities for her to speak in the House: she contributed to debates on defence, working conditions, education, agriculture, housing, transport, unemployment, local government, family law, and to the debate on the extension of women's franchise. Concerned for the estate, she devoted her salary of £400 a year towards the upgrading of the seventeenth-century vernacular houses in Dunkeld Square—now the property of the National Trust for Scotland—which had become dilapidated.

Kitty and Bardie celebrated their Silver Wedding during the summer of that year and later shared the celebrations with their own people on Atholl. The tenants on the estate combined to commission a painting of Kitty by Sir James Guthrie, and the estate workers a bronze bust by Serge Yourievitch, for which she gave sittings in London. Kitty and Bardie both addressed parties on the estate. Kitty said that since she had come to

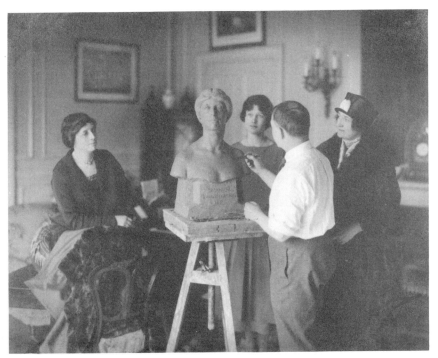

23   The Bronze bust, commissioned by the estate workers, 1924

Atholl she had received nothing but the greatest kindness and friendliness from every person on the estate and in the district. She had had the good fortune to be married to one who throughout his life had had the happy knack of being in the centre of things whenever anything special was going to happen and it followed that she had been rather in the centre of happenings herself. But if anyone had told her on the day of her marriage that she would spend her silver wedding as a Member of Parliament she would have told him in polite language to somewhere else and tell that to someone more credulous. She firmly believed that if there was anything that you were called upon to do you should do it, even if you felt that you were only a stopgap.

The Guthrie portrait was greatly admired. A critic wrote: 'It depicts the Duchess at the piano, turning round as if to discuss the merits of the piece of music she had been playing. The face is full of vivacity and the artist has lost nothing of the strength and intellect which characterises his model . . .'

It was presented by one of the tenants, Mr James Bowie, who observed in Gaelic that the Duchess was 'far prettier than yon picture'—a sentiment with which Bardie agreed in Gaelic before speaking in English of his pride in, and admiration for, Kitty. He went on to speak of his anxieties for the future of the estate and hoped that the friendship and sense of partnership which had always existed on Atholl might continue through a difficult period.

For Britain as a whole this was a difficult period. For some of the well-to-do it was an era of nightclubs, jazz, short skirts, oomph, champagne cocktails, racing cars and daring exploits in aeroplanes. The Prince of Wales and the Mountbattens were leading Society into a giddy new era. The youthful film industry was preparing its assault on the imagination of the world. There were motor cars, telephones; and above all there was the wireless, which was to bring 'information, entertainment and education' to an ever-growing audience. Kitty was initially nervous about the potential effect of the wireless, which might, she thought, be used as a political tool—as it later was in other countries.

The difficulties of the period were those of housing, pay, general living conditions and most particularly unemployment. Ramsay MacDonald's government introduced measures aimed at social reform at home, but it was in the field of foreign affairs that it had its greatest success. Germany was suffering from disastrous hyperinflation and MacDonald was instrumental in negotiating an American loan to Germany in order to stabilise the currency. He also managed to arrange for French withdrawal from the Ruhr, which they had occupied in protest against Germany's failure to meet its reparation payments; and he made a strong attempt to bring Communist Russia into full participation in international affairs.

The Liberals, divided between Asquithians and followers of Lloyd George, became aware that their supporters were deserting them—either joining the Labour Party in support of its successes, or the Conservatives in disapproval of the government. In October the Liberals triggered the Government's defeat over a secondary matter, as often happens: a motion critical of the Attorney General's failure to prosecute a Communist journalist over what was thought to be incitement to naval mutiny in Scotland. The Cabinet decided to treat it as a matter of confidence and with the Liberals against them the Government fell. The third general election in three years followed at the end of October.

This time Kitty enjoyed the campaign. She had gained confidence as a speaker and had learnt to deal with hecklers with good humour. At Doune, as she was hurrying off the platform to reach her next meeting in time, she was amused to find herself delayed with shouts of 'Here! We're no done wi' ye yet!' When supporters of Ramsay MacDonald interrupted her with shouts of 'Good old Ramsay!' she responded cheerfully that she used to be a Ramsay but now preferred her married name.

The campaign drew to a close and election day dawned wet and cold;

24   The Duke and Duchess of Atholl beside the gates given by the family

rain fell heavily all day and there was thick fog to add to the misery. Kitty's only opponent was a Socialist, Mr J MacDiarmid. The Liberals had been unable to find a suitable candidate and it was the first time Labour had fielded a candidate in West Perthshire. The lack of choice, according to a local newspaper, led a woman voter to remark 'I dinna ken hoo tae vote: on the ae side ye ha'e the Conservatives and on t'ither the Communicants.'

The 'Communicants' were unsuccessful: Kitty had a huge majority and in her speech from the window she said 'I am proud that I go back representing people of moderation and goodwill'—though she was almost drowned out by choruses of 'For she's a jolly good fellow'.

In the country as a whole, too, the Conservatives had a smashing victory, taking 419 of the 615 seats. Labour had done well, with 151 seats and the Liberals had been eclipsed, winning only 40.

Baldwin resumed the premiership he had lost nine months earlier and set about choosing his team. Ramsay MacDonald had made the first appointment of a woman as a junior minister in the previous government and it was felt that the Conservatives would do well to follow suit. Ironically, as it turned out, it was Neville Chamberlain, in conversation with the Prime Minister, who made the suggestion that the Duchess should be invited to become Parliamentary Secretary to the Board of Education.

In making this appointment Baldwin and Chamberlain were deliberately avoiding the more obvious choice of Nancy Astor. Nancy's unconventional behaviour in the House had not endeared her to some members. Baldwin was fond of Kitty and felt that she could be relied upon to be loyal and decorous; and her knowledge, experience and interest in the subject of education was without parallel. He wrote to her, offering her the post and assuring her that Lord Eustace Percy, who would be her Chief as President of the Board, would be very glad indeed to have her as his Parliamentary Secretary. 'Just say yes!' he wrote.

It was certainly a personal triumph for Kitty. West Perthshire rejoiced over her appointment. Kitty welcomed the new challenge as she accepted all challenges, confident in her ability to make a useful contribution. Thus, as 1924 drew to a close, she found herself installed at the Board of Education, the first Conservative woman ever to hold ministerial office.

Chapter 11

Education Minister, 1924-9

Kitty's chief, Lord Eustace Percy, was not a popular man. He was a younger son of the Duke of Northumberland, at that time thirty-seven years old, lordly in his dealings with others and careless of their feelings. He would stand up in the House, wag his finger at his fellow MPs and declare 'Mark this!' as if he and he alone were privy to the truth. Even as a young man he had been known for his pompous behaviour. In 1909 Harold Nicolson was in Paris 'cramming' and later recorded that he had been not a little disturbed by the arrival at the crammer's of fellow student Eustace Percy, who was so far above him, he imagined, in all subjects . . . 'and made me thoroughly ashamed of my own shortcomings'. Nicolson remarks that he 'always felt a little inferior before Eustace's noble idealism, deep religious convictions, knight-in-shining armour soul and high-minded scruples'.

As always, Kitty entered into her work with total dedication. Her philosophy was that if a job was worth doing it was worth doing to the best of her ability and without regard for her own health or comfort. It was noted by officials at the Department that she gave unstintingly of her time and effort. As a very new MP she had to learn quickly. This presented little difficulty and under normal circumstances she would soon have become an excellent minister: but the character of Lord Eustace Percy made this impossible and, as someone closely involved in her work at the time has remarked, it blighted her whole parliamentary career. 'There is no doubt that she would have done exceeedingly well. But Percy never favoured the idea of having a woman as his Parliamentry Secretary and made no attempt to hide his disdain.'

On one occasion, during a meeting with the Permanent Secretary and other members of the Department, the Duchess made a statement. Eustace Percy turned to face her and listened for a few minutes, until she had finished speaking: then, without a word of acknowledgement, he turned to the Permanent Secretary, Sir (Lewis) Amhurst Selby-Bigge, and said 'You were going to say?' Those present were angry and affronted on the Duchess's behalf, though she herself was too well-mannered to betray any sign of distress.

Lord Eustace's need to assert his authority and thus prove his superiority led him to deny Kitty the opportunity to take any decisions personally. She was given little or no power and was denied any encouragement whatsoever. This in its turn made her nervous and ill at ease. Answering questions in the House became a terrifying experience. The senior civil servants at the Department did their best to help her. Sir Amhurst Selby-Bigge and his wife were particularly attached to her and she sometimes spent weekend as their guest in Sussex. (Kitty had another reason for being grateful to them: Lady Selby-Bigge, as director of a fashion house, had been responsible for freeing women of the dreadfully uncomfortable clothing which had been fashionable at the beginning of the century and which Kitty herself had particularly resented.)

All the senior civil servants were fond of Kitty. They found her kind, shy and hardworking. Late into the evening she would be in her office at the Department, unaware of the passing time, until Bardie would arrive, concerned that Kitty was tiring herself out, and persuade her to come home, travelling by bus: the Atholls did not stand on ceremony.

But despite her popularity among the officials at the Department and those who knew her well in political circles, Kitty's nervousness in the House led to lengthy speeches of explanation on her part. She found it difficult to be short, sharp and to the point and on occasion the House made it clear that it was getting a little weary. This in its turn made her even less self-confident.

Certainly Nancy Astor, with her assertive personality and ready wit, would have dealt with Eustace Percy very much more effectively and would not have permitted herself to have been upstaged for one minute. He was cordially disliked on all sides of the House because of his manner in and out of the Chamber. Members greatly resented the way in which he would lean across the Despatch Box and hector the Opposition. Nancy would probably have made a laughing stock of him by imitating him mercilessly: having gained the upper hand, she would have made sure that she retained it.

Kitty, however, did not allow Percy's bullying manner to divert her from her principles and from the course which she felt the Board should be following. Percy and she had come to office with the promise of a reduction in the size of classes and of an expansion of secondary education. Percy had, almost immediately on coming to the Board, advised local authorities to review their requirements with a view to extending the length of schooling to the age of fifteen and the improvement of buildings and general conditions. By 1925, however, the Government found itself having to face the need to trim £40 million from the estimates for the following year in order to produce a 'balanced' budget, regarded at the time as essential. The cuts would have to be spread over all Departments, Education included. During 1926, in Cabinet, Eustace Percy was forced to agree to trim back his own estimates by £2 million.

One of the problems which both Percy and Kitty faced was the Chancellor's lack of interest in the subject of education. Churchill, who had—perhaps surprisingly in view of his very recent conversation to the Conservative ranks—become Chancellor in 1924, was by no means an academic, and indeed this applied to many members of the Cabinet, which was elitist in its composition. Of its twenty-one members, nine were aristocrats, all had been educated at public schools (nine at Eton) and sixteen had been to Oxford or Cambridge. Although highly educated themselves, they took their education for granted and—perhaps through lack of imagination and understanding rather than as a matter of deliberate policy—saw no reason to exert themselves over the educational opportunities of the working classes. However the Board's Consultative Committee, under its Chairman Sir Henry Hadow, was examining ways of improving elementary education and making it easier for the best pupils to pass from elementary schools to secondary school. That report was awaited.

Faced with the need for cutbacks, Percy set about deciding how it should be done without discussing the matter with Kitty or with the officials at the Department. One of his first proposals was that the age at which children should begin schooling should be raised to seven from the autumn of 1926. Kitty warned him that the entire Party would rebel against such a measure: the decision would be a betrayal of electoral promises and would be detrimental to the education of children. For the time being he dropped the idea.

Percy's next suggestion was that the principle of free elementary school education, which had been introduced in 1891, should be abandoned. Parents of elementary school children should be required to pay the sum of 3d. per child per week. At the same time the fees of secondary school children should be lowered to the same sum. This was regarded by Percy as fair all round and would create the saving of exactly the amount of £2 million which he required.

But elementary schools were largely attended by working-class children, secondary schools by middle-class children: the charges would fall on those least able to pay for them. Kitty rebelled again, pointing out that this plan was 'a violation of our pledges . . . open to grave objection . . . would have a disastrous effect on public opinion'. She believed that no great savings could be made in education at all, apart from an alteration in the basis of the grant to local education authorities, which could well be undesirable.

The 1925 summer recess arrived, bringing Kitty some respite from Percy and relief from the immediate problems at the Board. She was invited by the Foreign Secretary, Austen Chamberlain, to be 'the' woman member of the delegation he was taking to the League of Nations' annual meeting in Geneva. She travelled out via Aix-les-Bains to stay with the Prime Minister and Mrs Baldwin at their holiday haunt en route for Geneva. There, among other duties, she acted as hostess at a party for all Commonwealth delegates and their wives. During the conference she was able to take a leading part in the discussions, in particular in connection with an International Relief Union and in a discussion about aid for the Armenians. This gave her special pleasure; Armenia had particular appeal for her because of the old family connection with the country.

She returned to Westminster, when the House resumed, to find the first indications of the great economic difficulties in which the Board of Education was placed, and to a major confrontation with her chief. She was anxious to discover the direction in which Percy planned to take the department over the necessary reductions in expenditure. It is a matter of speculation how far Eustace Percy was simply flying a kite, but he now threatened the Cabinet that if he was forced to cut £2 million from the estimates he would propose total exclusion from schooling of all children under the age of six—a move which even Churchill recognised as undesirable. Following a debate in Cabinet, Percy produced a circular for local authorities proposing a complete halt in educational development for the next three years and the substitution of a block grant scheme for the existing percentage grant scheme.

A circular was despatched on 25 November 1925, despite strong opposition from the Duchess and officials to the Board. It produced shockwaves throughout the educational arena which extended far beyond those directly concerned. The country was appalled and the Government attacked for abandoning its pledges. Baldwin backtracked. The circular was, he said smoothly, issued in order to encourage discussion between local authorities and the President of the Board: such discussion would now be welcome.

During the debate in the House on 17 December the circular was vehemently attacked, not only from the ranks of the Labour opposition, but from Tory backbenchers. Percy spoke with less than his normal bravura. He had to admit that the circular had been issued in advance of receipt of the new estimates from local authorities, which he now realised were considerably higher than forecast. He guaranteed to withdraw implementation of the circular for one year. This did little to satisfy the critics.

It fell to Kitty to make the winding-up speech for the Government. She replied conscientiously to each point raised. In Percy's defence she drew attention to the fact that she had served on a local authority in

Scotland, where block grants had been in existence for some time and referred to the steady progress that had taken place there. She ended:

> I agree unreservedly . . . in regarding the children of this country as our best and most valuable raw material. Education is the last service on which I should like to see any economy made, but when the finances of the country are in the condition in which they are . . . I do not see how education can hope altogether to escape . . . what we want to do is to be able to hold our ground and to maintain existing services. Our education policy remains as it was stated a year ago; the improvement of opportunities for secondary eduction; the replacement of bad buildings and the reduction in size of the large classes. We hope to be able to give effect to this policy when the happy day comes that programmes submitted by local authorities can be approved. I earnestly hope that before long we may be able to proceed further with this policy, which we have been pursuing in the last year and which we continue to regard as vital to the interests of the children and the nation.

When she sat down, it was to cheers from her own side; and when the House divided she was cheered in the Government lobby. Sir Murdo MacDonald, the Liberal-National member for Inverness (the same eminent civil engineer whom she had met on the Suez Canal in 1916) wrote to her next day:

> Will you please allow me to congratulate you on the splendid appearance you made last night. As I voted in favour of the resolution I think you will agree that my opinion is all the more unbiased. In fact I can say I felt like King Agrippa when he said to Paul 'Almost thou persuadest me' and I was very glad to notice when you sat down that as happened to Horatius when he swam the Tiber and safely reached land 'Even the ranks of Tuscany could scarce forbear to cheer'.

Eustace Percy owed Kitty his gratitude, but he failed to show it, irked possibly, that her speech had served to emphasise his own poor performance.

One of the duties which Eustace Percy was happy to pass on to Kitty was that of attending school prizegivings round the country. The Board of Education applied to England and Wales; Scotland and N Ireland had their own systems of education which did not come under the aegis of the Board. On most Fridays Kitty found herself in some part of England or Wales delivering encouraging speeches to young people. It was extremely tiring, but she was glad to do it. She wanted to be able to impress on them those things which she herself valued in life: honesty, integrity, hard work and dedication. She always told them not to worry if their personal academic capability was not of the highest order—satisfaction in life lay in achieving one's own personal maximum. She constantly stressed that creative gifts were just as important, if not more so, as academic skills. If the children were slightly bemused by this earnest little woman, the staff were always delighted.

In the spring of 1926 Kitty was asked by Eustace Percy to take his place at an educational conference in Montreal. She and Ursula Morley-Fletcher, her secretary, set off by sea for Halifax. On board were a number of distinguished travellers from various countries bound for the same conference, including the Director of the Royal College of Music, Sir Hugh Allen, a genial, friendly and amusing man with whom Kitty naturally shared many interests. Kitty later recalled the look of incredulity on the faces of the French Minister for Education and one of his colleagues when they discovered Kitty and Ursula at the piano playing the baseline of 'chopsticks' alternately while Sir Hugh played his own amazing and dazzling version of the upper part, his fingers racing up and down the keys in a cascade of intricate melody.

The conference which Kitty was to address was one given by the Canadian National Council of Education every three years, attended by one thousand delegates. By now this was no strain and she enjoyed it. When it was over she received an honorary degree from McGill University and then she and Ursula crossed Canada by train to Vancouver, carrying out speaking engagements in Regina, Winnipeg and Vancouver. Kitty did not fail to note that the Scots abroad seemed to have achieved very senior positions in government, industry and the professions. She was warmly welcomed wherever she went, but found herself in an embarrassing position: the post of Governor General of Canada was vacant and Bardie's name, among others, was being mentioned. She found that her presence was being viewed with some curiosity. Lord Byng, the retiring Governor General, went so far as to ask: 'Why are you out here?' She was able to say with perfect truth that Eustace Percy had fully intended to come himself but had been prevented from doing so at the last minute.

However, as previously over Albania, Bardie was obviously interested in the idea. Kitty confided in letters to him that although she felt that they could do a great deal if fate sent them to Canada, she felt that they could not afford it: wages were so high and Government House conducted itself with such style that a large staff was required for entertaining on a grand scale. She thought on the whole the post would be better suited to someone with a long pocket.

Kitty and Ursula returned to a Britain paralysed by the General Strike. Bardie met them at the docks to greet them and to attend to the luggage personally. They returned to Eaton Place in a student-driven taxi: and

25   The Imperial Education Conference, 1927. (The Duchess of Atholl, centre, with Lord Eustace Percy on her left.)

Bardie to Scotland, where, as Lord Lieutenant of Perthshire, he was responsible for law and order during the strike.

In the autumn Kitty returned to the department, once again full of apprehension over Eustace's latest plans. Tawney, the Labour Party educationalist, had already dubbed the department the Ministry for Discouraging Spending on Education. Percy's utterances on the subject of education were not in accordance with his actions. There was a new plan on the part of the Government, under which all local authority funding from government, including education, would come in the form of block grants. Eustace Percy not only acquiesced in this but strongly pressed for it. Kitty objected vigorously and, although initially she was nervous about tackling her disagreeable chief, her righteous wrath brought her into a series of verbal battles with him. During the last of these, in December, she informed him that she had no alternative but to go directly to the Prime Minister to make her objections known to him.

The idea of a junior minister going over the head of her chief to speak directly to the Prime Minister seems unusual today, though there was, of course, no question of her doing it behind his back. In 1934 Eden, as Assistant Foreign Secretary, would similarly approach Baldwin (not, admittedly, then Prime Minister) over the head of his Chief, Sir John Simon, with whom he was at odds over matters of policy.

In January, Kitty saw Baldwin privately and put her case. He let her speak without interruption, pacing up and down the room as he listened. Her intervention was effective; as a result the education grants were excluded from the block grant scheme; percentage grants were retained, though spending was inevitably curbed. The morale of all those involved in education at all levels rose. Eustace Percy had paid lip service to the ideal of quality of opportunity for all and, although perhaps he had meant well, he had done his best to destroy it for a generation. Kitty had somehow managed to save the day so far as she could.

The school-leaving age continued to be a matter of debate for the next decade. Kitty thought it should be raised, with exemptions for those who preferred and were able to find employment. This was seen as an outrageously patronising attitude by many—Tories, Liberal and Labour alike—and perhaps it was a mistaken view. It was also a recognition of the fact that with high unemployment children of fourteen were often in a position to help their parents. This was still an era of domestic servants and of young agricultural workers. Children intending to go into these jobs often preferred to be free to do so at fourteen rather than staying at school for a further year. What Kitty looked forward to was a new curriculum for the non-academic children, in which they would be taught subjects which interested them: creative work—art, woodwork, music, embroidery, metalwork. Given these choices, she felt, children would enjoy staying at school. Until that was provided she felt that many would simply be wasting time against their will, others positively harmed by the experience.

The following June Kitty chaired the Imperial Education Conference in London, which lasted for three weeks and brought representatives of forty-five countries together. In the autumn she spoke at the British Association meeting in Leeds, choosing as her theme 'Broadening the Outlook in Education', which gave her an opportunity to explain more fully her belief in new forms of post-primary education. 'Schools exist for children, not children for schools,' she insisted.

Her last major act in connection with education was to chair a departmental committee on examinations for part-time students. Almost 800,000 young people over the age of fourteen in employment attended part-time schooling, either in the evening or at day continuation classes. It was felt that suitable curricula and examinations would provide 'incentives and opportunity for advancement'. The Atholl Report also recommended that there should be co-operation between representatives of industry, commerce, teachers, local authorities and the Board in arranging such curricula.

The five-year term of office of the Baldwin government was coming to an end and the election was held in May 1929. In a three-cornered fight Kitty retained her seat with a greatly reduced majority. The Liberal candidate on this occasion was a much respected local landlord and near neighbour, Dr George Freeland Barbour of Fincastle, the Socialist candidate a church minister.

During the campaign there was a complaint at a socialist meeting that at the end of the war the Duchess had visited working people's homes suggesting ways of circumventing the food shortage by such methods as making fish soup by including the fishes' heads. It was asked whether it was thought that her Grace would enjoy such a delicacy herself. This story may well have been true—and, since Kitty might have had some difficulty in boiling an egg without assistance, her temerity in delivering instruction in cookery is not without humour. The use of fish heads, though perhaps distasteful to many, is not unusual. (Andre Simon's *Encyclopedia of Gastronomy* contains a recipe for fish chowder in which head, tail and backbone are simmered to provide the basic liquid.) Bardie, *bon viveur* and chef, may well have primed Kitty before she set off on well-intentioned errands of instruction. It is possible that she caused offence by omitting to mention that the heads should be removed before serving the soup. (In the early days of the Second World War Kitty—now almost without staff—produced a rabbit stew for guests which proved to be quite uneatable. Questioned by Bardie, she replied that she couldn't understand what might have gone wrong: the meat should have been particularly tender, as the rabbits had been shot only that morning.)

The result of the election in Kinross and West Perthshire was: Duchess of Atholl, Unionist, 12,245, Dr G F Barbour (Liberal) 9,128, Rev W D Stewart (Socialist) 3,834.

The government was about to change: in the country as a whole the Labour Party won the election by a small majority. At the Board of Education there was real regret that Kitty would be leaving. The permanent officials were sorry to lose her and many wrote to say so. Eustace Percy wrote briefly, and with uncharacteristic warmth:

> Thank you for all you have done for me during these last four and a half years. I'm afraid you've found me a most trying Chief and I apologize for all the worry I've given you. But I think we can feel that we've done a job of work together that was really worth doing and you can certainly feel that, if we've left office with the goodwill, on the whole, of the educational world, that goodwill has been entirely due to your missionary work up and down the country and to the respect felt by everyone for your abilities and devotion to the work. You won't be sorry to have a rest—I know how much you need it!
> Eustace.

Eustace Percy may not have intended to be uncouth and domineering, though that is the impression he undoubtedly gave. Those consulted who remember him speak of him in such terms as 'cold fish' and 'pious prig'. Lord Home recalls that he was eventually dubbed 'Minister for Thought' and consigned to oblivion.

Chapter 12

Ted: and a DCL

Kitty's problems with Eustace Percy had an unexpected side-effect. When Percy's Circular 1371 was published in November 1925, Ted Butler, in a letter to his niece Ursula Morley-Fletcher, commented on its proposals. Kitty's secretary, Ursula—daughter of Ted's sister Queenie—passed the comments on as she knew that Kitty would be interested to read them.

Kitty and Ted had not been directly in touch in the twenty-five years since Kitty's marriage. Both married long since, Ted was now a grandfather. He had recently retired from his old school, Harrow, where he had been Senior Classics Master. He now lived at Monkton Coombe, near Bath. Anxious and depressed, Kitty felt the need to discuss the situation with someone detached and thoroughly knowledgeable in the field of education. In reply to his letter to Ursula she wrote to him:

> I feel I should like to say how interested I am to see your views on the Circular. I feel pretty certain that England is not getting as good value for money spent as Scotland. . . .

A meeting was arranged in March. Ted came up to London and over luncheon—which apparently took place at Lords—she confided in him about the disagreeable atmosphere and the difficulties she was encountering at the Board. As he listened, his thoughts went back thirty years to the summers at Wimbledon, to their adolescent friendship and affection.

A visit to Monkton Coombe was arranged. Afterwards he wrote:

> Monkton Coombe, 26th June 1926.
>
> . . . I am more glad that your visit came so soon. I had fancied, I think wrongly, that there was a little uneasy feeling between G and myself when I spoke of you or she knew that I had had a letter from you. Just before you came I spoke to her about this and told her that between you and me, so far as I was concerned, it must be all or nothing and that I should prefer nothing if I could not meet and write to you as my dearest friend. But now that she has come to know you and has seen us together I can see that she is glad that things are as they are . . .

Monkton Coombe, July 1926.

> . . . Now what I want to tell you: you have written exactly what I meant to write to you. Those three days were three of the happiest of my life. 'How fresh the splinters keep and fine!' I had just feared a little that, though in writing we had come near to each other again, it might not be so easy when we really met to pick up the threads again. You have led and are leading so much bigger and wider a life than I. But you were a dear, and all those years seemed to vanish away at once and I found that I had got my very dear little sister back again. Have you learnt a poem of twelve lines of which the central ones are:

> > How many loved your moments of glad grace
> > And loved your beauty with love false or true
> > But one man loved the pilgrim soul in you
> > And loved the sorrows of your changing face.

> You can apply those words as you like, but the last two lines have been very dear to me and, thank heaven, can now be truer than ever, openly and straightforwardly. But I do not want to see any sorrows, nor dark shadows under your eyes such as I saw at Miss Needham's and whilst we we were playing clock golf at Wells. You must not walk along the edge of a breakdown. What a metaphor!—Always your affectionate E M B

In the autumn of 1925 the Chancellor of Oxford, Lord Cave, had nominated Kitty for an Honorary DCL. She would be the first woman ever to receive the degree. However her pleasure at the nomination was tinged with unhappiness; other members of her family, notably her older sisters, felt that she should not accept it. Her father, who had died earlier that year, had never received an honorary degree from Oxford, despite his great contribution to history and his strong links with the university. There had been considerable comment about the omission and it was known that he himself had been disappointed. There was much pressure on Kitty to refuse and she hesitated, but her younger sisters and Bardie were able to persuade her to accept: a decision with which Ted agreed in retrospect:

> . . . as the daughter of a very distinguished Oxford scholar, with your position and work in education, you are just the person to receive it. I am very sorry you have had so much family bother about it. The more I thought about it, the more certain I was that you were right to accept, for the reason I gave you and also because I am sure that your dear old father would have been delighted that you should be honoured by his old university.

It was ironical that Kitty of all people—Kitty, the anti-feminist—was breaking the mould so effectively: trail-blazing almost by accident, certainly never by design. Despite her ever-lengthening series of 'firsts' it remained her view that

> a woman's primary interest lies in human welfare, of which in her home she is the guardian. Does not the very framework of a woman's body make her a realist? Is not the creation of life the greatest fact we know? Should not women, therefore, whose great task it is to carry on life, have an instinctive grasp of realities, of fact, of cause and effect, if they are true to themselves and to their fundamental instincts? (*Women and Politics*, 1932).

From this comment we may assume that despite her many personal achievements, despite the honours bestowed on her and despite her elevated social position, Kitty continued to regard motherhood as the most rewarding and fulfilling role for a woman and would infinitely have preferred it for herself. One might argue that she saw motherhood as the primary role and man's situation as that of supporter.

Monkton Coombe, 5th October 1926.

. . . The strange thing about you, Kit, is that at one moment you talk with the heart of a woman and a moment after—on business matters—with the brain and outlook of a man. I have met many women who do public work, but never anyone who combines these gifts as you do. And it is very attractive, if you will allow me to say so . . .

Now two small matters and I have done. You write that you have hard and bitter feelings, the cause of which I should understand. Well, I do not believe that you are capable of such feelings for any length of time on your own account. For wrong to others you might have been, but not for yourself . . . And as to courage once more, you know that the bravest people are those who do not think they are brave and whose nerves flutter before they go into any kind of action. Your whole public life shows that you have the right kind of courage. It must have been a tremendous step for you to enter the House and there to win the place you have won. And of courage in personal matters you gave, thank heaven, the highest proof when you said those few words to me at the end of our first meeting. I realize what they must have cost you and that emboldened me to tell you everything frankly about myself.

As you asked me to do so, my last thoughts every night now are to pray that you may have all the courage you require. But if there is any humour in Heaven, I suspect there are gleams of amusement in many eyes when prayers for courage float up from me to you. Anyhow, I feel the humour of it. Bless you.

As to what was said during that conversation—those few words spoken— between Kitty and Ted after their first meeting at Lords, we can only guess. It seems probable that she trusted Ted enough to tell him, truthfully and confidentially, of the difficulties and disappointments she had faced in her marriage: and perhaps, to tell him that, after all, although tenderness for the one had been overtaken by passion for the other during that summer of the Jubilee, recollections of that tenderness had long outlasted the passion. Her devotion and loyalty to Bardie remained: but it was, had been for many years and would remain throughout their lives, only the devotion of a loving, compassionate friend and partner.

Monkton Coombe, 4th November 1926.

. . . de la Mare's The Listeners is a difficult, but for me, a strangely attractive poem. I am not at all certain of its real meaning, but I think the Traveller is an old man, looking back on his early years and trying to revive old memories, old familiar faces, etc. He calls them up one by one, but they are only phantom listeners. No answer comes to him. It might have been so with me writing to you today, but thanks to you another 'Lords'-like date is going to be a happy one for me this year and there is going to be no 'stillness answering my cry'. Anyhow this year I am going to knock at your door and send through it much love and every best wish possible. If life can be likened to champagne, up to a few months ago it was somewhat flat; now there is a fizz about it, which makes all the difference.

Monkton Coombe, 4th December 1926.

My first writing with this beautiful pencil must be to you. I need not tell you how I shall prize it and how much it will mean to me. My birthday was the happiest one I have had for years. Exactly ten months have passed since a certain luncheon, and to me at any rate it has been going from rock to rock. Bless you for it.—Always your affectionate E M B.

Monkton Coombe, 30th December 1926.

I am glad you liked that book. I think I marked all my favourites. I didn't know your Mother had set 'Renouncement' to music. It must have been after ——. It is one of Alice Meynell's best bits of work . . .

Once more, much love and best wishes and a good deal of thankfulness and blessings. Stir them all up together and put them in your oven. What comes over will represent my message to you on Saturday. Bless you my dear for all your trust in me. Much love and good wishes. E M B

(*Renouncement*):
I must not think of thee: and, tired yet strong
I shun the thought that lurks in all delight—
The Thought of thee—in the blue Heaven's height
And in the sweetest passage of a song.

Monkton Coombe, 1st March 1927.

This letter is really to thank you for your lunch to me a year ago and for the few words at the end. 'A little more, and how much it is.' If I had been told this day last year that by now you would have spent two weekends with us, and I a week with you in Scotland, I should never have believed it . . .

Kitty's sister Agnata—Ted's stepmother, Ursula's step-grandmother—died in May 1931. After the funeral, he wrote to Kitty:

I was very glad to have a long, quiet talk with you yesterday. Kind and loving though my hosts were, the atmosphere was not congenial. You gave me just what I wanted. Now we must forget all that we hate so much in that creed, its seeming want of outspoken sympathy and natural affection and understanding. I am sure you understood that my sympathy for you was more than I could ever show . . .

This close, platonic friendship must have given Kitty at last the warm reassurance which had eluded her in marriage. She was too practical and too sensible to dwell on 'romance', but she would have been less than human if she had not reflected fleetingly on how life might have been for them both if they had married each other in those last days of Victoria's reign. It would have been a less glamorous marriage, might even have become a little boring: but it seems clear that together they would have 'mastered love's abiding stuff'. For her too, there would have been a home of her own, the opportunity—Ted would certainly have encouraged her—for fulfilment as a musician; and even, perhaps, children.

Ted died in 1952.

A possible explanation for Kitty's return to Scotland from the Royal College in 1896, before completion of her final term, could be that someone in the family, noticing the young people's fondness for each other, also believed that such a union would fall into the 'forbidden' categories of marriage as listed in the Book of Common Prayer. It does not state specifically: 'A man may not marry his stepmother's half-sister'; but someone may have thought that it was implicit in the instruction, believing that Kitty was, in the eyes of the Church, Ted's aunt. On this basis it may have been decided that separation was kindest under the circumstances. If this theory is correct, it is most likely that its source was Sir James, who was a staunch Episcopalian. It might also provide an explanation for the fact that Kitty and Ted did not meet again until shortly after Sir James's death. Obviously, despite his strongly held opinions and fiery temperament, he had inspired affection. (He was viewed by his son-in-law Bardie in retrospect as having been '. . . a mass of opposites—very hardy, yet hated bloodshed or roughness; quick-tempered yet childishly kindhearted; a wonderful brain yet unable to take in some of the simplest things that were practical.') If Sir James had intervened to prevent Kitty and Ted from marrying—and such a suggestion can only be speculation—clearly neither Kitty nor Ted felt any bitterness towards him on that account.

Chapter 13

Bardie on the Brink: and the Stirrings of Feminism, 1924–33

While Kitty was preoccupied with education and with politics in general, Bardie was fighting his own financial battles. His difficulties were unresolved and getting worse. One scheme for restoring his fortunes was the formation of a company known as Atholl Steel Houses Ltd. He personally designed these from an idea he had seen and he and Lord Invernairn, head of a leading Glasgow engineering works, Beardmores, set up a company to develop them. The houses were simpler, faster and cheaper to construct than those built by traditional methods and were both solid and durable. A few of them were built on the estate and quite a number were constructed on behalf of local authorities as council houses.

As with many of Bardie's ideas, this one was inherently sound: the steel houses which were constructed are still occupied and in good order today. He was convinced of the enormous potential sales to be made. In 1924 he was expecting to receive £10,000 worth of orders from Rumania and also from France and Italy. Despite his optimism, however, the contracts were never placed; within a few years his personal debt on Atholl Steel Houses had reached £20,000.

A further misfortune followed. Bardie and Lord Invernairn were persuaded by a Colonel Harrison to visit Jamaica with a view to inspecting a large estate and buying it in order to grow sugar and to set up a factory to refine it in Glasgow, with the additional prospect of helping employment on the Clyde. They were impressed by the potential development and after investigation were able to borrow money from government sources to buy it. As the years went by, however, poor local management, falling sugar prices and the world depression combined to make the enterprise financially disastrous. By the time the government called in its loan in 1930 Bardie's personal debt on Jamaican Sugar had reached the same figure as his debt on Atholl Steel Houses—£20,000. All his attempts to rescue the estate from disaster only combined to ensure that the disaster, when it came, would be even greater.

It is hard not to have some sympathy for Bardie, however, critical one may be of the means he adopted. He had inherited massive debts and great responsibilities at a time when the economic outlook in the country as a whole was grave. He continually rode out, hopefully and eagerly, like Don Quixote, to save the family fortunes: and always came a cropper.

In the early summer of 1926 his finances collapsed completely. He had for some time been a Director of the Union Bank of Scotland, but for the last few years had avoided attending Board meetings because of embarrassment over his own large overdraft. Now the local branch of the bank, from which the wages of the estate workers were paid, refused further facilities. In addition, the Chairman of the Bank, Norman Hird, wrote to him concerning the main account:

> It is quite obvious that in your own interest some definite scheme must be arranged for reducing expenditure and I have asked Mr Dickson to take this up with you at once. Failing that, the outlook for Atholl Estates a few years hence would be hopeless, as you cannot go on losing, as you are at present, at the rate of £20,000 per annum.

Estate workers and employees loyally continued to work unpaid for a time while the immediate difficulties were solved with the help of Douglas Dickson, Bardie's Edinburgh lawyer. Land and property were sold to reduce his indebtedness by some £114,000; but this was merely staving off the more drastic action which would be required a few years later.

The remaining lands on Atholl were valued at £600,000 and by 1928 it had become necessary to sell off one-third, to raise £196,000. Furthermore, in order to find ready money, Kitty's and Bardie sent many of their possessions to the salerooms of Spinks and Sothebys in 1928 and 1929. Christie's sold the emerald tiara for £6,500, a pearl necklace for £5,500, a sapphire and diamond necklace for £880, a ruby and diamond ring and various other pieces of Kitty's jewellery. Sothebys had already sold a three-row pearl necklace for £7,200, as well as Limoges enamels and other items from the Castle. Spinks sold a gold marriage medal which once belonged to King James VI and a collection of medals and coins.

It was hard to part with the land that had been part of the estate for generations and to lose valued personal possessions and still be in difficulties. Kitty's own lawyers wrote to her expressing anxiety over the proposed sales of land, since under the terms of her marriage contract certain of the lands might not be sold without her agreement. They pointed out that her own annuity, should she be widowed, could be gravely affected by the sales and they urged her to refuse permission. Kitty, however, was more anxious that the debts should be cleared and gladly gave her permission in order to help Bardie. Some years later, when her brother's finances at Bamff were in difficulties, she waived the entailment which would have provided her with an anuity from Banff which had been arranged in the event of her widowhood.

These large-scale sales in themselves would still not have been sufficient in the long run to prevent the sale of the entire estate, which had proved impossible to run on an economically viable basis. Salvation ultimately came from another, unexpected, source.

It had long been clear that Bardie's younger brother, Lord James (Hamish), heir to the Dukedom, would not marry and that after his death the Dukedom would pass to a distant cousin, Sir Evelyn Murray. The eventual heir would be Sir Evelyn's son Anthony. He was a frequent and popular visitor to Atholl.

In 1930 Anthony Murray married Angela Pearson, daughter of the second Viscount Cowdray—granddaughter of the first viscount, who had been a famous civil engineer and founder of the business empire built round the family company of S Pearson and Son. Although they naturally hoped that it would not occur for many years, the knowledge that Tony and Angela would one day become Duke and Duchess of Atholl gave Kitty and Bardie pleasure.

By chance Kitty and Bardie met Lady Cowdray, Angela's grandmother, at a musical gathering in Aberdeenshire shortly after the wedding and naturally discussed the prospects for the young couple in a polite and general way. However Bardie's cautious remarks alerted Lady Cowdray to the fact that a serious situation existed at Blair. She made a point of making further enquiries and arranged a meeting with Bardie in London.

Lady Cowdray was distressed to learn that part of what should have been Tony's inheritance was being disposed of piecemeal. She embarked on a series of meetings and conversations with Bardie with the intention of finding out if she could be of help. She had several other grandchildren to consider and had no wish to favour one more than another. On the other hand she was anxious that when Tony and Angela inherited the estate there should be something substantial remaining for them to inherit.

Lady Cowdray was initially given to understand that an injection of £50,000 would be sufficient to save the estate and the contents of the Castle. Gradually, however, as discussions and legal negotiations continued, the full extent of Bardie's debts were disclosed: the £20,000 on Jamaican sugar, £20,000 on Steel Houses, an overdraft at the Union Bank in Pitlochry of £47,000, overdrafts at the Clydesdale Bank, Lloyds

Bank, Barclays Bank, a claim for estate duty on timber sold, an advance from lawyers, etc.

The protracted negotiations continued for two years. Lady Cowdray was aghast to learn the final truth: the amount required to pay off all debts was nearly £400,000. She had become more and more appalled at each new revelation and was afraid that there might be yet more debts of which she had not been told. In January 1932 she wrote to Bardie:

> I feel my wish to help is impossible and that my offer should be withdrawn. When first thought of it was to be £50,000 to prevent the Bank from taking things from Blair. Then when things were looked into it was necessary to make it £100,000. Now it seems to be £150,000 to clear things generally: counting the charges £230,000, it makes £380,000. I am of course dreadfully sorry but your letter makes me sure I must withdraw. I am indeed sorry.

But perhaps against her better judgement or inclination, Lady Cowdray finally instructed her lawyers to draw up an agreement under which she would pay off all debts, while a company would be formed to take possession of all property and assets, including contents of the castle, houses and lodges. Bardie would become Company Chairman and would draw a salary of £2,000. Provision would be made for an annuity of £1,500 for Kitty in the event of Bardie's death. Bardie would sign an undertaking not to become involved in further financial speculation of any kind. Bardie and Kitty would occupy Eastwood House at Dunkeld, the Castle being let.

Lady Cowdray finally signed the documents relating to the agreement in March 1932. She made the stipulation that Tony and Angela were not to be told until she gave permission. She had acted in every way with noble generosity and the decision must have caused the old lady great anxiety. She went abroad immediately after signing the agreement and died suddenly and unexpectedly two weeks later. Her intervention had been providential. Her son, Lord Cowdray, had not known of the arrangement either and was probably initially dismayed by the discovery, but he and his legal and financial advisers immediately began to make the necessary arrangements to set up the new company: Atholl Estates would henceforth (and for the first time in its history) be prudently and, in time, profitably managed.

To Bardie it was a matter of great regret that the estate no longer belonged to him, but the strain of debt had been lifted from his shoulders for the remainder of his life. Kitty, who had remained detached from the proceedings, was overwhelmingly thankful and relieved that the financial troubles which had beset them throughout their married life were now over and that there would be stability in the future for tenants and estate workers also. Everyone concerned with Atholl Estates had reason to rejoice. Kitty was not least relieved, too, that Bardie would now be prevented from becoming involved in financial schemes of the kind that had caused her endless private anguish and acute embarrassment. She had buried herself in political issues partly at least in order to escape from the constant, gnawing anxieties concerning their situation.

There was one more hurdle to jump, however. In 1933 Bardie was involved in a financial muddle which caused him to appear in court and plead guilty to charges concerned with running an illegal lottery. It was a typical Bardie muddle—a mixture of financial ineptitude and carelessness. It concerned the London Clinic of which Kitty had laid the foundation stone in 1928 and which was opened by the Duchess of York in 1932. The lottery had been started in order to raise funds for the clinic but had been banned under the law pertaining to gaming and lotteries. Finding himself with a vast number of now useless printed tickets, Bardie proceeded to issue them as receipts for donations to a charitable fund for hospitals and nurses. When challenged by a member of the public who had believed himself to be buying a lottery ticket, not making a donation, Scotland Yard was called in. Bardie was appalled and Kitty noted in her diary: 'He seems dazed.' However it was a marginal case and he was let off with a caution, believing himself to be the victim of a badly framed law.

Whilst their financial affairs were passing through such turbulent waters during these years of the late 1920s and early 1930s, there had been more pleasant distractions. Work on the Scottish War Memorial was completed in the summer of 1927. It was generally regarded as the most eloquent war memorial in the world and a major achievement on the part of its architect, Robert Lorimer. Bardie planned the opening ceremony, which was to be attended by the Prince of Wales and included a parade of all the Services. With his habit of teasing Kitty, he rang her up on the day before the opening to ask her, casually, to bring her wartime VAD uniform from London. Slightly vexed by the request, she found it with some difficulty, packed it in her case and was mortified, on arriving in Edinburgh off the sleeper, to discover that Bardie intended her to lead the parade of Women's Services and would accept no refusal. She had never taken part in a parade in her life before, but the march to the Castle Esplanade was accomplished with her customary aplomb. She profoundly hoped that none of the onlookers would notice her knees knocking as she brought her column round with a command to 'Right wheel!' Kitty laid the wreath on behalf of the Women's Services and carried their Roll of Honour.

A day or two later the Atholls went to Fealar Lodge. Among Kitty's greatest pleasures were those summer weeks spent at one of the remote shooting lodges on the estate—and lovely Fealar in the hills between Glen Tilt and Kirkmichael was a particular favourite. Free of servants and obligations, Bardie cooked for their guests and themselves and they relaxed quietly, climbing, walking, fishing or reading, far from the worries of Westminster or the hauntings of bank managers.

One evening in the early autumn of 1927 Kitty and Bardie, now back at Eastwood, were sitting down to dinner. The chef at Blair had cooked and sent down a haggis, which was one of Bardie's favourite dishes. It had just been cut open when the telephone rang. It was Lady Muir of Blairdrummond, near Stirling: King Boris of Bulgaria had been staying with them and would be passing Eastwood the following day on his way to Balmoral. Might they bring him to luncheon? The Atholls agreed immediately and the haggis was returned to the kitchen to be sewn up again for the following day. History does not relate what Kitty and Bardie had for dinner—nor, alas, what King Boris thought of the haggis.

Bardie, ever mindful of his duties as a host, resolved to pay King Boris the ultimate compliment of having his National Anthem rendered on the pipes and accordingly called in Pipe-Major Wilkie during the morning and invited him to learn it. The Pipe-Major, though willing, was unfamiliar with the tune and had difficulty in memorising it in the half hour available. Nonetheless he duly entered the dining room in full blast when luncheon was over. Not surprisingly, perhaps, the King failed to recognise it, but observing everyone present standing up for some reason, promptly did so himself. It was left to his aide-de-camp to explain the nature of the salute.

A week or two later Bardie took Kitty and Ursula with him on his second visit to the sugar plantation in Jamaica, where they had a series of amusing experiences as well as a near disaster. Kitty, swimming in the sea at San Antonio, got into difficulties and by coincidence was saved from drowning by a fellow junior minister, Sir B M Eyres-Monsell, who fortunately happened to be swimming nearby.

After the holiday Kitty went to Washington to meet President Coolidge and to New York, where, amongst other visits, she called on Katherine Mayo, whose book *Mother India* had just been published. It had caused a minor sensation. It dealt frankly with the treatment of women in India, painting a picture of unbearable suffering, mental and physical; of small girls being subjected to sexual brutality; of the horrors endured by Indian widows; of poor medical services and of the taboos which surrounded the process of childbirth, making it a terrible and hazardous experience. Possibly the book was deliberately over-dramatic and colourful, and some of its allegations perhaps untrue or exaggerated, but the passages relating to child marriage at least were substantially true.

Mother India was a best-seller and ran to seventy reprints. It made a profound impression and aroused great indignation, both in Britain and America, particularly in feminist circles. One Independent feminist, Eleanor Rathbone, was so outraged by the account presented in the book that she resolved to stand for Parliament in order to campaign against such treatment of women and children in part of the British Empire. Churchill was another reader deeply affected by it.

Kitty found the book both sad and shocking, and said of Miss Mayo 'She seemed to me to have a wonderful power of getting to the heart of her very varied subject and her courage in exposing evils was amazing.' Eleanor, the feminist, and Kitty, the anti-feminist, would campaign together in the future.

When Kitty left office in 1929, Eustace Percy had commented that she needed a rest. Certainly the strains of office and her private anxieties had combined to produce an air of strain and an appearance of fragility. The shadows under her eyes of which Ted had spoken were always there now. She was no longer young, and her youthful enthusiasm for pretty clothes and bright colours had waned. She seemed to care little for her appearance. As with Queen Mary, her sense of style had become fixed in an earlier age, though in Kitty's case without the triumphant dignity of Her Majesty's pastel toques, fur collars, lace teagowns and cream umbrellas.

Kitty's clothes were simple, practical, thrifty, plain to the point of drabness, though she was always neat in her appearance. She usually wore a long tweed or tartan skirt, a long woollen jacket, woollen stockings and flat shoes, a single strand of pearls. She was said to have been the last woman to be seen wearing spats, which she continued to wear until the time of her death. Her long, still-dark hair was severely drawn into a bun, and topped if necessary by a neat black tricorn hat worn with a long brown mackintosh. 'Kitty has a soul above clothes!' Mrs Smythe of Methven would sigh to her daughter Barbara. Kitty's plain appearance and lack of style were noted and commented upon unkindly by male colleagues in the House, many of whom were neither youthful, attractive nor well dressed themselves.

There were others, more observant, perhaps, who were conscious of her as a beautiful woman. A schoolboy thought her so beautiful when she came to visit his school that he asked if he might dance with her—which she was pleased to do. Colonel Campbell-Preston, the present Duke of Atholl's stepfather, who only knew Kitty well after she had reached the age of sixty, has said 'Of course Kitty was always beautiful'. Others who knew her well have spoken in the same terms: the excellent bone structure, the brilliance of the eyes and the kind, if unbending, expression remained to create an aura of distinction which drab clothing could not destroy.

26   Chorus-line of women MPs, about 1930 (Nancy Astor sixth from the right, the Duchess of Atholl second from the right)

In 1929 Kitty may indeed have needed a rest, but she had no intention of taking one. She had been invited to write a book on the subject of *Women and Politics* several years previously, but lack of time had made her put the project aside. Now, however, she began work on it. It was meant to instruct women in political matters, which women at that time still tended to think of as a male domain.

Many women were uninformed, even ignorant, about politics. Canvassers for political parties would still be greeted with 'I'll have to ask my husband' when enquiring about political commitment. It was these attitudes which she tried to change. If there appears to be a certain air of condescension in Bernard Shaw's *The Intelligent Woman's Guide to Socialism* and in Kitty's book, this is because both writers felt that instruction of a fairly basic nature was necessary. Shaw's book is the more condescending.

Kitty's book is a reflection of her own personality: serious, honest, incisive, earnest and a little schoolmarmish. She dealt with the structure of government; gave instruction on how to discover the true facts of any political situation, discussed the equation between taxation and the funding of social services, and indicated the ways in which women could contribute to solving the nation's difficulties. It was a worthy effort, but once again her insistence on applying herself to the utmost in writing it exhausted her.

The experience she had undergone at the Department of Education—the crushing humiliation by Percy, the long hours of overwork, her difficulties in the House and the perpetual battle over matters of principle—had left her worn out mentally and physically. Bardie, Ted, Baldwin, Percy himself, colleagues in the House, friends and relations alike noticed and commented on her frailty and on the fact that at times she seemed noticeably absent-minded.

Kitty had never been interested in food and it is possible that now she was so busy and absorbed that she was not eating enough to maintain her health or vitality. It is also possible that she found it necessary to economise drastically on food for herself. The Scottish newspaper *The Bulletin* would later note and comment on the fact that she was the only member in the House who never stopped to eat a meal: and there would (also at a later date) be letters from her bank, sympathetically giving her warnings such as 'Your Grace has £2.5/6d in her account after the usual quarterly payment of £30.' She was in a state of perpetual anxiety over finances at Blair. On her birthday in 1930 Bardie wrote to her:

I have had a terrible financial year. Worse than you know but have been able to meet it all. Six months more, I shall see daylight I hope, but till then! rather horror. Dearie you have been very good this year about cash and I

27   The Duke and Duchess, Eastwood, August 1930

just hate having left you in the lurch. It was the beastly J(amaican) S(ugar) E(nterprise) that started the trouble—ie, the loan. That however (£6000) I hope to recover before very long and it pays 6% so is really not a bad investment. Trichrome may yet turn out useful, but above all I just hated taking your money. Don't worry about it—I am doing all that can be done and worrying over it only upsets one and doesn't mend matters.

Bardie's optimism in the face of potential disaster only served to add to Kitty's anxiety. Bardie complained that if he reported good financial news to her she responded that he didn't deserve it—if bad, that he did. She was wearing herself out with overwork and worry: and now national and international crises were succeeding each other like the mounting waves of a spring tide.

Kitty would never become a feminist, but she was meeting, mixing and discussing problems on a friendly basis with women who were. Rathbone, Wilkinson, Astor, Cazalet-Keir, probably Sylvia Pankhurst (the date of their first meeting is not recorded) and others began to influence her thinking. She developed a new rebelliousness and began to speak out against matters which the shy young Marchioness of Tullibardine of old would never have dreamt of mentioning. It was as if, together with her growing awareness of human misery—and of the depravity which was responsible for much of that misery—some streak

28   Kitty, 1931

of what might almost be called latent masochism had been uncovered. Now she would campaign on behalf of the underprivileged, the politically downtrodden throughout the world; and, as if identifying herself with them in particular, on behalf of women and children who had been physically or mentally mutilated.

In 1929, among all her other preoccupations, Kitty happened to attend a meeting in London held by the Church of Scotland Mission to the Kikuyu, in Kenya. One of the speakers was Mrs Hooper, the wife of one of the missionaries, and she spoke of the prevalent custom of female circumcision. It was a rite performed on young girls at the time of puberty. It involved extensive mutilation and lifelong suffering. Its purpose was to cause copulation to be so painful for a woman throughout her life that she would never actively desire it: a hideous means of ensuring fidelity on the part of a wife, it was a custom deeply rooted in the tribal system. Kitty was appalled to hear of it and immediately decided that it must be stopped. That the British

Government should countenance such brutal assaults on innocent victims in its colonies in the twentieth century seemed to her as unthinkable as slavery appeared to Wilberforce in the early nineteenth. She decided to act.

The first move was to set up a committee, a Committee for the Protection of Coloured Women in the Colonies. She invited Josiah Wedgwood, who had for some time been a resident magistrate in South Africa, to chair it, and he gladly accepted. Rab Butler became Secretary and the committee included David Ormsby-Gore, Captain Victor Cazalet, Eleanor Rathbone—now an MP—and several others: both MPs and co-options from outside the House.

The Committee began to take evidence from authoritative sources, medical and otherwise, over a period of months. Members were sickened by what they heard. There was evidence of an awareness among many of the Kikuyu themselves that the custom was barbarous and dangerous; missionary boarding schools to which young girls wishing to escape might be sent were overcrowded and had long waiting lists.

Eleanor Rathbone and Kitty co-operated. There were many similarities between these two courageous women, despite the dissimilarity of their political approach and despite Eleanor's feminism. They were almost the same age, daughters of intellectual and liberal fathers, highly educated themselves, each with a deep determination to use her gifts and abilities for the benefit of others. Both used their status as members of parliament to further humanitarian causes. Neither of them flinched from dealing with a subject which other women might have felt to be indelicate.

Eleanor was concerned with the entire status and treatment of women throughout Africa and in parts of Asia. Kitty campaigned in particular against female circumcision in Africa and against the suffering of girls in India (many of whom were married at the age of seven or eight to adult husbands: their internal injuries frequently caused them to bleed to death within a day or two of the marriage. Others suffered hips so severely dislocated that they would never be able to walk again.)

Colonel Wedgwood, Eleanor and Kitty, on behalf of the Committee, called on Lord Passfield (Sydney Webb), Colonial Secretary, to ask that a Select Committee be set up to inquire into the question of the Kenyan girls. This he refused, but he invited them to continue their work and to report to him in due course. Messages of gratitude to the Committee for the work it was undertaking were received from Kikuyu organisations, but there was evidence too of fierce opposition to it by the Kikuyu Central Association—of which Jomo Kenyatta was a leading member—which favoured compulsory circumcision of all Kikuyu women.

In December 1929 the House was discussing Colonial Affairs. Kitty and Eleanor seized their opportunity. Courageously they raised the matter of the treatment and subjugation of women in parts of Africa. Kitty spoke first. She launched into a description of the practice of circumcision. James Maxton, a Scottish ILP member, interrupted. 'Is this relevant?' he inquired angrily. Eleanor sprang to her feet in Kitty's defence. 'Women do not count!' she shouted sardonically. Maxton resumed his seat reluctantly and Kitty resumed her speech. There was no groundswell of support from fellow MPs. (An MP of the period, approached for his recollections of the Duchess, responded, chortling, 'I can only remember her for some campaign about female circumcision—a thing I should have thought impossible!')

The work of the Committee continued throughout the following decade. Eleanor kept up her stream of questions and the Colonial Office was bombarded with petitions and information, but despite combined efforts the practices continued.

Chapter 14

'No' to Indian Independence, 1929–35

From Kenya to India; and to the first of three major issues which would bring Kitty into direct confrontation with the Conservative leadership. If Baldwin had chosen her as the first woman Conservative minister on the grounds that she lacked Nancy Astor's rebellious spirit and would therefore loyally support the Party line at all times, he was about to be disillusioned. She had already shown her courage where matters of principle were involved in her refusal to be browbeaten by Eustace Percy and in her commitment to the cause of Kenyan women, but Baldwin was as yet unprepared for what was to come. For some of her Perthshire constituents, too, Kitty's opposition to official Conservative policy was to become an irritant.

In 1929 when the issue of self-government for India came to the forefront of the political scene there were very divided views. The nations now known as India, Pakistan and Bangladesh existed as part of a whole—the Indian Empire—and that Empire was part of the British Empire, coloured pink on the atlases of the day, covering one quarter of the earth's surface. British schoolchildren were taught to take pride in the achievements of the British explorers, missionaries, armed forces and statesmen who had contributed to the building of the Empire, often with heroism and at great personal sacrifice. To visit any British cemetery in India and wander round long forgotten and neglected gravestones is to recognise the personal contribution made to the epic of British Imperialism by countless young families, wiped out by cholera or typhoid as well as in fighting or disturbances.

The relatively short period of British rule in India had had a profound effect on its peoples. Amongst other 'blessings' it imposed for the first time a strong, unified central government and system of law on the sub-continent. With the development of railway and road systems, travel and interchange between the vast and widely differing regions became possible. It also permitted Indian people, who spoke 225 widely differing languages and dialects, to communicate with each other: English was adopted as the official language. An English-language daily press was developed, which educated Indians could read.

India was a complex pattern of differing religions and local governments, a continent which had never been a country. There were Parsees, Jews, Jains, Sikhs, Christians and others, but Muslims and Hindus were by far the greatest numerical groups, of which Hindus were the greater by a ratio of three to one. Overall, apart from five colonies ruled by the French, three by the Portuguese, and those ruled over by Indian princely rulers, the British government ruled with a system of justice which was firm and on the whole fair. Indians, however, viewed the Raj with mixed feelings. In educated circles the British political regime and British paternalism were resented.

The Indian National Congress began as a meeting of seventy-two high-caste Indian men in Bombay in 1885. It was the start of a concerted movement towards a new nationalism which would survive and develop into a great Indian national movement. In its early years it was dominated by Hindu lawyers, doctors and journalists and its proceedings were conducted in English. The All India Muslim League was founded in 1906. It too was founded on nationalism, but its purpose was to safeguard Muslim interests in a self-governing India.

In 1914 Mohandes Gandhi, a Hindu lawyer who had been working in South Africa, returned to India with the intention of devoting himself to the attainment of Purna Swaraj (complete self-rule) for India 'by all legitimate and peaceful means'. Gandhi's hope was that within a self-governing India all races, religions, castes, rich, poor, educated, illiterate, would be treated with equal respect. In the Hindu caste system practised by his contemporaries, children were born into a situation in life from which there was no escape, destined to exist as sweepers, cleaners of floors, emptiers of slops: forbidden so much as to allow their shadow to fall across the path of those of higher caste. He opposed it as repugnant and immoral. He also believed that the women of India were unjustly oppressed and dominated by men. He believed that the custom of child marriage was revolting and barbarous and he sought to prevent it. In all these matters he and the Duchess of Atholl would have found themselves in agreement: where they would diverge was in the matter of timing. Gandhi wanted Purna Swaraj immediately: the Duchess and others would wish to pospone it until it could be shown that Gandhi's ideals could be achieved.

Gandhi sought to heal the enmity of centuries between Hindu and Muslim and tried to create one people: free, separate and Indian. He led a concerted movement of non-violent opposition to the British regime in order to try to achieve his objective. Not all in those communities identified with the idealisitc aims of Gandhism, as his later martyrdom at the hands of a Hindu fanatic would prove.

The movement towards eventual independence of India began in earnest after the First World War, when the Montagu-Chelmsford reforms gave certain powers to the Indian people, with a promise of 'gradual development of self-governing institutions with a view to the progressive realisation of responsible government in British India as an integral part of the Empire'. A review of the situation was promised within ten years. In 1928 the Conservative Government sent out a Commission headed by Sir John Simon, a Liberal lawyer and politician, many of whose members had never set foot in India until that date. No Indians were included and as a result Indians of all religions refused to co-operate with it.

The Muslim leader, Mohammed Ali Jinnah, in early life a London-based barrister, always maintained that although Hindus and Muslims must unite to achieve Dominion status, there must be separate electorates and reserved seats in the legislatures for Muslims. The refusal of Congress to recognise this need led him to begin, as early as 1928, to despair of the possibility of unity. He already foresaw a parting of the ways and concluded that Hindus and Muslims must be organised separately in order to understand each other better. Jinnah has been severely criticised for the direction of his leadership, which ultimately ensured that India would be split into two (later three) countries. The alternative as it appeared to him was for minorities, including Muslims, to be permanently subject to Hindu domination.

It was against this bitter and confused background that the Simon Commission reported. Its findings were that there had been a deterioration in all transferred departments, much embezzlement, bribery, quarrelling and corruption. In spite of greatly increased spending, local education authorities were doing little or nothing to fight illiteracy. The experiment had not been a success and Simon said privately that they were dealing with a puzzle with no solution. On the principle that it would be impossible to set the clock back, the Commission recommended granting provincial autonomy. It recorded its doubts about the possibility of developing full, responsible parliamentary government at central level, but in the meantime recommended that all remaining departments in the provinces should be transferred to Indian ministries, even at the sacrifice of efficiency.

Without waiting for the report to be published—but with the consent of the new Labour Prime Minister, Ramsay MacDonald, and the leader of the Conservative party, Stanley Baldwin—the Viceroy, Lord Irwin (later Lord Halifax), tried to placate Congress by announcing that dominion status was the natural issue of India's constitutional development. On 23 October 1929 Baldwin told his colleagues in the shadow cabinet of the statement which Irwin was about to make and expressed his agreement with it. His own view was that, like himself,

29   With members of the India Defence League

most people in the country were more interested in home affairs than in
foreign affairs and would be glad to be rid of the troubles with India. His
colleagues did not agree. Three members of the team threatened to
resign. Baldwin backtracked smoothly, assuring them that his support for
the MacDonald line had been in his personal capacity only. Later he said
it had been his understanding that the Viceroy had prepared his statement
at the wish of the Simon Commission. In fact the Commission was
gravely affronted. There was immediate uproar in the ranks of the
Conservative Party, followed by calls for Baldwin's resignation.

Sir Samuel Hoare (who was to become Secretary of State for India in
1931) had to admit that almost no-one in the party—particularly in the
ranks of the party outside parliament—liked the idea of granting Indian
independence with what many felt was undue haste. Neville
Chamberlain supported Baldwin in public, but privately thought that he
was quite out of touch. Churchill deplored as mischievous and criminal
the suggestion of self-government for a country which ostracised a large
and vulnerable proportion of its population. Britain, he said, was
responsible for the protection of those untouchables. Churchill's motives
in opposing the government's plans were not, however, entirely
humanitarian: he was also an Imperialist by tradition and instinct. Two
years of increasing bitterness both in Britain and in India followed.

Churchill resigned from Baldwin's shadow cabinet in January 1931. He and a number of allies formed the India Defence League, largely financed by Indian princely rulers, who were apprehensive about their own future in a self-governing India.

Contrary to Baldwin's view, British people—including many in Kinross and West Perthshire—were deeply interested and concerned about the future of India. Kitty was one of the most immediate dissenters to the government's proposed policy. She had never been to India, but her own background predisposed her to take a particular interest in it. Apart from the influence of her husband—a soldier who had been under Kitchener's command—Kitty could never forget that she owed her very existence to the compassion and resourcefulness of the ayah who had rescued her mother, and to the bearer who had carried the child in his arms from Gwalior to Agra. The woollen shawl in which Charlotte had been carried was treasured at Bamff. Honoraria Lawrence, wife of Sir Henry Lawrence of Lucknow, had been Kitty's great aunt. She had died three years before the Indian Mutiny, but tales of the fate of the gallant Sir Henry, of Jane and William Stewart, of the deaths of men and the appalling final hours of women during the mutiny were part of family lore. India and its peoples were of great concern to Kitty.

Kitty's concern over conditions in India had already been expressed in her work on behalf of young women and children who were being cruelly ill-used. In 1929 Eleanor Rathbone had tried to persuade Kitty to sign a joint letter to *The Times*, protesting against the Indian child marriage laws and the low age of legal consummation, which had been raised, in the face of fierce opposition, to 13 in 1925. Kitty had declined: she wanted time to take advice from people who knew more about India on a subject in which racial and religious feeling were so much involved. For the next four years she made it her business to take advice from a great many people on the subject of Indian independence. Her informants were mostly senior members of the Indian Civil Service—British men who had spent their working lives in India. She and Eleanor had frequent meetings and social contacts with groups of Indian women, and a number of Muslim intellectuals were among her friends.

Kitty had many concerns over Indian independence. She was worried about the treatment of women and girls in India. She was determined to make sure that there would be adequate provision for the representation of minorities in a self-governing, predominantly Hindu, India. She was alarmed about the defence of India and about the effect on Britain's defences in the Middle and Far East. She was concerned about financial safeguards for the payment of the pensions of retired Indian civil servants. She also foresaw adverse effects on Britain's cotton and jute industries, on which employment, particularly in Lancashire and in Dundee, was dependent. She believed that the government was giving way unnecessarily to combined pressure from the Viceroy, the Secretary of State and Congress. The fears of the Muslims and other minorities, expressed to the three Round Table conferences convened by the government over the next few years, underlined the seriousness of the problem.

When the India Defence League was formed Kitty did not join it, though eighty MPs and many prominent figures in and out of politics did. She concentrated on bombarding ministers and newspapers with letters. In 1933 she wrote to Baldwin (since 1931 Lord President of the Council in an all-party National Government). He replied sympathetically:

> My dear Kitty
> I am sorry that you are perturbed but I am not surprised. The whole Indian question is the gravest and most difficult with which the government has to grapple. I have always felt that it was inevitable that there would be a real honest difference of opinion in our party and that the difference would be ultimately expressed in the Lobby. It cannot from the nature of the case be otherwise. I write frankly to you as an old friend for whom I have a true affection and a high regard. You will not expect me to write a long letter of an argumentative nature; you will I know act as you believe to be right and honest and whatever you do I shall take no exception to it. For myself, I view the future with some apprehension and doubt: but my doubts and apprehension would be increased many times if the course advocated by Churchill and any of his friends was taken. I am, with much affection and much regard,
> Your friend Stanley Baldwin.

At the end of 1933 Kitty published the fruits of her research in a pamphlet: The Main Facts of the Indian Problem. The foreword was written and the pamphlet warmly endorsed by Lord Islington, distinguished Liberal Under Secretary of State (for some time acting Secretary of State) for India from 1915 to 1919. He had been concerned with the drafting of the 1919 reforms, to which he remained entirely committed, but he warned:

> The deeper I probe into the various proposals of the White Paper the more convinced I am that a mistaken sense of political expediency on the part of its authors is placing India, Great Britain and the British Empire in grave peril . . . I urge on all Members of Parliament of all parties to consider most seriously the facts set out in this pamphlet and to bear in mind that as representatives of our nation a heavy responsibility rests on them.

Kitty could not have had a more balanced, responsible and informed ally than Lord Islington. He was by now an 'elder statesman' and becoming a little frail, but having visited and studied every Indian state and its people he knew the country as few of those engaging in the argument did. He had not retreated from his commitment to the principle of self-government, but was advising extreme caution in its implementation. This coincided with Kitty's position and despite a verbal battle with a former junior minister who accused her of wishing to abandon the Montagu-Chelmsford principle outright, she affirmed her commitment to it. In her pamphlet she pointed to the bitterness of communal feeling indicated by Hindu, Sikh and Muslim witnesses, the dangers of community pressures, the problem of illiteracy—88 per cent of India's people were illiterate—and the prevalence of corruption reported by the Simon Commission. She went on to deal with the proposals in the White Paper, commenting that putting proposals for federation and provincial autonomy into one Act, and giving Parliamentary commitment to the transfer of responsibility at the centre before provincial self-government had proved successful was in complete opposition to the Simon Commission's recommendations and to the 1919 Act.

She warned that Sir Tej Bahadur Sapru, chief Hindu delegate to the Round Table Conferences, had appealed to members of Congress to capture the machinery of the new constitution, since it would place a powerful weapon in their hands, suggesting that if necessary they should send those who opposed them to jail. She reported that Hindu newspapers in Bengal had said that it would be better for high-caste Hindus to remain for a few years longer under the present constitution than to give in to provisions which would adversely affect them—one of which would ensure fair representation for lower caste Hindus and the other of which would ensure Muslim majorities in the Punjab and Bengal.

She went on to speak of the Muslim proposal to set up an independent federation of the five mainly Muslim areas—the Punjab, Sind, the North West Frontier, Kashmir and Baluchistan—and noted that such a federation would include the bulk of the fighting races of India, that it would control her most vulnerable frontier and that beyond that frontier lay a continuous belt of Muslim states stretching to the Mediterranean. A greater political and military danger to India could hardly be imagined: it might mean civil war in India and an Afghan invasion with Soviet support, adding 'It should not be forgotten that as recently as the 18th century, Kashmir and the four provinces in question referred to today as Pakistan, actually formed part of an Afghan Kingdom.' (The use of the term 'Pakistan' in Kitty's pamphlet is the first documented record of that name noted by the India Office.)

Rudyard Kipling, Baldwin's cousin, who knew India more intimately than most, was all too well aware of the dangers of allowing legislation to be prepared by those who knew and understood nothing of the complexities of the country, and who had no love for it or its people. He endorsed Kitty's point of view, praising her pamphlet as 'a temperate exposition of some of the graver perils inherent in the proposed scheme'.

By 1934 attitudes had hardened all round. Kitty had become more closely identified with the diehards and she and a number of leading politicians, including Admiral Keyes, Lord Lloyd and Winston Churchill, published a commentary on the report of the select committee, ending with a Churchillian ring:

> We have looked in vain for convincing evidence that the majestic structure of the Government of India should be demolished at one stroke and the great partnership dissolved in order, so prematurely, to force unfamiliar and democratic institutions upon the ancient civilisation of India with its 360 million inhabitants for whom we are trustees.

Early in 1935 Randolph Churchill, Winston's son, annoyed his father and appalled the diehards by announcing his candidature as an Independent Conservative at a by-election at Wavertree, Liverpool. It was a safe Tory seat which was being contested by a Tory who accepted the government's line on India, and by Liberal and Labour party candidates. Young Churchill intended to make his name and win glory by exploiting the Indian controversy. Sir Patrick Donner, secretary to the Defence League, recalls that the League was obliged to support Randolph or be derided as paper tigers—'men who talked big but had not the courage of their convictions . . . we had no option but to take the train to Liverpool and to defeat.'

Randolph sought help from all who opposed the White Paper, including Kitty. She and Sir Patrick were the first politicians to travel to Wavertree on his behalf and they both spoke at a meeting on 25 January. Sir Patrick gives an account of it in his book, *Crusade*. Kitty took as her subject the matter of Hindu temple prostitution, involving the violation of small girls. The audience, which had been expecting a more orthodox political speech, were, to put it mildly, surprised. But Kitty's motives were neither to amuse nor to titillate. To her it was the heart of the matter and one of the principal reasons for her campaign: she expected the same compassion from others.

Randolph's intervention, as predicted, allowed Labour to win the seat. The rebel MPs who had supported him had been threatened with withdrawal of the whip. This was not carried out, but there was much criticism within the party, not least from members of Kitty's own constituency association. At the Eastern Divisional Council (all constituencies in the East of Scotland) held in Edinburgh, a resolution was put forward and passed, not specifically naming Kitty, but condemning all who had assisted Labour in winning Wavertree and calling for united support for the policies of the National Government. Curiously, the council apparently saw nothing inconsistent in then calling for the government to change its policy with regard to the price of oats, a subject closer to its heart.

It was undoubtedly politically inept of Kitty to have intervened at Wavertree: but she was never in her entire political career able to sacrifice principle for political expediency: that was to be her downfall. She believed that it was her duty to speak on behalf of those who were oppressed and unable to speak for themselves, and she did, as she would do again in another context, without regard for the political consequences to herself.

The India Bill received its second reading and was examined in committee of the whole House between February and mid May 1935. On 2 May Kitty, together with a small group of equally troubled Members of Parliament—none of whom were leading diehards—wrote to Baldwin regarding government policy on several counts, but their principal complaint was on the India Bill, on which if they received no assurance that there would be a modification of policy they would have no alternative but to renounce the whip. Churchill warned the diehards against such action at a meeting of the India Defence League on 6 May.

Baldwin, overwhelmed by official duties in connection with the King's Jubilee celebrations, pleaded for time in which to send a considered reply. No assurances being received, Kitty and five other MPs resigned the whip. It was a last defiant gesture against the India Bill which became the Government of India Act of 1935.

The Act was undoubtedly an earnest, well-meaning attempt to hand over power to India on a fair and equitable basis. It provided for an all-India federation, so long as half the princely states agreed to join. For the time being central government would remain under the Viceroy, with reserved powers, and there would be considerable devolution at provincial level. There was no mention of dominion status.

In the event, the India Act pleased no-one. It did not please the Hindus. It did not please the Muslims. It made the princely rulers apprehensive. It did not please those in Britain who had hoped for a speedy transfer of power. Worst of all, it failed in its objective of satisfying Indian ambition. Due to the outbreak of the war in 1939 it was never fully implemented.

Indian elections, held in 1937, were extremely favourable to Congress, although they belied the claims of both Congress and the Muslim League. Of the 450 Muslim members elected to the legislatures, only 26 were Congress, most of them from the North West Province. It was obvious that Congress had no real appeal for the Muslims. Out of 228 seats in the provincial assemblies 64 were reserved for Muslims chosen by Muslim electorates. Of these, 26 were won by the Muslim League, 28 by Independent Muslims, 9 by the National Agricultural Party and 1 by a Congress Muslim—fairly clear evidence that Mussulmen did not generally perceive themselves as Congressmen, though they had been prepared to identify with Congress in furthering the cause of self-government. Despite the warning inherent in these results, Congress used its overwhelming overall success to try to force dissolution of the Muslim League and incorporation of its members in Congress.

The historian John Grigg, whose sympathies lie with those in favour of immediate Dominion status rather than with the point of view of his grandfather, Lord Islington, has commented that the Act of 1935 was greatly watered down from the plan as originally intended in order to pacify diehard opinion, and that the framework of the elections of 1937 was set up in order to emphasize communalism—Britain playing her old game of 'divide and rule'. He believes, however, that lack of magnanimity on the part of Congress in handling its success was responsible for much of the animosity which was to follow. As it was, Jinnah and the League refused to bow to pressure from Congress and from that date onwards Jinnah directed Muslim political thinking towards an increasing sense of nationhood. By the time the Second World War began it was apparent to many that two nations would ultimately emerge: the Muslim community had already begun to think of itself as separate. Gandhi's idealistic goal of a united, secular India, for which he continued to work and hope, would never come into being.

The Hindu writer Rabindranath Tagore had said many years earlier that unless social conditions permitted intermingling through inter-marriage and participation in social and professional activities, the sense of belonging essential to the unity of a nation could not develop. A Muslim writer described his condition as a Muslim and Indian as being 'part of two circles of equal size which are not concentric'. It may, however, be of interest to note that present-day India is the second-largest Muslim country in the world.

One of Kitty's nieces, speaking of her aunt's campaign on India, has said that she remembers very clearly that Kitty's opposition was mainly due to her fear of terrible communal strife causing losses and suffering which would make the establishment of democratic and progressive government almost impossible. Unfortunately those fears of communal violence between the religious communities proved to be only too well founded: in the weeks following partition in August 1947 an unknown number of Indians of all religions—possibly up to 3 million—were slaughtered. A witness in Lahore stated: 'For days on end the nullahs (canals) ran so thick with dead bodies that you could have walked the length of them.' Some 100,000 small girls and young women, on whose behalf Kitty had been so apprehensive, were abducted and lost. It has sometimes been said that such tragedies are inevitable in the name of political and constitutional advance. Kitty did not share that opinion.

The whip which Kitty had resigned in May 1935 was restored to her in September on her application: the Abyssinian crisis, she felt, required that everyone should show support for the government. However, in the election which followed in November she invited electors to support her on the understanding that she could not be expected to support the government on foreign policy unless she believed it to be right:

> . . . I feel that, while recognising that some compromise is inevitable when supporting a government in which three parties are represented, I must ask to reserve my freedom where I may feel that a compromise proposed would be too injurious to the interests either of the constituency, the country or the Empire.

She felt that when the world was threatened with dictatorships it was more than ever necessary for members of parliament to preserve their right to full and free discussion and criticism, together with their right to obtain all necessary information from the government. Her election address included a promise to work for reform of the personnel and powers of the House of Lords in order to make it a more effective bulwark than it was at that time against a dictatorship either of fascism or socialism.

She ended her address with a promise that, if elected, she would take her share in the deliberations of the new parliament with a very deep sense of responsibility to her electors and to the country. Neither the electors of Kinross and West Perthshire nor the members of the Kinross and West Perthshire Unionist Association could say that they had not been warned.

Chapter 15

Communism, Fascism and the Roots of Appeasement, 1932–8

Although India was to take up much of Kitty's time and concern (and that of the government) during the period from 1931 to 1935, like many others she began to turn with increasing concern to what was happening in other arenas.

In Britain a political 'Paul Jones' had been taking place, during which there was much changing of position and allegiance. In August 1931 a government composed of prominent members of all three parties had come into being because of the rapidly deteriorating economic situation in Britain. Ramsay MacDonald, to the dismay of many of his Socialist colleagues, remained as Prime Minister and was expelled from the Labour Party. Three previous Labour ministers joined him in the Cabinet, together with four Conservatives (Baldwin, who became Lord President of the Council, Chamberlain, Cunliffe-Lister and Hoare). Liberals were represented by Lord Reading and Herbert Samuel, in the important positions of Foreign and Home Secretaries.

Kitty's opinion of Ramsay MacDonald was not high. She considered him to be a vain and foolish man, who represented nothing whatever but exhaustion and disillusionment. In her view his pretentious and weak leadership had been at least partly responsible for the internal crisis in which the country now found itself and she thought him unfit to lead a great nation in the difficult time ahead.

She viewed the growing external crisis with equal alarm. Russia's activities worried her deeply; her post-war sympathy for the plight of the German people did not affect her perception that the peace settlement had been marred from the outset by lack of goodwill between Britain and France and the withdrawal of the United States. She was afraid that Germany had all too swiftly realised that her conquerors had neither plan nor resolution to maintain their costly victory.

Whilst the Conservative and Labour parties were suffering from internal disputes, a further split within the Liberal party was also taking place. Sir John Simon, a leading Liberal, had led a breakaway revolt against the leadership of his party and become chairman of a new party, known as the Liberal Nationals. Following the general election which took place in October 1931, Simon replaced Lord Reading as Foreign Secretary and within a year his old leader, Herbert Samuel, and his supporters left the government over the issue of free trade. Thereafter the 'Samuelite' Liberals and the Labour party were in opposition to the coalition National Government. Simon's Liberal Nationals supported it, as did the Conservative party and members of the National Labour Party.

In 1931 no women were included in the team of Ministers. Because of the all-party nature of the government there was much competition and jockeying for position among the men. Even if that had not been the case, it is doubtful whether Kitty would have been considered: she was by now judged by her colleagues in the House to be a boring speaker and a promoter of slightly eccentric causes such as the treatment of colonial women. Despite Kitty's championship of this cause, Lady Astor made representations against Kitty's inclusion in the team in a personal approach both to MacDonald and to Baldwin, apparently on the grounds that Kitty was not a feminist.

Thus Kitty was free to give her mind to India and to the many problems associated with the developing international situation. Her constituency association was divided on the question of her line on India. In 1933 they passed a resolution backing her stand, but in 1935 some members voiced their concern when she gave up the whip. The chairman, Colonel Butter, declared himself to be 'far to the right of her' on the matter.

West Perthshire was a very 'county' constituency, with an unusually large representation of aristocrats, landowners and minor county figures among the constituents, together with many families who had chosen to retire there after an army or naval career. When, hard on the heels of *Women and Politics,* Kitty published a book on the situation in Russia called *The Conscription of a People* it struck a chord with many of her supporters within the constituency.

Since the revolution in Russia in 1917 and subsequent events there had been a growing apprehension of the Communist regime and of its avowedly expansionist aims. In capitalist circles in Western countries these fears had been accompanied by a deliberately fostered suspicion that the communists were largely backed by Jewish organisations. The American multi-millionaire and industrialist Henry Ford had been a particular proponent of this propaganda. While the stories of a sinister international Jewish plot could be discounted—and Kitty never believed them—the nature of the totalitarian Communist regime at that time could not.

Kitty's research was, as always, painstakingly thorough. She had been concerned over the Soviet government's policy of dumping cheap timber and agricultural products in Western Europe, causing hardship to British producers, including some of her farming constituents. In 1931 she was disturbed to read official papers published by the British Government giving details of conditions in Soviet labour camps in Siberia and of the inhuman treatment of innocent people. She protested vigorously. She had begun to meet and interview many refugees who had escaped to the west. *The Conscription of a People* was the result. She wrote:

> Russia has carried through revolution on a scale without parallel and after thirteen years is as ruthless as in its early days . . . national defence is planned to be promoted by developing chemical and heavy industries, the basis of munition of war . . . The Five Year Plan . . . is a plan tending to undermine capitalist stabilisation . . . a plan of world revolution.
>
> It is evident that the Russian people, undernourished, ill-clothed, and miserably housed, are toiling to make and export goods which they urgently need themselves. It has been denied by Premier Molotov that prison labour of any kind is used in the USSR—yet the British Government has published a selection of documents which shows beyond a shadow of doubt that Russian legislation has allowed forced labour of persons undergoing sentences of imprisonment and of unconvicted men and women.

Her evidence, based on official publications or on sworn statements of refugees from Russia, told of the oppression of the people—particularly with regard to the northern timber camps, to which many Kulaks (well-to-do peasants) had been conscripted against their will. She quoted a report which put at no fewer than 4–5 million the number of people deported to compulsory labour in the camps, from which refugees had given a terrible picture of overwork, bad feeding, insufficient clothing, insanitary accommodation and deaths from disease and cold. Failure to fulfil impossible workloads was punished by the withholding of food. Lack of fat in the diet, she said, led to a form of nightblindness which sometimes caused victims to stray off the path, for which transgression they were shot by the guards. The truth of many of Kitty's allegations has recently been officially acknowledged in Russia.

By November 1932 Philip Allan, the publishers, had sold 1,035 copies of *Conscription of a People* and 1,595 copies of *The Truth about Forced Labour in Russia* and reported that both were still greatly in demand, in addition to the newly published *Women and Politics*.

At the same time Boosey and Hawkes were arranging for the re-publication of Kitty's later songs in a uniform series which included works by Elgar, Roger Quilter, Vaughan Williams and Haydn Wood: distinguished company.

This led to a request by a well-known Scottish singer, Walter Burnett, for permission to perform them during a concert he was about to record for the BBC. Kitty, welcoming the respite of a return to her music, agreed, with the proviso that she should meet him in order to have a preliminary rehearsal. She made time in her busy schedule for an afternoon meeting in Edinburgh, during which they discussed the interpretation of the music. Kitty played the accompaniment for Burnett as he sang. After the broadcast he reported that the songs had been such a success that he would like to keep them in his repertoire: Kitty's songs, written so long ago for genteel Victorians, were now to be discovered and enjoyed by a very different audience.

The depression had given rise to a resurgence of Scottish nationalism. There was a feeling that English management, which was controlling more and more of Scotland's industry, had allowed Scotland to rot as steelworks, railway workshops, dockyards and shipyards were abandoned. Unemployment was high in central Scotland—much higher, proportionately, than that in England—and the population of the Highlands and Islands was declining dramatically. There was also a strong intellectual and cultural movement towards a revival of Scottish identity. The demand for Home Rule was growing in momentum and Kitty, like other Scottish members of parliament, was invited to support it. Her response, embodied in an article for the *Daily Record* in 1931, was that if Scotland were to be separated from the rest of the United Kingdom, Britain and the Empire would be deprived of the sturdy outlook and wisdom provided by Scots in parliament at Westminster. In addition, she believed that Britain's defences as a whole would be endangered. Although anxious to improve conditions for Scotland and determined to maintain the interests of its people in the context of Britain as a whole, for her unity of the kingdom was paramount. She was, and remained, a Unionist.

The government had abandoned the country's commitment to the 'gold standard' and had begun to tackle unemployment. Gradually unemployment dropped by over two million, real wages improved, nearly two million new houses were built and exports increased by £130 million. Ramsay MacDonald, becoming increasingly unwell—by the summer of 1934 he was barely able to cope with the requirements of office—left much of the guidance of affairs to Stanley Baldwin, who was approaching seventy, anxious about the division in his own party over India, not particularly interested in foreign affairs and unwilling to contemplate the possibility of a relapse towards further hostilities. Both in Britain and France the overwhelming mood of many citizens was for peace at any price.

Britain and France, in those crucial years of the mid 1930s, could have

30   Launching *The Duchess of Atholl* on the Clyde

forged an alliance backed by powerful and well equipped armed services. Instead, suspicion of each others' motives was allowed to develop. In Britain, France was regarded as unstable. Lord Home recalls that as young man after the First World War he was present at his home, The Hirsel, when Lord Haig said to his father (the then Lord Home) 'We must never trust the French again. they have been bled white by this war.'

Kitty, writing later about the period, said:

> Unfortunately the foreign policy of the Empire was still dominated by the theory that the ideal of 'no more war' could be attained and the international criminals restrained by the futile welter of debating in the League of Nations, which was incapable of reaching an honest decision or of enforcing it if it had reached it. For the continued domination of that theory the 'business' politicians typified by Mr Stanley Baldwin were responsible, heartily supported by Dominion and American politicians. It is difficult not to believe that they were influenced in this respect by two things—fear of social upheaval in Great Britain and the risk of loss of world trade. Fear, therefore, undisclosed but nonetheless real, dictated the policy of the British Empire instead of any resolute effort to attain positive and practicable aims at home and abroad. That policy was dangerous enough under a man of such notably fine personal character as Mr—now Lord— Baldwin. It became disastrous when he was succeeded by Mr Chamberlain, whose record, policy and choice of associates speak for themselves.

That summary was written in 1939. When Hitler came to power in Germany in 1933 few people in Britain recalled the fact that he was the author of a book written from prison between 1924 and 1925, in which he outlined his plans for the conquest of Europe. To many observers in Britain, Hitler seemed to be rather a good leader, with the best interests of the German people at heart. It was now believed by many British observers that the conditions imposed on Germany had been unduly punitive, though Germany had defaulted on her debt and borrowed ten times the amount she had paid. There was no sense of understanding in Britain of the natural nervousness of the French, with their long shared border with Germany.

The rise of fascism was, in fact greeted with considerable enthusiasm by many of the most influential people in Britain. That enthusiasm was to grow stronger throughout the decade, permeating the corridors of Westminster, the financial institutions of the City and the grouse moors of Scotland alike.

The redrawing of the boundaries of Europe under the terms of the Versailles Treaty meant that whereas before the war 50,000,000 people lived under an alien national regime, that figure had now been reduced to 20,000,000: there had been a genuine attempt at a fair rationalisation and redistribution, though inevitably grievances remained.

But ten years after the treaty Europe was seething with fresh troubles, or troubles exacerbated by the effects of the world depression. Political extremes of left and right were latched on to by desperate statesmen seeking immediate remedies. Italy was already ruled by a Fascist dictator. In Austria and Czechoslovakia the Nazis awaited an opportunity to profit from the instability of the situation. In Bulgaria the communists came to power, in Hungary the fascists. Rumania and Jugoslavia both succumbed to monarchist dictatorships. Greece and Spain swung like crazy pendulums between left and right.

As early as 1932 Churchill warned the House of Commons:

> All these bands of sturdy Teutonic youths, marching through the streets and roads of Germany, with the light of desire in their eyes to suffer for their Fatherland, are not looking for status. They are looking for weapons, and when they have the weapons, believe me they will then ask for the return of lost territories and lost colonies and when that demand is made it cannot fail to shake and possibly shatter to their foundations every one of the countries I have mentioned (France, Belgium, Poland, Rumania, Czechoslovakia and Jugoslavia) and some other countries I have not mentioned.

Although in 1933 Churchill forecast that there would not be a further war, he soon foresaw the need to prevent such a possibility by preparedness against it. As he had eliminated himself from influence with the party leadership due to his stance on India, few people were willing to support him publicly. Only a small number of Conservative Members of Parliament, a few diplomats and some Foreign Office officials agreed with him. Meantime the fascists in Germany began to re-arm fast in open defiance of the Treaty of Versailles.

Russia, faced with economic and internal problems, had laid aside any hopes for a world revolution and joined the League of Nations, to which body the Russian Foreign Minister Litvinov put forward a Convention for the Definition of Aggression which declared that 'every state has an equal right to independence, security, defence of its territory and free development of its state system' and went on to list five fair definitions of aggression by one state upon another. Russia, for the time being at least, was toeing the peace line and posed no threat to the world at large. The period of Stalinist purges within its boundaries was about to begin.

On the other hand Germany withdrew from the international disarmament conference, left the League of Nations and began to rearm.

As Kitty was quick to observe, there could be no doubt that German fascism constituted a more immediate danger than Soviet communism.

Robert Boothby, MP for East Aberdeenshire, described those who continued to see only communism as the enemy as 'rotten to the core—the only thing they cared about was their property and their cash'.

Hitler's Germany wooed Britain with success between 1933 and 1938, and that wooing and that success applied to all strata of society. It was as carefully planned and executed as any of Hitler's military coups—and with as little restraint or subtlety. Members of Kitty's own constituency association were among those to succumb.

The Anglo-German Association set up in 1929 intensified its efforts to attract members of all political parties. In 1933 an Anglo-German Group was founded, with Lord Allen of Hurtwood as Chairman, and composed largely of pacifist thinkers such as Philip Noel-Baker and Lord Noel-Buxton. In 1935 an Anglo-German fellowship was formed, aimed at the upper echelons: fifty MPs, three directors of the Bank of England, several generals, admirals and senior churchmen joined. The secretary admitted 'It is names we want, not numbers . . . otherwise how can we have influence with the government or the foreign office?'

Kitty and Bardie were exactly the sort of people the Nazis wished to attract: titled, apparently wealthy, influential. Senior Nazis Rosenberg and Ribbentrop were sent to Britain on visits aimed at cultivating the British elite: and it worked. British 'society' was led by a number of women who perceived themselves as influential hostesses. Harold Nicolson commented that the harm these silly women did was immense. Lady Londonderry, wife of the Secretary of State for Air from 1931 to 1935—herself a close friend of Ramsay MacDonald—befriended Ribbentrop and both she and her husband became warm advocates of closer relations with Germany. The Foreign Secretary until 1935, Sir John Simon, was said to be greatly under the influence of Mrs Ronnie Greville, a wealthy widow who also ran a salon. Mrs Greville befriended Ribbentrop and became strongly pro-Nazi. Through Lady Cunard, Ribbentrop became intimate with the Prince of Wales and Mrs Simpson. The Astors included Ribbentrop on their guest list. When Ribbentrop became German Ambassador to Britain in 1937 Chamberlain—then Prime Minister—let his home to him. Ribbentrop could hardly have expected a more signal proof of the country's warm approval and acceptance.

Press support for the Nazis came strongly from Lord Rothermere, who owned the *Daily Mail* and the *Sunday Dispatch*. At his insistence his newspapers strongly supported Oswald Mosley and his Blackshirt organisation. The editor of *The Times,* Geoffrey Dawson, was to be a consistent supporter of the government's policy of appeasement throughout the decade. Friendship for Germany was fashionable in Britain. German fascism was viewed by many as a welcome bulwark against the spread of communism, which they had been taught to fear. Many Conservative Members of Parliament joined in the chorus of approval and friendship—a number of them from Scottish constituencies.

The majority of members of the Labour and Liberal parties during this period favoured a blend of pacifism and collective security through the medium of the League of Nations and preached the doctrine of disarmament at a time when Germany was rearming as fast as her munitions and aircraft factories could manage. To them rearmament of itself posed a direct threat to peace: to be prepared was to precipitate war. In 1935 Attlee, as Leader of the Party, defined the position of the Labour Party as one of not seeking security through rearmament but through disarmament. In 1936 he stated that rearmament would only worsen the situation. By 1938 most of the party came to abandon its pacifist stance, though it continued to oppose conscription. By then too, most Liberals under Archibald Sinclair had begun to support rearmament. These parties were not, however, responsible for Britain's plight, since the National Government had an overwhelming majority in the House and were responsible for the defence of the realm.

If the government had any ideas of embarking on comprehensive rearmament in the mid 1930s it was deterred by financial stringency and by an apparent demonstration of the will of the people. The Oxford Union debate of 1933, a by-election win in 1933 at East Fulham by a pacifist candidate, a Peace Ballot which appeared to endorse collective security through the League as opposed to individual national preparedness, all apparently influenced Baldwin against the risk of alienating the electorate immediately in advance of a General Election. The men who had returned as young soldiers from the war were now middle-aged men with homes and young families: none of them wished a repetition of the horrors they had lived through, and there is no doubt that large-scale rearmament would have been unpopular.

At this time, until disillusionment set in, Kitty was a strong pro-Leaguer. Churchill was later to observe that war could easily have been prevented if the League of Nations had been used with courage and loyalty by the associated nations, as Kitty urged. But the British Government was not a strong supporter of the League. Baldwin himself was well disposed towards it but rarely used his influence to bolster it.

There was a strong women's pacifist movement in Britain, typified by the feminist writer Vera Brittain. Their arguments were persuasive and, to very many women, conclusive. Vera Brittain wrote and said what many women thought and felt:

Because we, as a nation, spend our money upon guns and battleships, the great majority of women have to live in wretched, inconvenient houses and manage with old-fashioned, second-rate tools. . . . Because English statesmen are still dominated by military ideals, many mothers who might be saved continue to die in childbirth . . . Our country's policy would soon change if no advocate of increased armaments could get a women to vote for him or invite him to her house. . . . I believe that what the women's peace campaign really needs is the sudden uprising of a movement as swift and dramatic as that of the militant suffragists. . . . Re-armament, whether undertaken in the name of the League or of naked nationalism, can lead us nowhere but the edge of the abyss.

During these turbulent years Kitty immersed herself more and more deeply in her work as a politician. India, the crisis over Japan (which had attacked Manchuria and northern China), the ill-treatment of Russian peasants, the international threat posed by Germany's military renaissance and soon the Italian attack on Abyssinia all caused her grave anxiety. She was in daily correspondence with people, personalities and newspapers on all these matters and was so preoccupied that her own welfare, health and comfort were ignored. *The Bulletin* commented on her style:

The Duchess of Atholl, that interesting critic of the India Bill, has set a spartan example to MPs who wish to concentrate on the causes they have at heart. She has attended the Scottish Grand Committee in the House of Commons at eleven in the morning and taken a prominent part in the discussion on the housing legislation, and from three o'clock to eleven pm has sat through the Committee discussion in the House on India for days in succession. She sacrifices an afternoon cup of tea and instead of taking an hour's relaxation from the discussions for dinner like every other member, she snatches ten minutes for a cup of coffee and two sandwiches.

Her name had begun to be known on the continent to refugees from the secret police in Germany as well as in Russia. Through contacts with such people as the exiled moderate Russian leader, Kerensky (whom she knew well and met from time to time for discussion over luncheon) and friendships with people on the continent, she received many pleas for help. In July 1934 she made a broadcast on behalf of Russian refugees. But as the Nazis became more entrenched their brutality towards Jews, communists and other opponents of the Reich increased and her help began to be sought by those in trouble under the Nazis in Germany. It was her ability to rise above all ideological barriers in aiding victims of totalitarianism which allowed her to perceive more clearly than others the dangers of Hitler's foreign policy.

One such appeal was from the younger brother of Klaus Fuchs, later notorious as an 'atom spy', who was himself a refugee from the Nazis. Klaus Fuchs was working as a research physicist at Bristol University and he sent her a translation of a letter from his brother in Prague. As a student, he had been a member of the Socialist Society of Berlin University and vehemently opposed to Nazism. He had almost finished his studies in law and economics, but had been forced to leave the university because of his political stance. Eventually he got a job as a chauffeur, but the Gestapo had begun to take notice of him. He had been able to leave Germany just in time, but his wife had been arrested and held hostage. She was pregnant and had given birth in the prison hospital, under circumstances of terrible suffering. The baby was now nine months old, separated from its mother, who was still in prison and about to be tried for 'constant Communist activities'.

Fuchs begged Kitty to make enquiries and to intercede on behalf of his sister-in-law. She spoke to Lord Cranborne at the Foreign Office, who advised her that an official approach would do more harm than good and suggested that she should try less formal avenues. Kitty then saw Lady Londonderry, asking her to use her influence with Ribbentrop on behalf of the Fuchs family. Three months later Kitty wrote to young Fuchs in Prague to say that she was 'very glad to hear that Frau Fuchs has been allowed out of prison and has been able to rejoin your child. I am sorry, however, to hear that she has not been allowed to leave Germany. I will see if I can get anything done about it.' The outcome is not recorded, though it is certain that Kitty would have done her utmost to help.

At a dinner in London Kitty found herself seated next to Sir Horace Rumbold, formerly British ambassador to Berlin, who added to her alarm with grim forebodings about the nature of the Nazi party, its treatment of Jewish people and its aims for the future.

Towards the middle of the decade Kitty received information about German remilitarisation, particularly in terms of the aircraft industry, from an anonymous informant. She never revealed his existence or disclosed his identity and it is possible that she herself never knew who her informant was, but it seems more likely that she did, and kept silent for his sake, since any hint of a particular knowledge on her part could have betrayed him to the Nazis. All that can be said for certain is that he was an Englishman living near the German/Dutch border and that he crossed into Holland in order to write and post his letters. However it is possible to speculate that he may have been Malcolm Christie, an English businessman who had been cultivated by the Nazis and who was on friendly terms with Goering and other high-ranking officials.

Christie was feeding Sir Robert Vansittart, Permanent Under-Secretary at the Foreign Office, with secret information. Sir Robert made it his business to maintain a private network of informants about

Nazi activities and was one of the first to warn of the growing menace of German air power. Sir Robert's warnings to the Foreign Secretary and to the Cabinet went largely unheeded and he himself was not always popular with the politicians. One of his contacts sent a note from Holland which 'Van' took the trouble to have copy-typed and sent to Kitty. It ended: 'You ask about "S". May I advise you to be careful. I am afraid he is sitting on the fence and takes money where he can.' There is no indication as to the identity of 'S'. The author signs himself 'M G', though this may have been a typing error. 'M C' would have indicated Malcolm Christie.

With so many problems on her mind, Kitty had time for little else. One of her nieces, Persis Clerk-Rattray (Mrs Edward Aglen, as she married the grandson of the Ramsays' old friend Archdeacon Aglen, rector of the church at Alyth) went to stay with her aunt and uncle in London during the early 1930s. She recalls:

> My aunt was very busy and I hardly ever saw her. She always had breakfast in bed, and I would call on her to say 'Good Morning'. Her bed would be littered with letters and newspapers and already she would be writing. Sometimes her secretary would be in the offing. As I knocked on the door she would call to me to come in and without looking up from what she was reading or writing she would direct token kisses in my direction ('Kiss, kiss, kiss . . . Dearie, how are you this morning?') Sometimes she took time to ask about my plan for the day, but not always. She was totally and dedicatedly bound up in her work.
>
> I stayed with them again a year or two later, when I was supposed to be 'coming out'. I had no wish to come out in the way thought suitable in those days. My uncle and aunt were very sweet and understanding about it and made everything much easier for me. My uncle was very 'spoiling'. He was so sweet and we had a lovely time together. I had made up my mind to train as a chauffeur; my aunt very kindly found a job for me at 10 Downing Street for a few weeks, licking stamps for an appeal Mrs Baldwin was running to help unmarried mothers.

Kitty was pleased when, in the summer of 1935, a change of leadership in the National Government took place. Stanley Baldwin and Ramsay MacDonald changed places. MacDonald became Lord President of the Council and Baldwin became Prime Minister. Her opposition to the government's line on India had made no difference to her friendship with the Baldwins. On one occasion at the end of 1933 she had written to him, addressing him as 'Mr Baldwin' and he had replied 'My dear Duchess', at which she protested. Baldwin wrote back:

> My dear Kitty
> Your letter thawed a frozen heart and cheered me very much. When you wrote to me as 'Mr' and signed yourself mine sincerely, I said 'Well, that's

hat and there's another chopped off' and I wrote 'Duchess' thinking it
would be agreeable to you. Thank God you hated it! Still, and as long as
you will, Affectionately yours, SB.

s later, on Bardie's death, one of the most tender and understanding
rs she was to receive was from her friend SB.

January 1935 France had signed an agreement with Italy and in
y, panic-stricken at the level of German rearmament, had concluded a
ty with Soviet Russia. In June the British Government, behind the
ks of the French and to their consternation, concluded a Naval
Agreement with the Germans, which permitted the Germans to begin
building submarines in contravention of the Versailles Treaty and to lay
down the hulls of two new warships. Coming from Britain, who had
repeatedly sought to persuade the French to reduce their army, this was
surely treachery: treachery which had been undertaken with the
authority of the retiring Foreign Secretary, Sir John Simon. (Hoare
replaced him on MacDonald's retirement in May.)

That month, May, Kitty met the Russian ambassador, Maisky, for the
first time at a dinner at Buckingham Palace. Despite her earlier outspoken
criticism of the Communist regime, the two were able to form a
relationship for the future based on mutual regard and respect.

During the summer, Kitty lunched once or twice with Vansittart to
discuss the international situation. In September she applied successfully
to have the whip restored—she had given it up in May. She applied
partly because of a growing apprehension that the strength of the
democracies could only lie in unity of purpose; but it was the developing
crisis over Abyssinia which chiefly prompted her return to the fold of the
National Government.

As early as 1934 Abyssinia had complained to the League about Italian
aggression. Mussolini, the Italian dictator, was planning to invade the
country, which fell within the Italian area of influence. Annexation of
Abyssinia was part of a scheme of self-aggrandisement on the part of
Mussolini. It would also meet the Italians' need for extra raw materials.
Preparations for the invasion had become obvious during the summer of
1935 and Britain and France were in difficulty as to how to react. Hoare
at the League of Nations gave ringing, though hollow, support to the
idea of collective security, but the French Foreign Minister, Pierre Laval,
had no intention of allowing Abyssinia to cause a rift in Franco/Italian
relations.

For the British Labour and Liberal Parties the issue was clear:
Mussolini must be stopped by and in the name of the League of Nations.
Abyssinia was a member of the League and as such was entitled to the
protection of other members. This much was beyond dispute. But the

League itself had no standing army; America and Germany, two major powers, were non-members. For Britain and France to stand up to their erstwhile ally Italy on their own would throw Mussolini into the arms of the other Fascist dictator, Hitler. The possibility of the imposition of economic sanctions was discussed at length. Mussolini riposted that any question of the imposition of oil sanctions—the only sanctions which could be effective—would lead to war.

Vansittart was strongly of the opinion that Britain and France must remain in total alliance and that at all costs nothing must be done to drive Italy into the arms of Germany. Kitty agreed with 'Van'. America would not act: if France would not join Britain in a show of resistance it would be impossible to restrain Mussolini.

When Italy invaded Abyssinia in October, economic sanctions short of oil sanctions were applied by the League. The Council of the League pronounced that by her action Italy had declared war on all members of the League. Yet the League was powerless and was shown to be powerless. British naval vessels were sent to the Mediterranean, without authority to intervene as Italian troops sailed unhindered through the Canal. Britain recognised that if there was to be a war it would be a war which Britain could not win—though Churchill believed that a strike by the British navy could have defeated the Italian navy once and for all.

Abyssinia was abandoned to its fate. The League, and Britain, had been challenged and had responded feebly. France was alarmed at Britain's willingness to cause estrangement between the Allies and Italy. The dictators in Italy and Germany noted Britain's unwillingness to risk war.

It was at this point, in November 1935, that a General Election took place. By common consent the coalition National Government sought re-election under Baldwin's leadership. There was, by now, some acknowledgement of the need to rearm, yet Baldwin shied away from making it a central issue of policy for fear of turning the British electorate towards the Labour Party. In a number of speeches during the election he linked the need for rearmament to the requirement of the League of Nations, which, he said, might well need to be rearmed; in this way he was able to steal the thunder of Labour's pro-League stance.

The chiefs of staff had wanted balanced rearmament in 1934 but, as Chancellor of the Exchequer, Chamberlain had said that the country could not afford it and had succeeded in cutting the defence budget by £30 million. Such rearmament as was permitted had been largely concentrated on strengthening the air force. Churchill, Amery, Kitty and others wished to see Britain's defences strongly reinforced all round (Churchill and Amery had demanded it at the party conference the previous autumn) and Kitty had not disguised the fact that in her view a programme of steady rearmament in Britain had been delayed for too long.

Thus it was that she came to face her electors in Kinross and West Perthshire, pleading for permission to preserve her freedom 'where I may feel that a compromise proposed would be too injurious to the interests either of the Constituency, the Country or the Empire . . .'

Her election address generally supported the government line on Abyssinia—that of

> fulfilling the obligations of the Covenant of the League of Nations to join in imposing financial and economic restraints . . . but not to take part in any military measures against Italy unless assured, not only that other members of the League will take their share, but that Germany, Japan and the United States who are not members of the League will at least give sympathetic support.

Few could have any hope that such support would be forthcoming.

This time Kitty's opponent was another woman: a Liberal, Mrs Coll Macdonald, wife of a Scottish Presbyterian minister living in the constituency. Mrs Macdonald was cast very much in the mould of Vera Brittain, who would certainly have approved of her election address, which was headed:

'For Disarmament, Peace and Social Reconstruction'—and went on to state:

> If you vote for the National Government you take the road which leads to competition in armaments, to bloodshed and economic ruin. If you return a Liberal Government you take the road which leads to peace, reconstruction, social amelioration and goodwill amongst nations. The return of a Liberal candidate for Kinross and West Perthshire would deal a staggering blow to rearmament and strengthen the League of Nations.

Mrs Macdonald was able to use Kitty's call for rearmament to suggest to the electors that she was a warmonger. She herself preached, in the words of Edward Grey: 'Arms do not produce security, but generate fear.' At the same time she called on members of the League to impose oil sanctions on the Italians.

Some of Kitty's meetings were stormy as a result of heckling by a number of Mrs Macdonald's followers. Kitty's supporters tended to be more restrained. After the election Tony Murray (heir to the Dukedom after Bardie's younger brother) wrote:

> My dear Kitty:
> Now that all the excitement is over and the victory won, I feel I must write a note to say how much I admired you during your election campaign. I had never seen you in 'fighting trim' before and it came as a

revelation to me. I thought it wonderful the way you bore the strain of motoring miles every day and speaking at the end of it and I don't think many women could have kept their colours flying at that last meeting at Crieff as you did.

In the event the electors of Kinross and West Perthshire failed to deliver a staggering blow on behalf of Mrs Macdonald and re-elected Kitty, on the clear understanding, as requested by her, that she had a mandate to criticise the Government on foreign affairs when she felt it necessary to do so. Her majority over Mrs Macdonald was 5,169.

On hearing the result Mr James Paton, Vice-Chairman (later to be Chairman of the Association), declared:

> One cannot wonder, for we all admire our member and she is the envy of people in many other constituencies. We are determined to stick to her as long as she will stick with us.

Mrs Macdonald and the Liberals, however, were strongly resolved to fight on and looked forward eagerly to the next election.

Chapter 16

Out of Step on Fascism and Spain, 1936

The National Government was back in office with a large majority: of the 585 candidates who had offered themselves to the electorate in the name of the coalition, 432 were returned. The Abyssinian crisis was still at its height. Baldwin was content to leave the general handling of it to the new Foreign Secretary, Sir Samual Hoare, but warned him: 'We must not have war!'

Hoare consulted his colleagues, Chamberlain, Eden, Simon and Runciman, over the question of the imposition of oil sanctions. Against Eden's wishes it was agreed to postpone a decision until Hoare could meet the French Foreign Minister, Pierre Laval, in Paris in early December. Laval was in league with Mussolini, and had already visited him in Rome. Speaking of that visit he said later: 'I recalled with Mussolini my youth as a socialist . . . something dear to us both. We began with an understanding instead of a misunderstanding . . . Of course I gave him Abyssinia.'

Abyssinia's fate, then, was already sealed when Hoare paid his visit to Paris. But between Hoare and Laval and with the tacit approval of Vansittart, who was in Paris and who saw Anglo-French co-operation as paramount, a pact was arranged under which three-fifths of Abyssinian territory would be handed over to the Italians. In return Abyssinia would be granted a narrow access corridor to the Red Sea. Hoare (known for various reasons as Slippery Sam) had not been given authority to make such a deal without consultation with London, but he sent back details of the agreement and went on to Switzerland in order to have a little holiday. At the age of fifty-six he nurtured a somewhat unlikely ambition to become an Olympic skater and whilst practising on the ice he fell and broke his nose.

As Vansittart guessed, it was probably Laval, past master at the double-cross, who deliberately leaked the details to the press, knowing that a storm of indignation would sweep Britain, as indeed happened. The British people were furious at what they perceived to be the abandonment of the Abyssinians. Eden threatened to resign. Baldwin repudiated the pact (as Laval and Mussolini had almost certainly intended). Hoare was sacked—unfairly, as he believed—and nursed his wrath and his nose for the time being. Eden became Foreign Secretary at the age of thirty-eight. Ironically, although it was a disreputable deal, the Hoare-Laval pact would have been to the advantage of Abyssinia, which was now to lose all its territory to Italy in a brutal war.

Kitty had recently read an account of appalling treatment of its own nationals by Abyssinia—of the brutal treatment of women and children and of the active encouragement of the Arab slave trade, which she understood Italy was trying to suppress. To this extent she felt sympathy for the Italian action. But she reasoned that Abyssinia was a member of the League and however much Britain might deplore internal cruelty in Abyssinia there could be no question of standing back and allowing an Italian invasion of that country without the strongest possible protest.

Kitty, as a pro-Leaguer, might have been expected to press for the imposition of oil sanctions by the League. In fact she did not: she accepted Vansittart's view that if the Italians carried out their threat to retaliate with war against any country imposing oil sanctions Britain would stand alone in a confrontation which, due to the disarmament which had taken place, she could not hope to win. She pointed out that France was confronted with a grave German menace and had just achieved an important pact with Italy. Other members of the League were not in a position to help and it must surely be unreasonable to expect Britain to be sacrificed in order to uphold the principles of the League, without military assistance from other nations.

Britain was exerting pressure on France to drop the pact with Russia. Kitty wrote to Leo Amery with grave foreboding:

> It seems to me that if France did this, Russia would sooner or later be driven into the arms of Germany. Germany's one weakness seems to me to be her lack of the minerals necessary for carrying on war. If she had Russia behind her with her vast natural resources it seems to me that she would be invincible.

She went on to press, in a statement to her constituents, for an amendment to the composition and procedure of the League in order to make it a more effective instrument for peace. She believed very strongly indeed in the ideals under which the League had come into being—the guarantee for the future peace of the world by the provision of a forum for the airing of national grievances; of co-operation and collective security, of large and strong nations supporting the security of weak and small nations in a covenant of international brotherhood. But it could only work if offending nations knew that the League was capable of strong and decisive action: which it palpably was not. It was one of the most profound disappointments of her life that the League proved in the end to have been a failure.

In the early months of 1936 a number of events occurred in quick succession which were of national and international importance. In January the old King, George V, died. Britain united in genuine grief at the loss of a good and kindly father-figure. He was succeeded by his son Edward VIII, whose personal problems would shortly distract the attention of the Prime Minister and the Cabinet from the first duty of government, defence of the realm. In February the Spanish people returned a democratically-elected left-wing government. It was not a Communist government: it was a Popular Front amalgam of Socialists, Republicans, Liberal Republican Unionists, Anarchists and a small number of Communists. It had gained office by a slender margin from an oppressive right-wing administration. In March Hitler, having observed the ease with which Mussolini was 'getting away with it' in Africa and having been assured by Ribbentrop from his researches at British government level that Britain would take no action, moved his army into the demilitarised Rhineland—the hitherto anaesthetised barrier zone between France and Germany—in direct contravention of the Treaty of Versailles.

One newspaper described the various reactions in Europe as: MOSCOW FURIOUS: FRANCE INDIGNANT: ITALY AMUSED: BRITAIN PAINED. Moscow might be furious, France had every reason to be indignant, Italy might be amused, but Britain was not entirely pained: a great many people approved. Kitty agreed with Eden in seeing at once that it was a move aimed at placing further strain on the relationship between Britain and France. Others saw it in a different light. Naturally Oswald Mosley and the British Union of Fascists approved. That was to be expected. In the opinion of Lord Londonderry the coup was a 'direct and understandable result of the Franco-Soviet treaty which was a move in the encirclement of Germany.' Samuel Hoare enquired why the Germans should not have sovereign rights in some of the most German territories of Europe. The newspapers generally took an ambivalent view and Lady Houston's weekly journal *Saturday Review*—though not typical—appeared with Hitler on the cover and a *Heil Hitler!* banner. Dr Dalton, on behalf of the Labour Party, declared that his party would not support any form of sanctions against Germany over the matter.

For Kitty it was again a matter of broken pledges and of the pathetic failure of the League of Nations. If a prompt and effective system of mutual assistance could not be achieved through a reformed League, she declared, it would be necessary to work to secure one outside it. But, as she recognised, the opportunity to deter the dictators once and for all had

31 Electioneering in the 1930s

been lost. From now on the dictators held all the aces. Lord Home, looking back, believes that the Rhineland was the last occasion on which action by Britain and France would have prevented war. (Interview with author, June 1985.)

On 13 March, a day or two after the Rhineland coup, Kitty wrote to the *Manchester Guardian* warning that it was perfectly clear from reading *Mein Kampf* that Hitler's aims went very much further than the Rhineland. He had actually stated that the annihilation of France would be the means of securing further territory elsewhere, as within a century Germany's 80 millions must increase to 250 millions and that new territory could only be acquired at the expense of Russia and the Border States.

Kitty had become seriously worried not only about Britain's defences, but about the attitude of mind of the country's leaders: their supineness, their complacency, their willingness to overlook the brutality of fascism and, while making public speeches deploring the actions of the dictators, making no move to deter them and even making friendly overtures to them.

Towards the end of 1935 Kitty had read *Mein Kampf* in its German version and was greatly troubled by it. An expurgated edition of the book was available in English translation, but it was merely a shadow of the original German version, which was recommended by the Fuhrer's press as a book which should be in every German household. As she pointed out:

> I am aware that Herr Hitler has recently reminded us that Mein Kampf was written some years ago, before his accession to power. But if it thus represents views which he has discarded, why is the book still being published with these statements in it? Above all, why is the English translation, first published in 1933, so expurgated that none of the passages quoted, or other similar ones, are to be found in it? That edition is only about one-third of the length of the original.

Together with a group called the Friends of Europe, Kitty was instrumental in having an unexpurgated version of the book translated into English. She consulted Ralph Wigram—sadly about to die—at the Foreign Office about the translation. In due course he replied sympathetically that he had had it vetted and the translation approved by members of staff and the Foreign Office, adding that, with regret, the fact that they had done so must not be made public. He stated that so far as the Foreign Office were aware there had been no changes in the German edition of the book since its first publication in 1926.

Kitty made it her business to see that the Prime Minister received a copy. She also sent copies of the two versions, unexpurgated and expurgated, to Churchill, who read them carefully. Other senior politicians were made aware of the publications, which were widely available. Chamberlain did not trouble to read *Mein Kampf* until *after* Munich, when he asked the Foreign Office to make translations of certain sections available to him.

Extracts of the most menacing and blatant sections of the book were published in pamphlet form by the Friends of Europe. Kitty, in the foreword, wrote

> Never can a modern statesman have made so startlingly clear to his readers his ambitions. . . . . The Third Reich must include Austria and all continental peoples of the Germanic race . . . Only by the power of a mighty sword can this policy be successfully pursued. France must be destroyed. . . . yet the crushing of France is only to be the means of securing German territorial expansion in other directions and for its achievement it is explicitly stated that considerations of religion and humanity must be set aside and diplomacy must not be scrupulous in its methods.

Kitty spoke strongly in favour of firm and united action in the face of Hitler's aggression. At the League of Nations, Russia, Poland, Czechoslovakia, Jugoslavia and Rumania pressed for united action. The Council of the League met to discuss the matter—most unusually—at Buckingham Palace, where King Edward took the opportunity of informing each of the delegates in private of his personal view that no action should be taken against Germany.

No action was taken against Germany. The French, who had urgently considered moving their own army into the Rhineland in retaliation, found the British Government, apart from Eden, hostile: a hostility largely generated by the attitude adopted by France over Abyssinia. Hitler proceeded to fortify the Rhineland frontier against France, which gave him the security to pick off the small nations of Europe one by one. France (referred to in *Mein Kampf* as a nation of niggers) could wait its turn.

Both Fascist dictators had reason to congratulate themselves on the success of their efforts during the spring. Hitler's Rhineland coup had passed almost without a murmur of disapproval—and for Mussolini May 1936 saw the final, brutal, defeat of Abyssinia. Bombs and mustard gas had been rained down on primitive and defenceless people in the final onslaught. It was obvious to Kitty that this was the beginning of the planned fascist conquest of Europe. Almost no-one seemed to mind.

On hearing the news of the fall of Abyssinia, Lucy Houston cabled to Mussolini: 'Bravo Bravissimo! Oh splendid man!' Lucy Houston and Kitty were at the time and for the next few months engaged in their own battle of words in the columns of the *Saturday Review* and *The Patriot, The Telegraph* and *The Morning Post*—a battle which continued until Lady

Houston's death in January 1937. She was an exceedingly wealthy widow, who, despite her overt support for dictators, personally financed the development of the prototypes of the Spitfire and Hurricane planes which proved crucial to Britain's defence when the need arose. Kitty was also involved in correspondence in many of the national newspapers on the subject of fascism. Her outright condemnation of the regime had begun to annoy some of her fellow politicians and some of her constituents—as much as her condemnation of communism had pleased them a few years previously.

Lord Londonderry was among those who found Kitty tiresome. In a speech in Durham in June, he said there would be 'a lack of statesmanship if in the event of war we should find ourselves on different sides from Germany'. Kitty wrote to protest and offered to discuss the matter but Londonderry declined.

The anti-Jewish propaganda circulating in Britain by mid-1936 seemed to Kitty to be not only distasteful but extremely alarming in view of all that she knew about the treatment of Jews in Germany. She raised the matter in Parliament, saying that while she had no case to bring forward of actual incitement to violence, there were unquestionably incitements to great prejudice. She quoted from a leaflet sent by the National Workers' Party:

> It is the Jews who have so misused the money system in their own interests with the avowed object of securing world power that they have deliberately produced war, civil commotion, crime and disease.

These were an echo of the allegations made in the 1920s by Henry Ford in the *Dearborn Independent* and reprinted in *The International Jew*.

She quoted the leader of the Party, Colonel Seton Hutchison, as having written:

> We will not permit the cream of youth of our country and of the Empire to be sent again to the shambles to line the purses of Jews and their puppets.

Kitty declared that that was a terrible suggestion to make, yet it was a doctrine being preached to gatherings of ex-servicemen. If statements of that kind were made in areas where there were many Jewish shops or Jews were employed, they might very well lead to violence against the Jews unless the police were vigilant.

During the spring and early summer of 1936 Mrs Coll Macdonald addressed a number of local Liberal Party meetings in West Perthshire, at which she expressed her great disappointment that oil sanctions had not been introduced and that disarmament had not taken place. At a peace demonstration in Crieff on 15 June she called for a Disarmament Conference to be convened.

In contrast to Mrs Macdonald's call for a Peace Convention, a great fascist march, one of a series, was held in London on 25 June. Thousands of fascists in uniform marched from the City, drums beating and colours flying, to a rally at Finsbury Park; a show of strength with more than a hint of menace. For the Government, Sir John Simon emphasised their right to free speech, adding that those who did not like what they heard and saw should stay away from the meetings. Later that year, however, under pressure from his Under-Secretary, Geoffrey Lloyd, Simon introduced the Public Order Act forbidding the wearing of political uniforms at marches and gatherings and allowing the police to ban marches for a period of three months.

Fascism was about to test its strength in another part of Europe. In Spain the right wing factions which had so narrowly lost power to the Liberal-Democrat-Socialist-Anarchist amalgam in February had been making plans. Having failed at the ballot box, a military coup was now the only way of regaining power.

Kitty as yet knew little of Spain, but when the rebellion began she made it her business to find out. As over India, she launched herself into a thorough analysis, seeking the fullest information from all sides. As she discovered, the cause of the situation was rooted in the past and in the condition of the people. A largely agrarian economy was dependent on an impoverished, downtrodden peasant class. For centuries, much of the population had been half-starved, whilst wealthy landowners reaped the benefit of their labour. Industrial workers had been exploited by rich entrepreneurs. The Catholic Church, though its power was diminishing, still wielded autocratic power over a simple, largely illiterate community, though in defiance many of the peasant people now embraced anarchism or fervent socialism in its stead. The army and civil guard completed the hierarchical system.

The last of a series of decadent monarchs had been forced to abdicate in 1931 and since that time the Republic had been ruled alternately by left and right-wing governments. King Alfonso had by no means abandoned hope of a return and one right-wing faction was committed to assisting him. He had taken almost £90 million with him when he fled and much of that money was now available to finance the coup. In addition Mussolini and Hitler had promised material aid. Business sources in Europe and America were also known to be willing to help. Accordingly one of the generals in the Spanish Army, Francisco Franco, had agreed to lead the coup. It was aimed at the restoration of repressive feudalism.

The coup began on 18 July, led by Franco from Morocco, using Moorish troops and battalions of the Spanish Legion, composed largely of renegades and criminals. They were transported across the Straits of Gibraltar in Italian and German aeroplanes and by Spanish navel vessels under commanders whose support had been guaranteed in advance. Franco and his fellow generals were confident that, as the army and civil guard would join the uprising, the coup would be effective and order restored under the new regime within a few days. They reckoned without the outstanding gallantry and fierce determination of the Spanish people to defend their recently gained freedom against an attack of unprecedented atrocity.

Within Spain the majority of the officers and just over half the troops joined in the rebellion. The Spanish government failed to take prompt and effective action. It was initially the trade unions and the working people, who, though at first unarmed, began to take matters into their hands.

The rising became known as the Spanish Civil War, though it started as a brutal insurrection from outside the country against a legally and democratically elected government and was conducted by rebel military leaders in charge, initially, of a foreign army.

Here was a cardinal point of principle and of legality. Kitty—still at that stage a supporter of the League of Nations—was quite clear that the democratically elected Spanish government was entitled to the moral support of other members of the League of Nations. That support was not forthcoming. Instead, members and non-members—twenty-seven countries in all—met in London in September to agree on the adoption of an international line of non-intervention. All nations would abstain from sending weapons, manpower or food to either side. Germany and Italy both agreed to be bound by the agreement, as did Britain, France and Russia.

Despite the fact that the pact sounded, on the face of it, to be honourable and even-handed, Kitty disagreed with it. If it had worked it would have been acceptable: but from the first moment of its inception it was neither. The Italians and Germans ignored it and continued to send arms and troops to Franco's support. Kitty believed that combined British and French fleets in the Mediterranean could and should prevent Italian reinforcements from reaching Franco.

France, whose new Popular Front government might have been expected to want to help the Spanish Government, backed non-intervention. The Prime Minister, Leon Blum, had suggested it, knowing that he had a slender majority and a large Catholic population. He was also afraid of Germany, following the occupation of the Rhineland. Dr Schacht, Governor of the German Central Bank, reported that Blum was anxious to be free of any 'Communist' tag and would thus prefer to be detached from overt or covert support for Spain.

In Russia Stalin had his own internal problems and had no wish to annoy fellow League members—or Germany—over Spain. America maintained a position of neutrality, which allowed the sale of arms and goods to both sides.

In Britain the government assumed a detachment which they did not feel: there was much sympathy for Franco's rebellion and a determination that whatever happened, the 'communists' must not be allowed to win. Baldwin was exhausted, unwell, privately worried about the state of the monarchy and longing to retire. It was largely left to Eden, Chamberlain, Simon and Hoare (now First Lord of the Admiralty) to guide British policy. All, including Eden at first, privately supported the rebel cause.

It was known and secretly acknowledged that non-intervention operated entirely to the detriment of the Spanish government. Even if Italy and Germany had observed the rules this would have been the case, since most of the army, with the weaponry, had now gone over to the rebel side. The Government side had relatively few weapons, few trained soldiers and a large population to feed. Under normal conditions of belligerent rights, as a legitimate government they should have been able to purchase arms and food in the world market. Not only were they denied that under the international agreement, but they were opposed by forces which were heavily supported by the two fascist regimes and the concerted assistance of international business.

Italy sent almost 300,000 troops, arms, planes and food supplies; Germany sent crack troops, aircraft and weapons. American business sources provided the rebels with massive aid: Ford, Studebaker and General Motors sent 12,000 trucks; Dupont provided 40,000 bombs. Texaco provided oil supplies throughout the war. British and European businessmen gave financial help on a large scale.

One of Kitty's first questions on the Spanish war in the House of Commons was to enquire about the financial assistance being given by Rio Tinto Zinc, who were supplying foreign exchange to the rebels at over twice the official rate. Thereafter she and Eleanor Rathbone, together with Members from the Liberal and Labour parties, kept a wary eye on all that was happening and kept up a stream of questions in the House to try to establish fair play.

Conservative officials were annoyed. It was to be expected that MPs of other parties should question the working of the pact—their sympathies were, of course, with the Spanish government. It was not to be expected that a Conservative member would become subversive. Kitty had three colleagues on the Conservative back benches who soon joined her in criticism of government policy on Spain: Captain J R J Macnamara, Major Jack Hills and Vyvian Adams. Churchill too, though never losing sight of his distrust of communism and fully supporting non-intervention, said that the British government must not be seen to be assisting the fascists to win in Spain.

In October Russia retaliated against Italian and German breaches of the pact by sending assistance to the Spanish Government, but it was a much more difficult matter to send ships and equipment from the Baltic than from Italy. Russian help never approached the level of fascist assistance to the rebels, but arms and money were sent. These permitted Russia to dictate terms and Russian advisers began to arrive in Spain in order to dominate the factionalised Republican political scene. This paved the way for the replacement of the Popular Front by a communist-led government the following year.

Questions which were being asked by Kitty and many others as the weeks wore on concerned the arrival of equipment from Italy via the Balearic Islands and of troops and aeroplanes from Germany or Italy. The British navy was sending home eye-witness accounts of such arrivals regularly: yet questions in the House met with consistently stone-walling replies from Eden, Hoare, Simon and other ministers in turn: 'I should be glad if the Hon Member would address that question in writing' . . . 'It is too soon to say' . . . 'We have as yet no confirmation . . .' etc. Ministers knew very well what was happening, but since they pretended even-handed detachment they could not admit to that knowledge. Eleanor Rathbone became chairman of an unofficial committee appointed to monitor and report on all breaches of the Non-Intervention Agreement.

In Britain, Socialists and Liberals in the main saw the struggle as one of the oppressed and exploited against the might of a tyrannical, privileged class of landlords and of the Church: of democracy standing up against the savagery of fascism. British Roman Catholics and Britain's business community supported the rebels, as did many Conservatives and Liberal Nationals. For some that support was lukewarm, as being perhaps the lesser of two evils. Others supported Franco with a fanaticism which gestated and bore a bitter fury. For the Catholics this was a Holy Crusade on behalf of Christianity. Both in Britain and America the Catholic minority was able to exert a political influence which was vastly disproportionate in power to its numerical strength. Equally for the business community it was a holy crusade on behalf of commercial interests. The *Daily Mail* was not untypical of the right-wing press in referring to the rebels as 'Crusaders of Righteousness'. Conversely, young men of all nationalities (including anti-fascist Germans and Italians) hurried to join the 'International Brigade' to fight on behalf of the Republic. All were idealistic, few knew anything of the carnage of war. Pitifully ill-prepared, woefully badly armed, many were killed or maimed.

The war developed into an explosion of brutality on both sides. The balance of cruelty was four times greater on the part of the rebels, whose leaders organised large-scale massacres of innocent men on the flimsy grounds of having left-wing sympathies or of membership of a trade union. As its leaders admitted, it was necessary to create a climate of fear.

The appalling accounts of the suffering of the Spanish people drew Kitty and Eleanor Rathbone to set up a National Joint Committee for Spanish Relief towards the end of 1936. Kitty became chairman and Eleanor vice-chairman. Although the committee was intended to offer help as required to both sides, Kitty's action was greatly resented at Conservative headquarters, where the committee was viewed as a Republican organisation.

Within the constituency many of Kitty's supporters were outraged. These included one of her oldest and closest friends, Mrs Stirling of Keir, a member of an old Scottish Catholic family and a sister of Lord Lovat. Mrs Stirling was a leading member of the executive committee of Kitty's association: she had been growing increasingly critical of Kitty's stance. As an old and valued friend she had already told Kitty of her anxieties several times in private, but this act of what she could only view as treachery was to end their friendship finally. Both women were equally hurt; the rift between them was never healed.

As Orwell later commented, the Spanish Civil War was a class war. If it had been won, the cause of the common people everywhere would have been strengthened. However annoying her previous eccentricities, rebellions and acts of defiance against the party leadership, Kitty had never before been seen to be betraying her own class.

Chapter 17

To Bucharest, Prague and War-Torn Madrid, 1936–7

On 7 August 1936 Kitty and Bardie held a reception at Dunkeld House. Those invited heard an address by Monsieur Charles le Simple, who had been a Consul in Germany for twenty-five years. He spoke of the Nazi regime as 'a religion in Germany' and warned the audience of Hitler's plans as explained in *Mein Kampf,* ending with a plea for British and French collaboration against German aggression. In her speech of thanks to M. le Simple, Kitty said that the international situation had not been out of her waking thoughts since Germany reoccupied the Rhineland. She reiterated her previous warnings about Germany's expenditure on armaments, and went on to express her anxieties about the anti-Jewish mail she was receiving. Neither speech was what some members of the audience wished to hear. In their opinion the French were unreliable and Leftist, the Jews financial upstarts—whereas the Germans were proving to be a reliable bulwark against communism.

At the time her Perthshire colleague, the Conservative Member of Parliament for East Perth, Thomas Hunter, was making it known that the House of Commons was pro-German in outlook and that the time had come for Germany to get a fair deal, adding that Mr Chamberlain had also complained of Germany being held up as a bogey-man. These were the opinions with which Kitty's guests agreed and many departed more convinced than ever that Kitty was becoming rather left-wing herself. They wished that she would stick to agriculture, health, education and matters concerning the constituency, instead of meddling in foreign affairs and creating fear and anxiety without cause.

Later on that month, a Fascist rally took place on the North Inch, a public park in Perth. Some 4,000 had congregated there by the time a 'Black Maria' containing the Blackshirt leaders arrived at the scene. The Socialists and Communists had arranged for a reception and as the Blackshirts ascended the platform sections in the crowd began to sing cheerfully and loudly: so loudly that the speakers could not be heard. They made several attempts, bawling through a microphone that 'The

British are fed up with democracy and desirous of a lead!' but were forced to retreat to the van, pausing only to give the Fascist salute in the direction of the Union Jack.

That month too, the Conservatives held a fete at Dunira House, near Comrie. On this occasion the speaker was Mr W S Morrison, Financial Secretary to the Treasury, spoken of by the local paper as 'a strong tip as next Prime Minister'. During her reply Kitty spoke strongly against the proposition being floated in response to demands from Hitler to return mandated territories in Africa to Germany.

> I feel bound to say that so long as Germany is governed under a system disposed to racial discrimination, which has led to the persecution of Jews in Germany, it would be a gross betrayal of our trusteeship to hand over natives and helpless races to their rule.

In September Sir John Simon addressed a rally in Perth, at which he said that communism and fascism were equally unacceptable to the British nation. Speaking in her own constituency ten days later, Kitty pointed out that although both regimes were equally unacceptable, Germany was now a much greater menace than Russia.

> Eighteen months ago we learnt that Germany was tearing up the clause forbidding conscription for the army. Her army was limited to 100,000. It is now 500,000. Next came news that she had a very large air force. Then she tore up the clause limiting her to a certain size of battleship. Now she is spending £800,000,000 on arms each year. In March she tore up two treaties and marched into the Rhineland. France and Russia have now formed a pact to help each other if attacked. They have invited Germany to join it: Germany has declined . . . Hitler is full of hatred for Russia and France.

Although she did not speak of it, she had received an unsigned, pencilled letter written in capital letters from Holland. It said simply 'Berlin's object is to put a wedge between Paris and Moscow and if this move is successful then look out for war.'

She reiterated that she did not retract one single word that she had said regarding the tyranny of Russia, but there had been indications of mitigation to some extent during the past three years (in this she was mistaken) while dictatorship in Germany was every bit as real as in Russia: anyone criticising the German government was liable to meet with arrest and there was a widespread system of espionage. She went on to call for rearmament in Britain and for the reformation and strengthening of the League of Nations, adding 'If Hitler starts on Eastern Europe he may pick off one country after another until he reaches the Black Sea and then turn back to Western Europe with a force which no-one can withstand.'

A few days later the Liberals held a rally in the constituency, which was addressed by the leader of the party, Sir Archibald Sinclair. He declared 'Liberals are . . . not prepared to envisage an endless vista of international rearmament. Peace would crack under the strain. We must shake our statesmen out of their pre-war mentality or replace them by men who see disarmament as the only policy by which civilization can be assured.' Mrs Coll Macdonald responded with what, under the circumstances, may seem to have been a slightly infelicitous choice of metaphor: 'We Liberals must buckle on our armour to win!'

The subjects of the Spanish War and that of the threat of fascist aggression in Eastern Europe were constantly intertwined in Kitty's thoughts and speeches at this time. She spoke in her constituency and in the House about the need for corporate strength:

> However much we may dislike the Soviet regime, we cannot do without their co-operation in the work of trying to keep the peace . . . It would be ultimately suicidal if we said that we had no obligation to the Czechs, that we would leave south and east Europe to its fate and only bother about the west.

Returning to the topic of Spain, she spoke of her fears about the consequences of an insurgent victory. She noted that access to the Mediterranean would be controlled by fascist powers, and she re-emphasised the unfair working of Non-Intervention against the constitutionally elected government, which had the support of a much larger part of the Spanish people than the rebels. She saluted the courage of the men and women who had gone into the firing line without adequate equipment and repeated her conviction that the extreme elements in Spain were anarchist rather than socialist or communist. Such sentiments were anathema to the National Government and to the Conservative Party.

In the House on 5 November, Kitty spoke on what was, to her, the most urgent topic of the day: that of international co-operation against all aggressors. She highlighted the plight of the small Eastern European countries with inadequate defences which were now clearly under grave threat of invasion.

Following that speech her friend Jan Masaryk, Czech minister to Britain, wrote to her:

> On my return from Czechoslovakia I hasten to thank you for the words of encouragement which you gave us . . . Your spirited appeal on behalf of Czechoslovakia has been a great encouragement to our people in these anxious days.

In an interview for a Czech paper a few days later, Kitty said that she and many of her parliamentary colleagues were regularly receiving, gratis, pro-Nazi literature and that in the last six months two pro-German periodicals had been launched in London. 'Soviet propaganda, I have no doubt, is also active, but I do not know of any free distribution of Soviet literature on a comparable scale. Nor do I know of any Soviet activity to compare with that of a van, painted with a swastika, which may be found handing out anti-Jewish literature by night in the streets of London.'

She added that she believed that if all nations which valued freedom were prepared to bring each other prompt support under the Covenant of the League it should be possible to confront a potential aggressor with superior force and so prevent war or at least ensure that the aggressor's aims were unsuccessful.

The difficulty remained that a defenceless League could do little but talk. Britain's government, whilst paying it lip service, had a cynical disregard for it.

Kitty's speech of 5 November resulted in an invitation from the Rumanian Council of Women to visit their country. She was glad to accept and Vansittart at the Foreign Office was extremely gratified to hear of it. She proposed to make up a small delegation of women who would travel together. With Van's help and encouragement arrangements were made for the visit to be extended to Jugoslavia and Czechoslovakia as well. Kitty invited Eleanor Rathbone and Lady Layton, wife of the proprietor of the *News Chronicle*. Lady Layton and her husband had been early members of the Anglo-German Fellowship, but had resigned quickly on discovering the nature of the Nazi regime. All three women were deeply committed to a policy of altering and strengthening the composition of the League.

The visits to the three countries went well. Kitty's title and position were by no means a handicap on occasions such as this: they provided an entry to the upper echelons and gained them the ear of those who might otherwise have disdained to meet a small group of British women, however worthy. They took part in an exhausting tour of travel, receptions and meetings, which they were expected to address.

With her usual disregard for matters sartorial, Kitty forgot to suggest that they should include in their luggage more than the simplest and most practical of clothing. On several occasions they felt slightly embarrassed at receptions when their hosts and fellow-guests arrived in formal evening dress with decorations and/or dazzling jewellery to find the three British ladies very plainly clad. Kitty acknowledged that it had been a miscalculation, but it did not trouble her, since the purpose of their visit was to meet as wide a section of the public as possible, to discern the facts, and to give what encouragement they could to those in a state of grave anxiety for the future of their country.

Each of the three countries faced different problems. In Rumania, which contained rich oil fields and would be an important acquisition for Hitler, the president of the Council spoke to Kitty in private, expressing the view that European peace would be assured only if Britain were to join France and the Little Entente in defending the Czechs against attack. Rumania was at that moment a particular target for Fascist propaganda and a number of Rumanian newspapers were being used for this purpose. Some took the opportunity to try to discredit Kitty:

> The Duchess is old, ugly and speaks French like a crocodile . . . in the delirium of Macbethic instincts she tries to expiate the sins of her diseased heart inherited from her devilish ancestor Lady Macbeth. Why does she do it? To overcome her physical ugliness. Now the most ardent Communist missionary, she lives at the most elegant hotel with hot and cold water, a bath and a male masseur. She also finds a few old fools who are willing to declare that she is pursuing a crusade against anti-semitism . . .

In Czechoslovakia the trio met Dr Benes and other government ministers, who discussed their country's problems earnestly and urgently. They were also able to meet Herr Henlein, leader of the Sudeten Germans, whose grievances against the state were being exploited by Hitler as an excuse to make menacing demands on the Czech government.

Czechoslovakia had been re-created when the map of Europe was re-drawn at Versailles. It included the historic states of Bohemia, Moravia and part of Silesia, together with Slovakia. Centuries before, these states had been swallowed up by the Austro-Hungarian Empire and its peoples forced to play a subservient role. The post-war rationalisation which had taken place meant that several million German-speaking 'Sudetens' who had previously lived in Austria now lived in Czechoslovakia. They had never been German citizens and at the time of the preparation of the Peace Treaties, although Austria had protested against their incorporation into Czechoslovakia, the German government had advised them to accept it. The Sudeten Germans, backed by Hitler, were now making impossible demands, including partition of Czechoslovakia. It was obvious that the intention was for ultimate incorporation of the Sudeten area within the German Reich. The Czechoslovakian boundary with Austria had been highly fortified against invasion and the Sudetenland contained the important Skoda munition works.

The delegation returned from Eastern Europe more convinced than ever that what was required was a firm commitment of mutual support on the part of all members of the League. Lady Layton and Eleanor Rathbone returned to Britain, whilst Kitty made a personal visit to Dr Schuschnigg, the Austrian Chancellor. He discussed with her in private his anxieties for the future of his country. Eight months previously he had been forced to sign an agreement with Germany recognising that Austria was 'a German State' in exchange for a promise that Germany would respect its neighbour's sovereignty. He and Kitty both recognised this as a temporary ploy. Hitler's intention was to occupy Austria as soon as he thought the moment was ripe. After her talks Kitty came away feeling reassured that Austria's leaders were not, as she had feared, already in Hitler's pocket.

If ever there was a moment for international consolidation in the face of general danger it must have been then. Yet Britain continued to refuse to undertake any commitment other than that of guaranteeing the French border with Germany.

Kitty's attempts to change the government's thinking on these matters were not appreciated. She was liked by those members of her own party who knew her personally, but they now viewed her political judgement with scepticism. There were a number of reasons why this should be more pronounced in her case than in the case of the other anti-appeasers. Firstly, she was a woman: for most of the men, the trade of politics was still an exclusively male domain. Secondly, she was viewed as being old and dowdy. This too was unfair, since many MPs were themselves older and much dowdier than she was—Chamberlain was several years older and not a handsome sight. Churchill, with his best years ahead, was exactly her age and not even his wife would have described him as good-looking. But because they were men their age and appearance caused no comment. Thirdly, Kitty—and to an extent Churchill too—were seen to have deserted their fellow-aristocrats at a time of crisis: this was almost the most heinous crime of all in the eyes of elitist MPs and of the aristocracy in the country. Businessmen too were up in arms over what they saw as a betrayal of their interests. Kitty remarked bitterly: 'Nothing matters now except business.'

Almost immediately on her return to Britain, Kitty prepared to take part in an all-women delegation to Spain. To her own satisfaction the Foreign Secretary, Eden, had recently said that the character of the future government of Spain was less important than that the dictators should not be victorious there. Unfortunately other members of the Cabinet were not equally enlightened.

The Spanish visit had first been mooted by a doughty little Socialist MP Ellen Wilkinson in January 1937. Kitty and Eleanor agreed to go in their capacity as Chairman and Vice-Chairman of the National Joint Committee for Spanish Relief. The party also included Dame Rachel

Crowdy, late Director of the Social Welfare Section of the League of Nations. Kitty and Dame Rachel intended to visit both sides in the war. It was Kitty's view that relief should be given wherever the need existed, since humanitarian needs were paramount. However, whether deliberately or not their applications for permits to visit rebel territory were delayed and arrangements could not be made in time.

On 13 April they travelled to Toulouse by train and flew on the next day to Barcelona. It was Kitty's first flight, and under those uncertain conditions it must have been a little unnerving. They spent several days in Barcelona, where they were officially received by Government representatives. The atmosphere was strange. Barcelona was as yet remote from the fighting. While the poor went short of food, there were hotels where life seemed almost normal, with those who could afford it eating well and still buying luxury goods in the shops.

Catalonia was a strongly anarchist region and the anarchists had adopted a code of ethics and a way of life which was based on idealism and brotherly love. In the anarchist areas the concept of ownership and of individual property had been abandoned. Individual landholdings had been confiscated. Money had been abolished. Wages took the form of food and the necessities of life. Marriage had also been dispensed with: relationships were free and without commitment. Communal peasant and workers' enterprises were established. Those too lazy to contribute to the general work were not punished and were equally rewarded, but were subjected to a general air of disapproval.

Dining with Rockefeller shortly after her return, Kitty apparently gave an account of the anarchist philosophy in action, which caused him some pain. Her diary reads: '23rd May. Dined at Rockefellers. Horrified him???'

Antagonism and bitter internecine disputes between anarchists on the one hand and socialists and communists on the other were to prove disastrous to the Government cause in Catalonia.

The party from Britain met leaders of both factions and went on to deal with the most important task from their own point of view, that of meeting the victims of the war. They visited hospitals and schools and noted that among the population generally food was very scanty. A subsequent article by Kitty in the *Sunday Express* in which she reported on her findings was resented by Orwell, who complained that English visitors were inclined to flit through Spain from hotel to hotel without observing anything of the real atmosphere.

From Barcelona they went on by car to Valencia, an industrial city at the southern end of the Republican zone. The rebel armies were only a few miles away and the city was full of refugees who had walked for many days and nights. The roads into the town from the south were strewn with the dead who had been ruthlessly machine-gunned as they struggled towards safety.

Kitty's party was impressed by the courage and resolution of the people in their misery and by the sympathetic and efficient way in which the injured were being cared for. In view of rumours that the government side took no prisoners, they visited prisoners of war and met a great many, including Italians, who wanted to talk and who said that they were only too glad to have been eliminated from the fighting. Many of them said that they had understood they were on their way to Abyssinia and were shocked to find themselves in Spain.

From Valencia the party went on to the capital, Madrid, which was under constant attack from the air and from shell fire as the rebels were encircling it and moving closer daily. There they encountered severe privation among the people and an acute food shortage. Whole areas of the city had been destroyed by shell-fire. Part of the hotel the party were occupying was damaged, with fatal casualties. while they were there. They travelled about the city freely, visiting the relief organisations and noting their requirements. Everywhere they went they were surprised by the courage and equanimity of the people during the bombardments. Here too they were able to meet political prisoners, who had few complaints except for the shortage and monotony of food. After talking to them, Ellen, Eleanor, Rachel and Kitty were agreed that they appeared to have been treated with consideration.

But it was the plight of the refugee children which outraged Kitty. Some were being evacuated from Madrid by bus and lorry (these vehicles were funded by her own relief organisation) to safer areas, where they were being well housed and educated. Others were being evacuated to live in caves near the city; but to her dismay Kitty saw that there were still many children at great risk and there was a need for further funds for transport, though she had much sympathy for the many mothers who were reluctant to part with their children.

Kitty went to a Protestant Church Service on the Sunday in Madrid and reported that it had been very well attended; the Pastor of the Church said that the setting up of the Republic in 1931 had, in fact, brought a religious liberty which had not existed previously. The Pastors in Valencia had told her the same thing, though they said that some pastors and evangelists had been shot in Franco-held territory.

The delegation also met members of the International Brigade, who told them that they believed themselves to be fighting for the liberties . . . 'not of Spain, but of Europe.'

While Kitty and the other members of the delegation were staying in Madrid, the Scottish Communist MP Willie Gallacher turned up at the same hotel on his own visit of observation. In his memoirs he recalled that when he entered the diningroom Kitty and Ellen rushed up to greet him. He had the impression that the little Duchess was happy and relieved to find a fellow Scot in those rather frightening surroundings. He was on his way to be introduced to Hemingway, who was sitting at another table, and excused himself to go and talk to the American author.

Gallacher tried to persuade Hemingway to broadcast to America on behalf of the Republic, but Hemingway refused on the grounds that he had his public to think of. Gallacher privately thought him a 'big sap'—an opinion evidently shared by the Republicans themselves. Kitty and Eleanor did not refuse. Both made broadcasts on behalf of the refugee children.

In a later conversation, Kitty discovered that Willie Gallacher intended to go up to the front line and immediately proposed that she and Ellen should go with him. Gallacher, knowing the danger, was appalled. He told them that they would require to get permission from the military authorities. Kitty pressed the matter, saying it could not be any more dangerous than Madrid itself, where they had already been to a point from which they could see the fighting going on and the shells bursting in the park of the Casa del Campo. However to Gallacher's relief permission was refused.

During their visit to Spain Kitty and her companions had been able to meet and talk at length to many of the chief personalities on the Government side: Companys, President of Catalonia; President Azana; Prime Minister Caballero. But the most arresting and compelling personality they encountered was, in Kitty's view. Dolores Ibarurri, the Communist Deputy, who, because of her remarkable gift for instilling courage by her heroic oratory, was known as La Pasionaria. Kitty had at first been reluctant to meet her 'as her name suggested to me a rather over-emotional young person . . . I have never ceased to be glad that I did so, for the only person with whom I felt La Pasionaria could be compared was the woman I had always regarded as the greatest actress I had seen, Eleanora Duse. She had Duse's wonderful grace and voice, but she was much more beautiful, with rich colouring, large dark eyes and black wavy hair. She swept into the room like a queen, yet she was a miner's daughter married to a miner—a woman who had had the sorrow of losing six out of eight children. I could understand nothing that she said, and she talked with great rapidity, but to look and to listen was pleasure enough for me . . .'

Orwell was right in suggesting that 'fact-finding' visits from Britain or elsewhere were too short and the propaganda too well focused for detached observation. But Kitty and her friends had seen enough to be certain that substantial aid was needed for hapless Spanish children who were the innocent victims of war.

Chapter 18

The Rift with the Party, 1937-8

Kitty returned from the war in Spain in April 1937 profoundly convinced that the elected Spanish government and people who supported it stood for a free and representative system of government. She was also determined to devote her energies towards raising massive aid for the victims of war.

That determination was reinforced within two weeks of her return by the news of the bombing of Guernica. The narrow strip of land on the northern coast of Spain was inhabited by the Basques, people who came of different stock from either of their neighbours the Spanish and French and who spoke a different language. They were Catholic, but vehemently anti-Franco and anti-fascist. Franco's troops had occupied the Spanish interior to the south of the Basque region, almost to the outskirts of Madrid and were pushing up to Madrid from southern Spain to encircle the capital. To the north, only the Basque region stood against them. Catholic Basque resistance to Franco was obviously an affront to the rebels who claimed to be fighting for the Catholic cause.

For some time the rebels had been trying to starve the isolated Basque region into submission with a naval blockade of the northern coastline against all imports from abroad. The rebel blockade received the tacit support of the British Government and the Chiefs of Staff, on the grounds that Britain could not intervene without breaking the non-intervention agreement which had been signed. As one backbencher, Sir Henry Page Croft, declared openly 'We are not going to support the feeding of Red children.'

A ground attack across the mountains by Spanish rebel troops supported by Germans had begun in March 1937. On 20 April a small British vessel carrying food and supplies broke the blockade against instructions by the British navy, and triumphantly arrived in Bilbao, bringing a small measure of relief against the famine and providing proof that British Chiefs of Staff had given false information about the existence of rebel mines at the entrance to the harbour.

The rebels were not long in meting out vengeance. In the afternoon of 25 April the beautiful little market town of Guernica, ancient capital of the Basque Province, was bombed, first by a single German plane and, as the people emerged from shelter, by a squadron of bombers. As the townspeople rushed to escape across the fields they were machine-gunned from the air. An hour later three squadrons of German Junker planes arrived out of the early evening sky and annihilated the town and its people in a two-and-a-half hour blanket bombardment. The anguish of Guernica aroused the compassion of the world. Vatican sources denied the story.

The resources of Kitty's relief fund were fully stretched. During the summer there was a hugely successful rally at the Albert Hall on behalf of the Basque children, which Kitty addressed. She also spoke twice at important functions in Paris. Lord Cecil, with whom she shared her passionate support of the principles on which the League of Nations had been founded, invited her to speak at an International Peace Campaign on the occasion of the opening of the Peace Pavilion at the Paris Exhibition. Her second visit was as a member of an inter-Parliamentary delegation.

In June Kitty was verbally attacked by a Catholic member of her Constituency Association's Executive Council, Colonel Rupert Dawson from Braco. He publicly accused her of speaking at meetings in London and Paris supported by communists. Kitty took the trouble to deny the story, pointing out 'Neither in London, Paris, nor anywhere else have I addressed meetings organised by any political party other than the Conservative and Unionist Party; surely, however, no-one can object to members from different political parties speaking from the same platform on behalf of humanitarian purposes such as Spanish Relief or for a great and good cause such as the League of Nations and collective security.'

Unfortunately many did object. Since support for Spanish relief came from non-Conservative sources, and support for the League largely from left-of-centre, a great many Conservatives regarded such participation as perfidy. As a result Kitty began to find herself more and more frequently appearing on platforms with politically unlikely speaking partners. It did not trouble her. As always for Kitty, the pitiable condition of the children came before political considerations. She was willing to stand on a platform with anyone who had compassion. The only way in which she could express her love for children was by the emotionally detached business of fund-raising on behalf of the stricken.

Matters in the constituency were becoming increasingly uncomfortable. Colonel Dawson had decided to take his complaints to the Executive Committee and he asked for a special meeting to be called. He addressed fellow members about his 'very unpleasant purpose'. He said he was convinced that so far as the Member's activities, speeches and publications on the subject of the situation in Spain were concerned, she had ceased to represent the principles and interests of the Conservative Party. She had taken the hand of friendship of communists and even of anarchists. 'Victor Cazalet MP has assured us that the Spanish people regard Franco as their Saviour from the terror of Bolshevism . . . we have in Nationalist Spain an earnest of future happy commercial relations such as would make for the common prosperity of both countries . . .'

Finally Colonel Dawson put forward the following motion: 'That the declared sympathies of the Member in this instance of the Spanish War are at variance with the principles and interests of ourselves as Conservatives.'

In reply, Kitty said that she had shown sympathy with a government of which members of the Communist and Anarchist parties formed a part, in their fight against fascist dictatorships, which she regarded as a great menace to the peace of Europe and to this country. She had never expressed sympathy with either communism or anarchism; as to what Colonel Dawson had said about the Conservative Party standing for a cautious evolution of society, if there had been such evolution in Spain she did not think there would be civil war there today.

Having failed to find a seconder for his motion, Colonel Dawson stormed from the meeting and resigned from the Executive, though not from the Association. Although he had not succeeded in gaining support, his intervention was a straw in the wind. Before the end of the year Colonel Dawson, Mrs Stirling and Sir Kay Muir were to resign from the Association in protest against Kitty's views on Spain.

Bilbao fell to Franco's troops in mid June and Kitty received reports that hundreds of Basques were fleeing for their lives, hundreds more dying of starvation. The port at Santander was overcrowded, there was little food and there was fear of imminent epidemic. Pressed in the House of Commons over British help for refugees, the new Prime Minister, Neville Chamberlain, responded that he was 'not sure who they are or how many or how we could help'. Pressed further, he agreed that if necessary Britain would give protection to ships carrying women and children to safety. Kitty's committee arranged to transport Basque children to safety abroad—to France, to Mexico (the Republic's only real friend) and later, when the government gave permission, for the arrival of 4,000 to Britain, where they were sent to camps near Southampton. Kitty's committee liaised with a committee organised by the TUC and the Salvation Army as well as a Catholic Bishops' committee.

The starved, homesick children were made as comfortable and as happy as possible. The committee felt that it was essential to keep them together in camps and not to permit them to be separated in individual homes, since the committee were responsible for their safety and also because it was hoped to be able to return them to their parents as soon as conditions improved. The arrival of the children was unwelcome and much resented by sections of the community.

Colonel Dawson had taken the trouble to have his diatribe against Kitty at the June meeting of the Executive published as a pamphlet and circulated in the constituency. It had also been published in *The Patriot*— whose editor, as Kitty pointed out, was a strong Catholic and anti-Semite—where it was alleged that Kitty had undertaken not to pursue her pro-Red speeches and activities outside the House of Commons. As this was offensive and untrue, Kitty's solicitor registered a complaint and an apology was printed. But the impression was now firmly established in the minds of the party, the local association and the general public that Kitty had gone communist. It was easy for those who favoured the rebel cause in Spain or the fascists in Germany and Italy—and this was the position of many influential members of the party in 1937—to distort her position. She was referred to openly as 'Red Kitty' and as 'The Red Duchess'. These epithets wounded her deeply, but she gave no sign of it and bore mounting criticism with dignity. A point of principle and of human justice was at stake.

In a letter to Sir Edward Grigg, who shared her views on the government's policy *vis-à-vis* the dictators, she wrote: 'I agree that the issue is whether we are able not only to preserve our liberties in the near future, but to hand them on unimpaired to those who come after us.'

To his own relief Baldwin had resigned as Prime Minister after the coronation of King George VI and Queen Elizabeth in the summer. He had been replaced by Chamberlain who, unlike Baldwin, was passionately interested in foreign affairs and believed in his own ability to come to terms with Hitler. As a businessman, Chamberlain still perceived Communist Russia to be Britain's principal enemy. Disapproving of his Foreign Secretary, Eden, he quickly surrounded himself with ministers with whom he worked independently of the Cabinet. The head of the Conservative Research Department, Sir Joseph Ball—a former intelligence officer, inscrutable and furtive,—was committed to running the Party as Chamberlain wanted it to be run. He made certain that a campaign was undertaken to discredit those opposed to Chamberlain's policies.

Grizel Warner, Kitty's niece, on graduating from Oxford, had been appointed tutor at the Conservative College at Ashridge. She recalls that after Chamberlain became Prime Minister the atmosphere changed. Previously it had been the custom at the College for speakers holding all points of view to be invited to present their case and for discussion to take place: now only Conservative speakers promoting the Government line were invited; Conservatives opposing the Government were regarded with open and undisguised hostility.

Although rearmament was stepped up, Chamberlain did not wish to upset the Germans by seeming to overdo it and as late as 1938 he remarked to Hitler that too much money was being spent on rearmament when it could be used to build better homes and hospitals— with which sentiments Hitler agreed.

By now Hitler's designs on Austria and Czechoslovakia were becoming clear. Britain urged the Czechs to come to terms with the Sudetens as a matter of urgency. Chamberlain's view, expressed in November 1937, was that it seemed desirable to try to realise an accord with Germany on Central Europe . . . Lord Halifax, Lord President of the Council, accepted an invitation to go to a hunting exhibition in Berlin. This opportunity for him to meet Hitler and Goering had been carefully set up by Sir Nevile Henderson, British Ambassador in Berlin. Halifax returned with the reassurance that the Germans had 'no wish to make war . . . of course they wish to dominate Eastern Europe and want as close a union with Austria as they can get and they want the same things for the Sudetens as we did for the Uitlanders in the Transvaal'.

Although Kitty was almost the only Conservative to oppose the working of the Non-Intervention Pact in Spain, she was not the only Conservative to oppose the Government line on other matters. A small but vociferous body of MPs and others considered that Britain's policy of appeasement of the dictators was not only mistaken but suicidal. These included Churchill, Harold Macmillan, Duff Cooper, Sir Edward Grigg and Robert Boothby.

Apart from Churchill, who was her exact contemporary—they were born within two weeks of each other—these were younger men who knew Kitty rather vaguely, though Boothby knew her well as a Scottish colleague. These MPs had also earned the displeasure of Conservative Central Office and the Conservative Whips, and were beginning to feel pressures within their own constituencies. However their electors and constituency committees were very different in character from Kinross and West Perthshire, with its dominant 'county set'. Churchill at Epping, Edward Grigg at Altrincham, Macmillan at Stockton, even Robert Boothby in Aberdeenshire, had much more 'down to earth' members to deal with—members less right-wing and less likely to challenge their sitting member of parliament.

Throughout 1937 and 1938 a series of Blackshirt meetings were held in Kitty's constituency: at Crieff on a number of occasions, at Aberfeldy and at Auchterarder. There is no record as to the organiser of these events, though it is possible that they were the work of a Captain Luttman-Johnson, who came to live near Perth about that time. He was an organiser of the pro-Fascist January Club which had been founded in order to hold functions for important and influential establishment figures in the hope of persuading them to join the movement. Whether or not he had any political influence over them, he quickly became an accepted figure with the 'county'. He was interned during the early part of the war. Interviews were sought with a small number of people who were believed to have attended these meetings; even in 1988 they were unwilling to admit to having done so.

Kitty was being assailed by extremely offensive letters from members of her Association. Colonel T W S Graham of Rednock House, Port of Menteith, considered that her visit to Spain should never have taken place and accused her of 'propaganding all over the country . . . It is by no means in the best interests of the country that all and sundry should broadcast their views . . . The Russian Army is no doubt enormous . . . I would hazard the conjecture that the Germans, the most magnificent fighters on Earth, would go through an armed mob of this sort like a hot knife through butter.' He ended with a comment that the heart was being taken out of landowners who were having to struggle with high taxation.

Colonel James Dundas of Ochtertyre wrote: 'You have far outstepped the action that is right for a private member to take in a matter of foreign policy . . . you will lose the seat at the next election to any reasonably good Liberal . . . and all for what—to preach a doctrine which the bulk of your constituents care little about . . . It all seems so utterly unnecessary'.

Kitty did her best to heal the breach with her dissident flock, making personal visits or writing polite, explanatory letters to those known to be annoyed by what they believed to be her pro-communist stance. She called on Sir Kay and Lady Muir in particular and had a friendly talk, though she 'found his mind very closed'.

As it happened, many of the dissenters lived within a few miles of each other to the south of the constituency—Mrs Peggy Stirling, the Muirs, Colonel Dawson, Colonel Graham of Menteith, Mr and Mrs Alistair Dixon, Mr William McNair Snadden, Mr and Mrs P C Dickson. Mr Alistair Dixon, of Ledcameron, Dunblane, complained that he had understood he had been voting for a National Government supporter and his branch at Dunblane refused to allow her to address any further meetings there under its auspices. However Kitty still had some loyal supporters. Bardie was President of the Association and he, of course, supported her totally. She also had a knight-in-shining-armour at Auchterarder, Will Hally. At meeting after meeting of the Executive or of the Association, Will Hally spoke in her defence. A Mrs Ramage-Dawson at Kinross was also loyal; she frequently wrote letters of encouragement and warning: 'The situation is becoming difficult for those of us who are working for you as so many people feel that your support of the Spanish Government is wrong.' Miss Patrick, Chairman of the Young Conservatives (known as the Junior Unionists) was also a warm supporter both personally and on behalf of the entire Junior Unionist Association in the constituency.

In the summer of 1937 Kitty spoke at a meeting of young people held in Manchester in aid of Spanish Relief. She believed that almost 25 per cent of them were communists, but they all loudly applauded her appeal on behalf of the Catholic Basques. She made a point of telling them what a mistake Russian Communism had made in persecuting religion.

Annoyance over Kitty's behaviour had now given way to anger. Fellow MPs greatly resented her interventions in the House, her speeches in the country and her letters to the press on Spain and on the need for collective action to thwart the dictators' plans. Apart from Boothby, she was without support among the Unionist MPs in Scotland. Particular opponents were Captain A H M Ramsay, Sir Thomas Moore and Captain J H F McEwen, all of whom represented constituencies in the south of Scotland. Ramsay was interned during the war; Moore was spoken of by Hitler with warm admiration. Revulsion for communism led to support for co-operation and friendship with Germany by some prominent members of the Border landed gentry and aristocracy.

Kitty had become so conscious of her position within the Association that she sent a circular letter to all her constituents in September, pointing out the massive aid now being sent to Franco from Italy and Germany . . .

> If we condone clear aggression how can the League of Nations again hope to prevent or restrain an act of aggression—and if the League collapses what hope is there of maintaining our liberties?

Meantime in the House Captain Ramsay enquired whether the Basque children might not be sent back to Spain; Samuel Hoare, as Home Secretary, replied that in his view 'the sooner these children go back to their families the better.'

That autumn Kitty paid another visit to Austria to visit Schuschnigg, whose position was daily becoming more precarious. Until recently Mussolini had been the stumbling block to Hitler's ambitions, but apparently Mussolini was now willing to trade Austria's freedom for international recognition of his own territorial gain in Abyssinia; or so it was rumoured. Whilst there Kitty heard what was, to her, a much more encouraging rumour: America might be about to emerge from its isolationist stance and take an active part in solving Europe's problems.

The rumours with regard to Roosevelt were correct. In mid-January 1938 the Foreign Office heard, through Sir Ronald Lindsay, the

Ambassador in Washington, that Roosevelt was offering a personal initiative which would involve calling the Diplomatic Corps in Washington together and reading the riot act—redefining the rules relating to international law and aggression and setting up a committee from the smaller states to examine the situation. Lindsay strongly recommended acceptance. Unfortunately the Foreign Secretary Eden was abroad at that moment. Chamberlain discourteously spurned the President's offer without waiting to consult Eden. He was convinced that he could pull off an agreement with Hitler—though it might involve sacrificing Czechoslovakia and Austria—and he had no wish for Roosevelt to steal his thunder. Eden returned immediately and attempted to rescue the plan, but he was too late: the President retired, hurt. As Hitler's threat to Austria became clear, Chamberlain prepared to make a deal with the dictators. The Cabinet—apart from Eden—agreed. Eden resigned. The date was 20 February 1938. Halifax, fresh from his German visit, became Foreign Secretary.

Kitty immediately sent a letter of condolence and congratulation on his stance to Eden. Few people in the country were aware of the reasons for his departure, since he never divulged the Roosevelt initiative. There was considerable speculation in the press over the matter. Kitty, though, almost certainly knew of Chamberlain's duplicity because of her recent meeting with Schuschnigg and her contact with Vansittart. Churchill, too, knew of the background to the resignation and wrote of his sense of sorrow and grim foreboding when he heard the news.

Kitty was one of the speakers, with Lord Cecil and Sir Archibald Sinclair, at a League of Nations Union rally at the Queen's Hall in protest at the departure of the Foreign Secretary, whose resignation had been followed immediately by that of his Under-Secretary, Lord Cranborne, who made a much more vigorous and explicit resignation speech than Eden. Sir Joseph Ball saw to it that their reputations were damaged and that their Constituency Associations took the matter up with them. Eden challenged his Association to a vote of confidence and won. Cranborne had greater difficulty with his, but managed to survive. Grizel Warner, at Ashridge, noted the bitter and hostile atmosphere which developed against them—and the others. Churchill (who was constantly described as always drunk . . . totally finished), Brendan Bracken, Duncan Sandys, Kitty and others. Twenty-five Conservatives abstained in the debate on Eden's resignation.

On 22 February Chamberlain said that he did not believe that the League could provide collective security, adding: 'We must not try to delude small weak nations into thinking that they will be protected by the League against aggression.'

Hitler moved into Austria on 9 March. Dr Schuschnigg and thousands of others were immediately imprisoned by the Gestapo. Chamberlain regarded the coup as 'an unfortunate and unpleasant business which could have been avoided if Halifax had been at the Foreign Office earlier.' He and Halifax then granted the Italians recognition of their conquest of Abyssinia. The agreement was signed on 16 April.

Kitty told her electors that Chamberlain's declaration of 22 February had shown Hitler that if he attacked Austria, Britain would not try to get the League to stop him. He had repeated the statement with a slight change on 7 March and four days later German troops had seized Austria. 'The seizure of Austria brings Germany to the Italian frontier and so makes fascism extend right across Europe. . . . If we give further rebuffs to Russia there is always the danger that she may withdraw from the League, from her pledges to help France and Czechoslovakia, and think only of her own immediate security. In that event I do not see how Herr Hitler could be prevented from getting to the Rumanian oilfield and the Black Sea. In that case all Europe sooner or later would be at his feet.'

A small group of people of all parties had begun to meet for luncheon at intervals to discuss pressing aspects of foreign policy. These included Winston Churchill, Kitty, Violet Bonham-Carter, Norman Angell, Wickham Steed, Philip Guedella, Eleanor Rathbone and other anti-appeasers. One such luncheon was held in April 1937.

On 28 April Kitty wrote to the Prime Minister to complain that the conditions of the pact with Italy included an agreement that no further Italian troops would be sent to Spain: yet Italian troops were continuing to arrive, and she therefore, with great regret, suggested that she might have to resign the government whip. She also complained about other matters and Chamberlain replied that as he was sure his answer to her letter would not satisfy her, he had instructed that the whip should be withdrawn from her.

Kitty wrote to her constituents to explain: the Prime Minister had retreated from the policy adhered to by Mr Eden—the principle of the Covenant of the League—at a time when Britain and other countries should be consolidating mutual agreements against aggression. This should apply equally to Eastern European countries and to the North Sea nations, all of which were at risk. Now that Hitler had seized Austria, thousands had been robbed or arrested and thousands more were said to have committed suicide. All European countries were under threat. Although fully aware of the defects of the Soviet regime, Britain should discuss joint security with Russia and not risk alienating it. She warned her constituents that the government policy on Spain was extremely dangerous. To allow the Spanish government to be defeated for lack of arms and food was, in effect, to take sides or 'intervene' in the Spanish war. She ended by reminding them that she was, as their MP, a representative, not a delegate. She believed that the safety of the country was endangered by the government's policy and that nothing else mattered in comparison.

The Patriot commented: 'The Duchess of Atholl has resigned the government whip and she is opposing the government's foreign policy, which is a question of overwhelming importance. The association is supporting the government, the Member is opposing it.'

For the Liberals and Socialists Kitty was still the Duchess of Atholl, the well-known aristocratic warmonger—though some had begun to warm to her over her stance on Spain and others were revising their own approach to rearmament as a result of the international situation.

On 12 May a rally of the Friends of Nationalist Spain (of which Mrs Peggy Stirling was a leading member) was held in Perth. This was organised by Captain Luttman-Johnson and was well attended. It was first addressed by Sir Norman Stewart-Sandeman MP, who spoke of the necessity for discipline, national or individual, and went on to say: 'We hear a great deal about Nero and his murders. I have made a careful investigation and have discovered that Nero certainly had not murdered any more than five hundred people. There are many more savage persons in the world than Nero was.' He praised Chamberlain and went on to say that a lot of nonsense was talked about Guernica—people did not know the difference between a bomb and a landmine and much of the damage had been done by retreating Reds. And he had been talking to a Holy Father in London about the Basque children and the priest had told him that everyone was frightened because they had broken every window in the place.

Sir Walter Maxwell-Scott then informed the meeting that on his visits to Franco's Spain he had been allowed to go anywhere he liked and had had a very good time. He had also gone to Spanish Morocco and had found that Franco was adored by the Moors and that they called him the Holy Man. Sir Walter lost his temper and referred to hecklers as 'scum'.

Mr Arthur Loveday, late President of the British Chamber of Commerce in Spain, spoke of what was probably at the heart of the matter: that there had been great losses by British trading interests. One British firm had lost as much as £20,000. To shouts of 'whose money?' he shouted angrily: 'You have no compassion and fill me with disgust!'

Many members of Kitty's Executive would have been pleased indeed to have seen her supporting the platform at this meeting, which she did not attend. She went to speak at a meeting organised by the International Peace Campaign in Glasgow three days later. This was the organisation for which she had spoken in Paris and which was supported by Lord Cecil, at whose invitation she went, though, as was to be expected, since the purpose of the meeting was to complain about the Government's

Spanish policy, most of those attending on this occasion were from left-wing organisations.

Subsequently Colonel Dawson received a report (for which he had presumably asked) on Kitty's conduct at the meeting from a woman who had attended it. Her report included the allegation that Kitty had listened to speeches criticising the government and had then remained on the platform for the playing of 'The Red Flag'.

An Executive Council meeting was called for 27 May to discuss these allegations. It was, as those responsible for calling the meeting were aware, a date on which Kitty would be unable to be present, as it was the date of the Caledonian Ball in London. Kitty was anxious to attend the meeting and sacrifice the Ball, but for once Bardie put his foot down: the Ball must take precedence over Association matters. Kitty might frequently neglect her social duties because of her political commitment, but on this occasion they would attend the ball together as they always did, as the President and his lady.

Kitty's absence from the meeting was unfortunate. She wrote a letter of explanation: she had certainly heard a tune being struck up as she was leaving the platform, but had had no idea what it was and had certainly taken no part in singing. However, the allegations had aroused further indignation.

The meeting was attended by Colonel Pat Blair, secretary to Sir James Stuart at the Scottish Whips' Office. On his advice the Executive made two decisions: (1) to begin to distribute Government literature and to invite speakers taking the Government line to address meetings in the Constituency and (2) not to re-adopt Kitty as candidate for the next election.

Kitty was informed and was shaken by the news, but it in no way altered her judgement as to the rightness of the cause or the mistaken policies of the government—which, as she pointed out, she had received permission from her electors eighteen months previously to criticise if and when she felt it necessary. She would continue to do so.

Meantime hostility towards the presence in Britain of Basque children grew and developed to such a pitch that Kitty found herself under great pressure to send them back. Kitty realised the nature of those who were attempting to bully her. She was determined to expose the way in which the Spanish Government's case was being distorted and to present the truth. She had met Gerald Brenan, a British writer and academic who had lived in Spain for many years. Captain Brenan's own political stance was not left-wing, but he vehemently supported the justice of the Spanish Government's case and as an academic and observer he had made it his business to discover the facts of the matter. Kitty learnt much from him and from several other detached sources, such as Liddell Hart, Military

Correspondent of *The Times,* as well as from observers with more left-wing sympathies such as Arthur Koestler.

In the summer of 1938 Kitty's Penguin book *Searchlight on Spain* was published. It dealt at some length with the conditions of extreme poverty and the intransigence of the ruling classes which had inevitably led to the growth of left-wing philosophies among the workers and peasants. In later chapters she demolished Francoist propaganda about the beginning of the rebellion and about the conduct of the war. It was demonstrably untrue, she said, that Franco had nobly stepped in in July 1936 to prevent a Communist uprising, since the coup had been planned as early as 1934 with the connivance of Mussolini and Hitler and there was evidence of Nazi activity in Spain for at least a year before the rebellion began.

She emphasised the danger to Britain of a Franco victory in Spain, quoting Liddell Hart as saying 'The danger is so obvious that it is difficult to understand the eagerness with which some of the most avowedly patriotic sections of the British people have desired the rebels' success.' Kitty's campaign was for fair play for the Spanish government: her demand was that they should be permitted to buy arms in the world market on an equal footing with the insurgents, who were being given favourable treatment in every respect, under cover of a spurious non-intervention treaty. At no stage did she advocate British support for the Republic.

Searchlight on Spain was an immediate best-seller and the first edition was sold out within a week. Two further editions were printed and over 300,000 copies—priced 6d—were eventually sold. It was also translated into French, German and Spanish. It caused a sensation throughout the country: those on the side of the Spanish Government were gratified to have their case supported with such factual evidence and conviction. On the other hand Francoists were further incensed by its publication. It was referred to in *The Patriot* as 'a farrago of pernicious absurdity . . . those who know the chivalry and noble nature of that great gentleman and patriot, Franco, must boil with indignation at this foul aspersion . . . and deplore that any women of culture and position can repeat these infamous lies.'

Tom Johnston, a Labour Member of Parliament, said in a newspaper article,

The *Red Duchess* is a complete misnomer. She is a quiet, unobtrusive, rather pale and tired-looking old lady. She possesses infinite courage of conviction. She is absolutely and fanatically sincere. What she believes she says. There is no facing both ways about Her Grace of Atholl. And now she has fallen foul of the Tory machine at Westminster. She has the powerful landed aristocracy in West Perthshire dancing with fury.

In June 1938 Kitty, Walter and Dorothy Layton and Dr Wickham Steed, a former editor of *The Times,* were invited to attend the Solol Festival in Prague: a visit much frowned on by the British Government. The British ambassador told the Foreign Office that such a visit 'might help to stiffen Czech resistance to Hitler, rather than convincing the Czech government of the importance of making far-reaching concessions'.

Since the Anschluss in Austria Walter Layton, like Kitty, had spent his energies—and those of the *News Chronicle*—in trying to alert the British public to the Government's deplorably weak policies. Their visit lifted and sustained the spirits of Dr Benes and the beleaguered Czech Government. The Sudeten Germans were now making impossible demands and the Czech army had been mobilised. The Russians had declared that if Czechovakia were invaded Russia would come to her assistance, provided France gave the same undertaking. (Lord Home has commented 'France would never have fought.')

Kitty and the Laytons were still pressing for united co-operation under the Covenant of the League, believing that Britain, France, Russia and the small nations acting in unison could still deter German aggression. The Soviet ambassador, Maisky, had told them there was growing resentment in Russia towards Britain and France, since Britain seemed totally supine and France was under British domination.

Some weeks later Layton received secret information that Hitler's plan was to take over Czechoslovakia in the autumn of 1938, Hungary in the spring of 1939, Poland in the autumn of 1939, Jugoslavia in the spring of 1940, Rumania and Bulgaria in the autumn of 1940, France in the spring of 1941, Russia in the autumn of 1941. Layton did not publish this information for some months after receiving it, but it is certain that he would have shared it with Kitty and Wickham Steed.

Kitty and the Laytons returned to Britain in depressed mood. In July Kitty made what was to be her last appearance in the House of Commons. It was not a pleasant experience. At the close of business she was accused by the member for Bury St Edmunds (Captain Heilgers) of recruiting men for the International Brigade, thereby infringing the Foreign Enlistment Act. The accusation brought a forthright denial. The following day Kitty returned to the subject: 'I am glad to have this opportunity of emphatically refuting the suggestion made by the Hon and Gallant Member for Bury St Edmunds . . . He suggested that I had taken a share in recruiting men for the International Brigade in Spain . . .' She went on to produce a letter from Professor J B S Haldane inviting her, on behalf of his wife, to become a patron of the International Brigade Dependants and Wounded Aid Committee. Kitty produced her own reply to Professor Haldane, which said: 'I shall be very glad to be patroness of the proposed appeal, if it can be worded in such a way as not to make an attack on our Government'. Kitty added, 'It is perfectly clear from the letters I have had from Mrs Haldane that her Committee had nothing whatsoever to do with recruitment.'

Once again, however, an unfounded charge had been levelled at Kitty which had the effect of condemning her further in the minds of those who already profoundly disagreed with her.

Chapter 19

The December By-Election 1938

Kitty's work on behalf of the Spanish children had not gone unnoticed in America, where feeling on their behalf ran high. In the summer of 1938 she received a number of invitations to speak at fund-raising events there. Her would-be hostesses assured her that her presence would greatly enhance their ability to raise money for the cause. She agreed to go, with the proviso that she might have one free day each week.

Firm arrangements were made in June and she left for Canada in early September, already half regretting the fact that she would be out of the country as the situation in Europe was becoming more critical: during the summer, reports of German preparations for war against Czechoslovakia had been growing. Britain was warning Germany against aggression and at the same time pressurising the Czechs to give in to German demands. Kitty would have preferred to have remained in Britain to watch events as they unfolded. However she had given her word to the Americans and the cause for which she was undertaking the tour was of paramount concern to her.

The situation was already becoming more ominous, however. When she was still aboard the Duchess of York on 8 September, she heard the news that the Sudeten Germans had broken off negotiations with the Czech Government. She wrote to Bardie

> It seems clear that Hitler does not want a settlement with Czechoslovakia . . . I am truly sorry not to be with you at a time like this, but there is work to do here if I can manage it. Bless you, dearie. . . . If this tragedy happens . . . do get extra vegetables put in wherever you can . . .

She arrived in Toronto on 9 September. Bardie tried to persuade her to return immediately, but despite the knowledge that she might be trapped there if war broke out her conscience would not allow her to disappoint her American friends, or to let down the Spanish children. She began a gruelling two months' tour round coffee mornings, luncheon clubs, official dinners and meetings which would take her from Toronto to Chicago, Ohio, Philadelphia, Baltimore (where she was given an honorary degree), and New York. These were attended by record-breaking crowds—in some cases thousands of people came. In addressing these gatherings she was scrupulously careful, while supporting the position of the Spanish Government, not to criticise the British Government.

Wherever she went she was received with warmth and gratitude. Tributes were paid to her 'excellent crystalline transparence and convincing argument'. Money and gifts of foodstuffs poured in for the children's cause. But the situation was developing and changing daily and even hourly in Europe. She never strayed far from a wireless and listened to news bulletins with foreboding.

On 12 September Hitler made his Nuremberg speech, demanding self-determination for the Sudetans. On 15 September Chamberlain flew to meet him at Berchtesgaden. Hitler demanded the incorporation of the Sudetenland within Germany. On 16 September Chamberlain returned to London to consult the Cabinet on Germany's demands. The Runciman Commission—set up to report on the situation in Czechoslovakia—left Prague. Lord Runciman of Doxford, a Liberal-National member of the Government, had enjoyed the hospitality of a number of German princes and aristocrats during the visit, though he complained that there had been no time for partridge shooting. He announced.

> . . . the Sudeten Germans have been ruled with tactlessness, intolerance and discrimination and I regard their turning for help towards their kinsmen and their eventual desire to join the Reich as a natural development . . .

In reply to a cable from Bardie warning her that she must re-apply for the whip in order to avert trouble within the Association, Kitty responded on 17 September that the situation was too dangerous. She felt one possible course for Hitler might be to patch up an agreement over Czechoslovakia and then work away in Spain until the Loyalists were defeated. Then France would have enemies on three sides and could do nothing if Hitler then attacked Czechoslovakia. She felt that it was vital for her to keep her freedom to speak out.

On 17 September officials in Washington met to discuss the extent of the proposed sell-out of Czechoslovakia by the British and presumably the French. They guessed that Czechoslovakia would still try to fight and they thought the British were trying to bring America into the picture 'so that they shared responsibility for the sell-out'. Those present decided that there was very little chance of that happening.

On 18 September the French were consulted in London. Benes in Czechoslovakia still trusted that they would honour their mutual pact.

The French Prime Minister M. Daladier had stated that war could only be avoided 'if Britain and France made their determination clear to maintain the peace of Europe by respecting the liberties and rights of independent peoples'. Sir Eric Phipps, British Ambassador in Paris, had reported in the spring that the French were convinced that if Britain spoke with sufficient firmness Hitler would collapse.

Meanwhile Nevile Henderson in Berlin wrote to Sir Alexander Cadogan (who had succeeded Vansittart as Permanent Under-Secretary at the Foreign Office) urging him to try to get *The Times,* Camrose and Beaverbrook press to write about Hitler as 'the apostle of peace . . . It will be terribly short-sighted if this is not done.'

When consulted, France agreed to the Berchtesgaden proposals and it was indicated to the Czechs that if they refused to co-operate they would be 'on their own'. At a second meeting, at Godesberg on 22 September, at which Chamberlain intended to concede agreement to the Berchtesgaden demands, Hitler furiously insisted on altering the terms. German troops must be allowed to occupy the Sudetenland within a week and all property (including the Skoda arms factories) within the area must be handed over to Germany intact.

Chamberlain returned home to a country in which public opinion was hardening against further concessions. Yet still the allies refused to send a collective ultimatum. Chamberlain sent Horace Wilson to plead with Hitler, who cynically offered to guarantee Czechoslovakia's 'new frontiers'.

Chamberlain had invited Mussolini to intercede with Hitler in order that a conference might be held. On 28 September Hitler agreed to meet Chamberlain, Daladier and Mussolini in Munich on the following day. When the announcement of the forthcoming meeting was made in the House there was an outburst of cheering from all sides.

No Czech representative was present at the meeting of the four heads of government at Munich on 29 September, when it was agreed that the Czechs should evacuate their Sudeten territory on 1 October, and complete it by 10 October, and there there should be a plebiscite to decide on the future of the 'doubtful' territories.

Kitty, in America, listened to the news as it came in with dismay on behalf of the Czechs. She had written to the British Ambassador, asking if an arrangement might be made for her to meet the President or Mr Cordell Hull, to which she received the following chillingly polite reply:

> British Embassy, 26th September 38.
> Dear Duchess
> If you come to Washington my wife and I hope that when you have settled on your dates you will let us know and it would be a pleasure to see you at luncheon or dinner. But as Parliament has been convened I presume you

will go back to England immediately. I do not feel at all confident that Mr Hull and still less the President would have time to see you these days.

Meantime if you are making speeches I dare say you will have realised that most Americans have a violent dislike to being propagandised and so much so that they may well regard as propaganda what is not intended as such. It is natural that as the papers give them very full information on all that is passing in Europe they should prefer to make up their minds for themselves on the issues presented. As you ask for my opinion I should say that public speaking by English (*sic*) people just now was particularly dangerous and liable to have an effect quite different from what the speaker expects.

Yours sincerely . . . R C Lindsay.

Kitty had, in fact, just given a Press Conference at which a *Daily Telegraph* representative had been present, during which she gave Chamberlain full credit for his efforts on behalf of peace.

President Roosevelt was, however, delighted to have an opportunity of meeting and talking to Kitty. He neatly upstaged the British Embassy by arranging for a small luncheon party in Kitty's honour at his country 'cottage', Hyde Park. Kitty travelled by train and by taxi to a point where a group of people were gathered round a car. Full of apprehension in case she should fail to recognise the President, she walked over towards the car. The group of men fell back and she was able to see the smiling President at the wheel of the car, holding out his hand in welcome. He invited her to climb in beside him and drove her to Hyde Park. She was seated next to him at luncheon and afterwards they spent some time in earnest and private conversation. She remarked later that she had been unable to interest him in the Spanish question. On the subject of the European situation as a whole Kitty found Roosevelt deeply concerned, though perhaps less worried by the menace of Hitler than she had hoped. She left Hyde Park feeling uplifted by the meeting, by Roosevelt's friendliness and by the warmth of his personality.

The US ambassador to Spain had met the same response as Kitty; he had tried unsuccessfully on many occasions to urge the President to help the Spanish Republicans. Roosevelt later acknowledged that failure to do so had been a miscalculation. His Under-Secretary of State, Sumner Welles, subsequently described America's lack of attention to the Spanish question as having been 'disastrous'.

After the news of the settlement at Munich, Kitty, in Philadelphia, made a speech attempting to allay the strong criticism of Britain and France which was widely expressed in America by pointing out to the audience the weakness of their position with regard to arms and

equipment, though she found it difficult to hide her dismay. She wrote to
Bardie:

> Oh, dearie, what an agonising week this has been—we have had the radio
> on practically all day and Mrs Curtis or I have been 'on guard' from 7 or
> 7.30 a.m. to listen to the news bulletins from Europe. It was of course an
> immense relief to have the immediate fear of war removed on Tuesday, but
> I am afraid I feel that the Czechs have been left in a terribly dangerous
> position . . .

Bardie's advice to her in reply was that she must at all costs support the
Munich agreement and be seen and heard to do so: 'I really do feel you
should support Chamberlain. I shall feel terrible if one shot is fired and
you are against a Government which even the Labour party supports.'

Bardie had his ear close to the ground in the constituency and was
aware that criticism of Chamberlain would damage her further in the
eyes of the Association. Since she was fundamentally opposed to the
agreement she found his advice impossible to take and, though she was
careful not to disclose her personal opinion while abroad, she noted that
American sentiment continued to rise against the Chamberlain policies.
The Hearst press, however, continued to take a pro-Fascist line.

Kitty returned to Britain in late October—a Britain still steeped in
post-Munich euphoria. Only a few dissidents stood back, aghast at the act
of treachery which they had witnessed in the name of peace and in the
name of Britain. Duff Cooper had immediately resigned his post as First
Lord of the Admiralty in protest. Churchill called it an 'unmitigated
defeat'. Eden, Sandys, Bracken, Grigg, Amery, Nicolson, Boothby and
Eleanor Rathbone were among a small number of vocal dissenters.
Macmillan declared that the situation was more terrible than at any time
since the beginning of Christian civilisation.

There had, for some months, been talk of forming a new, breakaway
party. Kitty, had been approached to become one of its leaders. She had
replied, asking for further information as to its aims and policies, but had
not received a reply. Eden, for his own reasons, chose to distance himself
from Churchill and the other anti-appeasers and shortly afterwards went
to America. The others found themselves in deep personal trouble in
their own Associations. Kitty was in deepest trouble of all. The nature of
her Executive in particular and her Association in general meant that
Chamberlain's policies were warmly welcomed: there was still warm
sympathy for Germany, and the government's actions in distancing itself
from the Czechs 'who had no right to the Sudetenland in the first place'
were regarded as praiseworthy. Of recent months the composition of the
Executive had changed; Bardie and Kitty's old friend and neighbour,

Colonel Butter, who had for the last year or two found himself increasingly uncomfortable in his position as chairman of the Association, had resigned. He had been replaced by a Kinross farmer, Mr James Paton, who was not bound by old ties of friendship. Mr Paton had, only three years previously, expressed his complete loyalty to, and admiration for, the Duchess.

During Kitty's absence abroad, as Bardie had feared, the Whip's office had been making a concerted effort to stamp their authority—and that of the government—on the Association. Colonel Pat Blair, secretary to Scottish Whip, James Stuart, was guide and mentor to James Paton throughout the weeks which followed. As resolved by the Executive during the summer, party literature was bought and circulated by the Association throughout the constituency and a series of meetings was addressed by top level speakers, including five Ministers.

One of the most influential members of the Association was the Earl of Ancaster. The Earl had, in 1933, become father-in-law to Nancy Astor's daughter, Phyllis. Nancy herself was strongly in favour of Chamberlain, as was her friend Lord Lothian. Nancy had, in recent years, clashed with Kitty on a number of issues and had made no secret of her disapproval.

As part of the Association's campaign in support of the Government a rally was planned to take place in the grounds of Drummond Castle, Lord Ancaster's seat at Crieff, to be addressed by Sir Thomas Inskip. Bardie spoke to Inskip personally on the subject of the rally at a chance meeting. Inskip expressed surprise and said that he had no knowledge of the difficulties the Duchess was experiencing with her Association. Since the Duchess's difficulties had been widely reported in the national press for months and had undoubtedly been discussed at top level within the party, this was patently untrue. Inskip promised to think the matter over and subsequently wrote to say that as he had been invited to address the rally he would do so, though he would certainly refrain from referring to the Duchess. As it happened, the rally had to be cancelled on account of the national crisis.

The ground had been well prepared, then, when Kitty returned to Scotland and at their request met some members of the Executive. They asked her directly for her views on the Munich settlement, which she gave equally directly. She later published them as a pamphlet. Having noted that she was firmly opposed to the Government on the matter, those present went on to accuse her of talking the government down during her American tour. This she denied, pointing out that the furthest she had ever gone in reference to the situation in Europe was, prior to Munich, to review the situation as it had developed over the years and to point out the dangers to democracy of allowing Germany to swallow up Czechoslovakia, making Hitler the master of Eastern Europe. She had also felt it quite fair to stress the sacrifice of the Czechs in agreeing to give up the Sudetenland and to point out the liberal treatment which the Sudeten Germans had received at the hands of the Czech Government, as she had personally observed.

At a stormy meeting of the Executive on 21 October it was decided to put forward the name of another candidate at the Annual General Meeting, due to be held at the end of November.

Kitty, meantime, was actually much more concerned with the country's position than with her own. In the middle of her personal crisis she met M. Maisky, the Soviet Ambassador, at the House of Commons. He requested an urgent meeting with her and she wrote a report of the encounter to Churchill:

> Maisky said he had seen a member of the Inner Cabinet who had greatly surprised him by talking with great confidence about the present international position. Czechoslovakia had been a danger spot, but now was no longer! No account was apparently being taken of the great increase caused to German military power by its dismemberment.
>
> The war in Spain was apparently not regarded as constituting a danger. No account was apparently being taken of the effects that an insurgent victory might have on Germany's strategical position. M. Maisky therefore got the impression that the government, being confident of the success of the appeasement policy, were not pushing ahead with rearmament as he would have expected.
>
> He believed, I think, that this was the reason for the refusal to set up a Ministry of Supply and was obviously concerned about the position.
>
> M. Maisky went on to tell me, in a very matter of fact way, as if he were quite certain of his figures, that the German Air Force was 10,000 strong and consisted almost entirely of new machines. He believed ours to be not more than one third of that, including, of course reserves, and said that not more than about 900 of ours were up to date machines.
>
> He also said that Germany was building 800 aeroplanes a month and that she might increase that figure in the course of this next year. He thought that by the end of the year we might have about 5000. He was obviously very anxious about this. I forget what he thought our output of aeroplanes was per month and I daresay he doesn't know, but President Roosevelt six weeks ago with great assurance told me that the German rate of production was three times ours and six times that of the French.
>
> On the other hand M. Maisky told me that the strength of the Russian air force was equal to that of the Germans and Japanese combined, with something to spare. I don't know how far these facts can be relied upon, but his estimate of the relative strength of the German air force and ours is very much the relative rate of production given by President Roosevelt and if these figures are anywhere near the truth they are so serious that I feel I must pass them on in confidence. They seem to me to form a very strong argument for a Ministry of Supply. Before our talk ended I asked him if he

thought that any awakening of sturdy public opinion in this country would have an effect in creating greater confidence in the South East of Europe. He replied at once that it would have an immense effect and added what I did not feel I could ask, that it would stop the drift to an isolationist policy in Russia which had been increasing so much since Munich. The importance of this seemed to me to be very great.

Kitty's anxieties regarding Russia were all too well founded. Stalin was watching, ready to jump in either direction. He would certainly have preferred an alliance with Britain and France, but lack of enthusiasm or even simple diplomatic courtesy on the part of Britain over negotiations and the knowledge of Britain's weakness ultimately pushed him into the arms of Hitler, whom he hated and despised. Britain was shocked and pained, but British 'diplomacy' was responsible for what happened. While Britain openly snubbed Stalin, Hitler wooed him, enticing him with the offer of a half-share in Poland.

Churchill replied to Kitty's letter by telephone and there is no record of the conversation. It was probably then that he advised her against the step she was contemplating—resigning her seat and fighting a by-election. He had been encountering his own problems at Epping, though as he had not had the whip withdrawn he was in a rather stronger position. His advice was to hold on and take no precipitate action; the situation could easily change, and perhaps sooner rather than later.

Bardie was of the same mind as Churchill, as were most of Kitty's friends and advisers. Two by-elections were already under way at which the Government's foreign policy was being put to the test: at Oxford the Master of Balliol, A D Lindsay, standing as an Independent, failed against the Government candidate, Quintin Hogg, but at Bridgewater in Somerset in November the Independent journalist Vernon Bartlett succeeded in defeating the Government candidate. Despite Bartlett's victory Kitty's friends believed that it would be politically unwise for her to chance a by-election at that point.

Kitty, however, viewed the matter differently. She did not act out of pique or wounded pride. Nor, apparently, was there any question of a death-wish on her part: she firmly believed that she would win. She was also a fatalist: if it transpired that she lost, she would have lost in the best of all causes. As always with Kitty, it was a matter of honour and principle; but above all she believed that the publicity surrounding an election campaign would provide an important opportunity to highlight the issues. Flying in the face of all political wisdom she might be, but her talk with Maisky had served to underline the urgency of 'reawakening sturdy public opinion in this country'.

When the Annual General Meeting of the Association confirmed the Executive's decision to seek another candidate with some urgency, Bardie

32   At the time of the by-election

resigned as President of the Association and left the meeting. His place as President was taken by the Earl of Ancaster. Kitty immediately applied for the Chiltern Hundreds and a by-election was called. The last act in the drama was about to be played out.

Polling Day was fixed for Wednesday 21 December. At that time Christmas was not recognised in Scotland in the way that it is today; many people worked on Christmas Day—shops and offices were open for business as usual. It did not seem as surprising a choice of date as its proximity to Christmas makes it seem today.

Chamberlain, Ball, Stuart and the senior political figures in the National Government were determined that this was a by-election which they must not lose. If Kitty's honour was at stake, Chamberlain's prestige was equally so.

The Association began interviewing candidates without delay: an Edinburgh lawyer was almost selected and withdrew at the last moment. William McNair Snadden, a wealthy local farmer with a wide knowledge of agricultural interests, who had been a quiet, long-serving member of the Executive, found himself being steam-rollered into accepting nomination.

Mrs Coll Macdonald was delighted at the prospect of having another opportunity of defeating Kitty. It was, after all, what she had been working for and planning for three years. Her meetings and rallies—reports of which appeared regularly in the columns of the local newspapers throughout the period—had drawn large and appreciative crowds. This time she had, she believed, a very good chance of winning; with the Tories divided and the Labour Party apparently not fielding a candidate, she could inherit all the Labour and Liberal votes and possibly disaffected Tory ones as well.

More sophisticated Liberal politicians viewed the by-election rather differently. However much they disagreed with Kitty in the past over her diehard attitude on India, her patrician attitude to the employment of children of fourteen, her early advocacy of rearmament, they realised that on this occasion she was right. She was standing on a matter of principle and displaying admirable courage. Both the Liberal and Labour Parties had shared in the general sense of relief that 'Peace in Our Time' had been guaranteed, but some were now beginning to look at the small print with which that guarantee had been underwritten.

The question of a new political alignment of all-party dissenters to the Munich agreement was again under discussion. Thirty Conservatives who had withheld approval of the Munich agreement in the House might indeed have been expected to join such a party. But the Tory dissenters were split among themselves, nor could Labour and Liberal party members find enough enthusiasm for a Popular Front Alliance.

Liberals throughout the country pressed the Leadership for withdrawal of any opposition to Kitty on their part. Sir Archibald Sinclair, their Leader, agreed and without actually instructing Mrs Macdonald to withdraw, he made it clear that in the view of the Party she should do so. She did—but with such obvious reluctance that her followers were confused. Had she made a gracious speech of withdrawal, explaining that although she had disagreed with the Duchess in the past and continued to reserve her position on rearmament, the issue involved was such that she wished to recommend her followers to vote for Kitty, there is not doubt that Kitty would have romped home. Mrs Macdonald did not do so. She made it clear that she would not be voting for either candidate. That position was adopted in consequence by many other Liberals.

Another influential Liberal, local aristocrat and landowner Lord Mansfield, whose home was the historic Scone Palace near Perth, deplored Mrs Macdonald's withdrawal and in the later stages of the campaign advised Liberals on this occasion to vote for the National Government candidate, Snadden, adding that in his view Winston Churchill was Public Enemy No 1. Ramsay MacDonald's son Malcolm added his voice to the chorus of support for Mr Snadden, as did another former Liberal candidate, Colonel Seton-Hutchison.

By contrast, Kitty's Liberal opponents of the 1929 and 1931 elections— Dr George Freeland Barbour and Mr Atholl Robertson—generously supported and actively helped Kitty in her campaign.

The Labour Party also felt a sense of loyalty to Kitty for her stance on Spain and for this reason, and because they knew that a Labour candidate could not win and could only add to the chances of a government victory, they were not intervening in the election, though a putative socialist candidate appeared on the scene for a day or two to add to the confusion.

Nomination Day revealed only two candidates: Katharine Atholl, Independent, and William McNair Snadden, National Government. Katharine's papers were signed by Sir James Wilson of Invertrossachs, Callander, and Sir William Haldane of Cloan, Auchterarder.

William McNair Snadden fought a fair campaign, insisting at his meetings that no direct reference should be made to the Duchess. He did, however, allow himself to repeat at his meetings allegations that policies such as those she advocated could only lead to war now and war again and again—recurrent wars had always been the result of such policies, he maintained, whereas Chamberlain's policies would lead the world to peace.

The Conservative Research Department and the Chief Whip's Office saw to it that literature and speakers flooded the constituency in an unprecedented campaign of support. Pamphlets paying tribute to the

Man of Peace dropped through every letter-box—describing the efforts of the ageing man who, although he had never flown before, had three times hurled himself into the breach, unsparing of his time, uncaring for his health and safety, to bring permanent peace to the world; a man who had succeeded in his mission and whose name would be recorded among those of the great men of all time.

Kitty had lost the organisation which had been built up over the years. Her agent was no loss personally, as he was a Uriah Heep who had earlier connived with the Chairman to add to her difficulties with the Association by methods such as deliberately packing Association meetings with non-members, but he held all the vital information, such as the canvass results of former years. She had also lost her branch chairman and secretaries, her canvassers and most of her helpers. Although many individual members of the Association resigned in order to stand by her, she was now forced to rely on help of a rather more amateurish nature: but these people made up for their lack of experience in enthusiasm. The list of sub-agents for each district appointed to act for Kitty reveals them to be, in the main, solid bourgeois—farmers, tradespeople, retired professional people, rather than members of the 'county' set.

Her canvassers of former years now called on everyone as before, but this time with the purpose of persuading voters not to support her, categorically warning electors with startling, patronising simplicity: 'If you vote for the Duchess there will be a war and your sons will be killed.'

But it was the sheer volume of help thrown into the constituency by Conservative Central Office which really swung the election in Mr Snadden's favour. Night after night MPs and top party workers poured into the constituency to address meetings. In those times there was no cover on radio, and evening meetings gathered large audiences.

Leaflet after leaflet was distributed through every letter-box. A letter went to every elector in the names of seventy listed Members of Parliament, stating: 'We believe that Mr Chamberlain acted in the best interests of Europe and the whole of humanity in preventing the terrible calamity of another universal war. For that reason we believe that those who share our opinion should unhesitatingly give their vote to Mr McNair Snadden and against the Duchess of Atholl.' The signatories included Nancy Astor and her son in law.

Kitty responded that it was not difficult to excite fears of war and spread such ideas without justifying the statement. . . . 'There is no indication that they understand my policy. It seems to me a very cheap and unworthy form of electioneering.'

On Kitty's side Bardie was laid up at Eastwood, Dunkeld (where he and Kitty were living) following an injury to his back. But she was supported by many notable and distinguished personalities of the day who came to speak and help her. Her niece Persis drove her throughout the campaign. Her friend Eleanor Rathbone came, of course; Lord Cecil; Josiah Wedgwood (who sadly suffered a heart-attack during the campaign, at his hotel in Dunkeld); Vernon Bartlett, the victor at Bridgewater, Dr Lindsay, the loser at Oxford; Lord Lloyd; Dingle Foot; Richard Acland; and Shiela Grant-Duff, a remarkable young journalist who had been living and working in Czechoslovakia for the past four years. She had, on the very day of the Munich agreement, published a Penguin Special on the subject, *Europe and the Czechs,* in which she pointed to the strength of Czechoslovak defences, the willingness of the Czechs to fight, but above all the necessity for a united defence on the part of the Powers to block the Nazi plan of aggression. She joined the campaign at the behest of Sir Archibald Sinclair and stayed with the Haldanes at Cloan.

Kitty's friend from the Spanish War, Gerald Brenan, came to help. He bought himself a new dinner suit for his visit, only to discover to his disappointment that there was no time to dine as they were off speaking somewhere in the constituency every evening. Brenan observed Kitty at home and in action throughout the campaign and wrote later that the better one knew her the better one liked her.

Messages of support included those from Churchill, Viscount Cecil, Sir Charles Trevelyan, Provost Dolan of Glasgow, Lady Violet Bonham Carter, Sylvia Pankhurst—Kitty had travelled a long way since her anti-suffragette days—Lord Listowel, Captain Liddell Hart, Professor Seton-Watson, Lord Strabolgi, Lady Rhondda, Lady Layton, Sir William Haldane, Lord Davies, Professor Sir Bernard Pares, Professor Gilbert Murray.

These internationally admired and distinguished personalities and intellectuals did not cut much ice in the constituency. Churchill considered coming to speak, but as Kitty had chosen to stand as an Independent rather than as an Independent Unionist as he had advised (possibly a miscalculation on her part) and had in any case precipitated the by-election against his advice, he contented himself with telephoning to her every evening. He did, however, send a strong letter of support which was circulated throughout the constituency:

> In the face of the challenge which has been offered you by your Association I do not see what other course you could adopt but to appeal broadly to your constituents. It is the course which I have always proposed to follow myself should circumstances require it. I therefore feel the fullest sympathy with you at the present juncture. . . . The issues raised by your candidatureship go far beyond ordinary questions of Parliamentary or Party

affairs. You stand for the effectve rearmament of our country and for an end to the procrastination, half-measures and mismanagement which have led us from a safe position into a state of woeful unpreparedness and danger.

He applauded her call for a Ministry of Supply and added

> Your victory as an Independent member adhering to the finest principles of the Conservative and Unionist Party can only have an invigorating effect upon the whole impulse of British policy and British defence, and will be a signal from Scotland of the strong and growing resolve of the British nation to remain a power for good among men.

Kitty's letter from Churchill was a trump card: and she had another ace which she was looking forward to playing. She had had the promise of one speaker who was well known to her audiences—the gruff-voiced fellow anti-appeaser from East Aberdeen, Robert Boothby. Unlike Churchill, who had never suggested a personal appearance, he had offered to speak for her immediately on hearing of her intention to call a by-election and she looked forward to his intervention. In the event, she was to be disappointed. James Stuart now threatened him with withdrawal of the whip if he supported her.
He wrote from London:

> A good deal has happened here since you went north! When it was announced in the press that I was going to speak for you I was given to understand that if I did so the authorities would take such a serious view that it would probably involve my being deprived of the whip. I might have been prepared to leave the Party on this issue although as you know it is a serious step to take. But the Chairman of my Association is Gardie Duff, whom I think you know. He is also Chairman this year of the Eastern Divisional Council. He is also my oldest and best friend. He told me that, while he personally deplored the action of your Association, if I came out in open support of you he would feel obliged to resign. Frankly I cannot face this . . . I know you will understand . . . I am in negotiation with the Whips' Office with a view to achieving a compromise under which I can send you a letter—for what that may be worth.

To his Chairman Boothby wrote:

> In my private letter of explanation to the Duchess I said that while I might have been prepared to risk a row with the Party, I could not face the possibility of your resignation. You may or may not be flattered by this!

Kitty politely thanked him for his letter and for his offer to negotiate the sending of a letter . . . 'but I fear I could not use it'—pointing out that had he been prepared to resign the whip it could only have had a most beneficial effect so far as the main cause was concerned.

Press coverage was of great importance. It was, on the whole, not in Kitty's favour. Post-Munich satisfaction with Chamberlain's 'bargain' still hung in the air. Although the *Yorkshire Post, Manchester Guardian, Glasgow Herald* and *News Chronicle* had been sharply critical, most of Fleet Street (the Beaverbrook and Rothermere press in particular) continued to support Chamberlain. The daily newspaper which arrived in most households in Perthshire would have been one which was running stories and editorials in sturdy support of the government.

Wickham Steed accused a section of the Press of succumbing to government pressure—an accusation which a Royal Commission on the Press later discounted as 'not proven', though the chief leader-writer of the *Yorkshire Post* advised that the Foreign Office was providing 'information necessary for guidance' to a number of newspapers.

The Catholic Press, which had begun to attack Kitty bitterly during her intervention in the Spanish War, strongly continued its attacks.

Naturally local newspapers in Scotland covered the story in considerable detail. The most widely read locally was the *Perthshire Advertiser* which as a Liberal paper was critical of the government but was ambivalent in its advice to readers as to which way to vote. It commented 'The lairds will vote for Snadden. The result will depend on how the Liberals vote.' The *Perthshire Constitutional,* as a pro-government paper was in no doubt, as was the *Strathearn Herald.*

The *Dundee Courier* also held back from supporting Kitty outright. Two journalists (one of whom was probably James Cameron) visited Kitty's brave supporter Will Hally, himself a journalist, in Auchterarder during the election. They both expressed the view that Kitty *ought* to win, but were doubtful as to whether she would win. James Cameron, was at the time, a junior reporter for the *Courier.* His recollection of the election forty-five years later was 'We all thought that the Duchess was splendid, marvellous! But she spoilt it all by her rather boring manner.'

Cameron, if indeed it was he, remarked to Hally that he felt—or hoped—that people were solid for the Duchess, barring the old aristocrats . . . and some new ones!

One newspaper carried brave, if slightly maudlin, verses in Kitty's support, composed by a Mr John Dick of Woodside Road, Glasgow, the final lines of which read:

> Defy the Fascist hordes
> With challenge strong and clear
> Though loud their drums and bright their swords
> They're sick at heart with fear.
> Scorn Hitler's blatant noise

And Mussolini's bray
And when they hear a manly voice
The cads will slink away.

They listen on the air
In Berlin, London, Rome;
Then tell the rogues these mountains bare
Are still the Freeman's home
The world is on the rack
O Scottish hearts be true
And send the noble lady back
Or—endless shame on you!

Kitty had not improved as a speaker over the years. One newspaper referred to her a 'prosy speaker', adding prophetically 'and dullness can cost dear'. Her voice was a rather monotonous drone, her speeches were too long and her appearance was uninteresting. Wherever she went she took with her a map of Europe at which she pointed with a walking stick. Perhaps because of her very earnestness and sincerity, she failed to capture her audiences.

On the other hand Snaddon's meetings were addressed by the most practised and sparkling speakers available (including fifty Members of Parliament) which obscured the fact that Mr Snadden was by no means an orator of note himself, though on the subject of oats, cattle, sheep and silage he could wax eloquent. Among the phalanx of speakers for Snadden was Lord Dunglass—now Lord Home—who was pressed into service by Central Office. He had no reason for loyalty to the Duchess, whom he hardly knew, but as Chamberlain's Parliamentary Private Secretary he was bound to support him. In his speech at Auchterarder he spoke of the Prime Minister's 'gallant and courageous stand for peace' and denied the suggestion that Hitler might have been bluffing. (You don't bluff with six million lives!')

The core of Kitty's appeal was, as she declared:

The foreign policy for which I stand is not only the policy of Mr Eden, Mr Churchill and of most Unionist members of Parliament who have devoted time to foreign affairs, but also the official policy of the Liberal and Labour parties. I am standing as an Independent so that Unionists, Liberals and Socialists may be able to support me without voting against their several parties. Real unity will be founded on a readiness to put country before party. Munich has not brought appeasement. On the contrary, Hitler's speeches and the officially controlled German press have become increasingly aggressive. And there has been a renewed persecution of Jewish people of unparalled brutality.

(She was referring to the Kristallnacht pogrom which took place in mid-November.)

The women's vote was a critical factor. There were more women voters than men on the electoral roll. If Kitty was to win she must have their support. Unfortunately Kitty's reputation as a warmonger had stuck. Women were genuinely afraid—as had been so carefully explained to them on the doorsteps—that a vote for Kitty meant a vote for war and that their husbands and sons would be off to the army and dead within the year.

Much publicity was given to a rumour that the Communist Party had offered its assistance to Kitty. It was untrue and Kitty denied the story in the newspapers, adding that had it been true she would have refused. But once again the mud stuck. The offer was said to have been received at the office of Mr Snadden's agent in Crieff—Kitty's former agent. (Kitty's agent's office was in Dunkeld.) It is easy to start a false and damaging rumour: very much more difficult to deny it, as she discovered. Though outwardly cheerful, she was forced to agree with Will Hally's comment that they were up against bitter unscrupulousness in their opponents.

One other, more sinister, factor was that of the landlords. It was widely rumoured that on a number of estates, including that of the Earl of Ancaster, there had been extra money in the pay packets at the end of the previous week, with a note reminding the estate workers to vote for Snadden. Although the ballot was secret, many men and their wives felt themselves to be under moral pressure which almost amounted to blackmail, since there were hints that Kitty's supporters would no longer be welcome as employees—and jobs were hard to find.

On the Muir and Ancaster estates there was said to have been an abatement of rents to farmers and tenants after the election had begun, and Snadden car stickers enclosed with correspondence concerning the rent. Bardie later remarked that as both these proprietors were very close in their dealings it was a matter of general surprise that such generosity should be shown. Such pressure is against electoral law. Had it been proved, legal action would have followed. 'Treating' and 'Influencing' are corrupt practices, subject to fine or imprisonment. The rumours were so widespread throughout the constituency that although no written proof now exists it may be thought that they were not without foundation. Bardie was informed of it by an Ancaster tenant and was so incensed that a few days after the election he drafted a letter on the subject to Douglas Dickson, his Edinburgh lawyer. Kitty, however, persuaded him not to send it and the draft remains, neatly filed, among her papers at the Castle.

On Atholl the tenants and estate people were strongly in favour of their Duchess. Elderly people on the estate still remember the election and say today: 'Aye, she was right, she was right. And there's millions dead that shouldn't be dead; and they knew she was right!'

It was reported by Will Hally at Auchterarder that many of the tradespeople were afraid to support Kitty for fear of losing the accounts of landowners such as Sir James Roberts of Strathallan (the local landowner) though Hally thought it undoubtedly applied throughout the constituency.

The 21 December was a day of appalling weather in Kinross and West Perthshire. It was early for snow, which more frequently arrives in Perthshire in January. A blizzard blew from the north all day and the roads were covered with rutted ice. Many of Kitty's supporters were country people who would have to struggle along difficult tracks and roads for some miles to reach the poll. It was estimated that the official Unionists had five times as many cars as Kitty's team at their disposal to ferry supporters to and from the polling stations. In the event, many of Kitty's supporters simply did not make the attempt to vote.

Kitty set off from Dunkeld at 7.55 a.m. on a tour of the constituency which took her to twenty-two small towns and villages, gave her half an hour for lunch and permitted her to return to Dunkeld at 8.55 p.m.

Kitty and Mr Snadden met in their cars at Aberfoyle, one leaving the polling station as the other arrived. Mr Snadden courteously raised his hat: Kitty politely bowed.

The count took place on the following morning. Not until 1963, when Lord Home himself was candidate at an important by-election in that same constituency, would the eyes of Britain be fixed with such fascination on the returning officer for Kinross and West Perthshire.

Kitty arrived in good time—looking, for once, rather dashing in a high, brimmed, velour hat with a sprig of white heather stuck jauntily at one side, a multi-coloured silk scarf at her neck, a smart, dark coat and a red white and blue rosette on her collar. There had been protests from members of the British Legion at her use of these colours during the campaign.

The poll had been rather low: fewer than 67% had voted. Of these 11,808 had voted for the government candidate, 10,495 for Kitty. It was a close-run thing.

After the announcement Kitty gallantly accepted defeat and acknowledged Mr Snadden's victory in a fair fight. The candidates departed with their followers: he to euphoric celebrations at the George Hotel, she to receive commiserations at the Salutation Hotel, where she apologised to friends for having let down the cause and all those who had helped her. She felt sadness, but no personal bitterness.

Afterwards, she drove home to Eastwood and to Bardie, thinking perhaps of that other by-election in 1872 which her father had lost before proposing to Charlotte—which in a sense is where she began. As always, she had bravely suppressed her own feelings in front of others; but in the evening, after dinner, she went to her beloved piano and played two Beethoven sonatas. Instinctively, perhaps, she chose the 'Waldheim' and the 'Apassionata' from Beethoven's so-called 'Heroic' period, written at a time when he too was recovering from a period of profound despondency.

From his sick-bed Josiah Wedgwood sent a telegram of commiseration—a fitting epitaph on Kitty's political life:

> To Socrates they gave hemlock. Gracoleus they killed with sticks and stones. The greatest and best they crucified. Katharine Atholl can hold up her head in good company. Let the victors when they come, when the forts of folly fall, find thy body by the wall.

In Government circles joy was unconfined. Chamberlain sent a fulsome message of congratulations to William Snadden. For their part Mr and Mrs Snadden declared that this must be the finest Christmas present they could have given to Mr Chamberlain.

Ivor Cobbold (brother in law of James Stuart, who had large landholdings and property around Loch Rannoch but whose home was in Suffolk) sent a telegram to Kitty:

> Am delighted you are out. Hope my Rannoch people voted against you. Now you may find time to remove your Basque children from Suffolk.

James Stuart himself, encountering Churchill in the House, gleefully taunted him over the result and challenged him to be next to resign the whip.

Three months later Hitler occupied the whole of Czechoslovakia. Nine months later, after the German invasion of Poland, the Second World War began. The appeasers, guilty of monumental folly, had betrayed the British people. So far as is known, no-one ever apologised to Kitty for having been wrong when she was right.

Epilogue 1939–60

Kitty's efforts to alert the British people to the dangers ahead and of the threat to democracy were unsuccessful. It was not until Hitler's entry into Prague in March 1939 that the country awoke and a large section of the press, for so long muzzled by Chamberlain, began to re-exert its freedom to criticize the government. Hitler's hopes of an alliance with Britain were dashed by the impetus of British public opinion, roused and united at last. For their part Chamberlain and his Inner Cabinet, assisted by Ball, continued to seek to appease Hitler. Even in the early part of the war there were those in high places who sought to conciliate and negotiate a peace pact.

Kitty herself bore no grudges. The main thing was that she kept faith with the cause and with her conscience, though as Josiah Wedgwood remarked, that course usually leads to trouble. Kitty was politically resilient and remained determined to continue to play her part in detaching Britain from its subservient stance towards the dictators. It was her profound wish to see Churchill and Eden returned to the Cabinet. When war broke out in September 1939 she gave her energies to war work on behalf of the Red Cross. She and Bardie turned several of the Atholl shooting lodges and part of the Castle into hostels for evacuees from Glasgow, not all of whom enjoyed the experience of living in the isolation of the glens.

She had been adopted as Independent candidate for the Scottish Universities' seat in 1939, but resigned in 1940, when Winston Churchill replaced Chamberlain as Prime Minister. She wrote at once to congratulate him and to inform him that she was now gladly rejoining the Conservative and Unionist Party, with whose philosophy she felt at one, adding: 'In agreeing to stand as an Independent I did not renounce my Unionist faith, either then or when I stood in the by-election here two years ago.' Now, to her immense relief, she could once more trust the leadership. Churchill expressed his pleasure and welcomed her back to the Party.

When, to her profound sorrow, Bardie died in 1942, she was overwhelmed with letters of condolence and tributes to his many fine

33 Bardie's funeral 1942 (Kitty behind the carriage)

qualities—among which, undoubtedly, were his personal kindness and his sense of humour. No longer away from home on political business, she had sat at his bedside reading to him in the weeks before he died. His last words to her before losing consciousness were 'You must be very tired.' She felt greatly honoured to be invited by the King to become Honorary Colonel-in-Chief of the Scottish Horse in his stead and she took great pride in their achievements in Italy and Normandy.

There was no retreat into quiet widowhood. Kitty remained active and occupied. She had been asked to serve as Honorary Secretary on the Scottish 'Invasion Committee', part of whose duties was to attend to the blocking of roads and digging of trenches in the event of an invasion. The argument mentioned in the introduction to this book—when she dismounted from her bicycle in Dunkeld in 1942—was probably a continuation of the argument which had been going on for over a year on the question of the digging of trenches in the area, which she believed to be of the greatest strategic importance. Few of the local people sympathised with the idea, Dunkeld being a small inland village on the edge of the Scottish Highlands and far from any military or civil targets. The arguments continued endlessly and this was considered to be 'just one more wee bee in Her Grace's bonnet'. She had, a year or so earlier, recruited a number of helpers to begin digging on the land at Dunkeld House, but to her disappointment word had come from military HQ in Edinburgh that no digging of trenches was to be permitted.

There was perhaps some logic in her argument: a small invasion force parachuted into North Perthshire could have cut the north-south railway and divided the country in half, cutting the mainland link with Invergordon and Scapa Flow. With the massive Highland hills behind them they could have struck southwards into Central Scotland—as had happened in 1698 and 1745.

During the remainder of the war Kitty spent much of her time in London, giving her energies and more money than she could spare towards assisting refugees from Europe. Towards the end of the war she began to hear of atrocities and mass deportations taking place in Eastern Europe: of the sufferings of the peoples of Poland and the Baltic States at the hands of the Russians. With Foreign Office support in October 1944 she broadcast a message of encouragement to the resistance in Warsaw shortly before their surrender to the Germans. Stalin had left them to the mercy of the Germans because of their opposition to communism, and the Red Army entered Warsaw only in January 1945.

Shortly afterwards she became Chairman of the British League for European Freedom, dedicated to giving assistance to all countries in which freedom was threatened, particularly following the partition agreements signed in Tehran and Yalta. The League published a number of leaflets documenting deportations and attempted to persuade the new Labour Government in Britain to prevent the forced repatriation of thousands of Eastern Europeans, also sending a resolution to this effect to the first meeting of the United Nations. Kitty wrote: 'Gratitude for the Soviet army's help during the war had persuaded many people to blink at the truth, and few of them knew of the terror many Russian war prisoners showed on being sent back to their country.'

At the request of the Polish Government in London, Kitty published another Penguin Special: *The Tragedy of Warsaw and its Documentation*, all proceeds from which were given to a Polish Relief charity. It was an attempt to piece together the reports, press notices and broadcasts available in order to give information and an account of the heroism of the people involved in the Warsaw Rising of 1944. Kitty's tireless humanitarian work on behalf of exiles and displaced persons continued for many years.

Tony Murray, heir to the Dukedom, was tragically killed in the last moments of the war in Italy in 1945, a matter of grief to the people of Atholl and to Kitty personally: Lady Cowdray's granddaughter did not become Duchess of Atholl. Her son inherited the title on the death of Bardie's brother Hamish (Lord James Stewart-Murray, ninth Duke of Atholl) in 1957.

Angela remarried: her husband was Tony's friend, Colonel Robert Campbell-Preston. They, with Kitty's own nieces, were watchful and caring as Kitty's own ability to care for herself declined with age.

Kitty's niece, Persis Aglen, who was in the Sudan with her husband until 1955, recalls the final years:

> When we came back after the war on leaves it was to a very different world and to situations that we found strange. There were gaps; Uncle Bardie, our Mother, Tony Murray and others had died. We visited our aunt at Iverna Court in London, where she was living. We found her totally occupied with Poles and other European refugees. She worked for the League for European Freedom in Elizabeth Street and brought to that work the same total involvement that she had given to any work she had undertaken throughout her life. She was deeply and personally moved by the tragedies and disasters of the individuals she met and she was generous with her help and hospitality to them. Sometimes this was rather badly abused by some of her less worthy protégées.
>
> When we came back to this country in 1955 we began to be aware of the changes that were taking place in her. She still lived at Iverna Court during what would have been, to her, the parliamentary sessions, and she came to Blair at intervals during what would have been the summer recesses. She was comfortable at Iverna Court and I am sure she was comfortable and

34   Glasgow, February 1959

happy in her flat at Blair. Lord James had a flat there too and he started the work on re-opening the Castle to the public. She took a great interest in this work and she used to enjoy showing it to our children and telling them about some of the treasures in it. She used to love to show us the room where she slept the first time she came to Blair with her mother.

But she was beginning to fail and to lose her memory and although she had a very devoted housekeeper in London, in the way that sometimes does happen with faithful and devoted retainers, Miss Smith became rather overbearing and there were moments when we thought that Aunt Kitty was unhappy.

Angela asked if I would help to bring her back north so that she could be nearer to us and we persuaded her to do this. though we knew what a sad step it was for her. She came and stayed with us in Edinburgh for a little while and then Angela arranged a flat for her. But really the move had come too late. She had always needed a cause and to have no cause left a void that couldn't be filled.

In the spring of 1953 Kitty arrived at Ardchattan Priory to stay with Colonel and Mrs Campbell-Preston. Some time later she mentioned that she had been in some pain all day. Mrs Campbell-Preston quickly realised that the pain, spoken of so casually, was severe; the local doctor was summoned and pronounced an acute appendix which was about to burst. He arranged for Kitty's immediate admission to hospital in Oban. Kitty chose to travel there in Colonel Campbell-Preston's car in preference to ambulance, and as they drove she chatted to him about the book she was writing. On arrival, Kitty walked into the hospital. The nurses, unused to having a duchess as a patient, lined up like a guard of honour. The surgeon, coming into the corridor, gasped in horror at the sight of the small figure walking towards him: he rushed forwards, picked her up and carried her in.

Some time after the operation, Matron told Colonel Campbell-Preston that Kitty was dying: there was no possibility of recovery. The Scottish Horse Ball due to be held at Blair was cancelled and the estate prepared to mourn their duchess. A day or two later came news that she was sitting up in bed, working on her notes.

Kitty's memory began to fail more noticeably in 1958. She began to have difficulty in remembering words, which made her laugh. Colonel Campbell-Preston recalls an earnest and lengthy search for a word for 'things that sting' ending with Angela, after a number of attempts to help, hitting on 'nettles'. Gradually the forgetfulness became worse, so that she would appear to be unaware of the conduct of conversation. Persis's husband, Edward, recalls that, as a result 'One might be holding a conversation without including her in it, when suddenly she came right back and was her old forthright self again.'

Kitty's own account of her life with Bardie, *Working Partnership*, was published in 1958. At the publisher's party to launch it, she told her audience: 'I have enjoyed the battles of my life'. I think she did.

Kitty died in 1960, after fracturing her femur whilst climbing over a wall. She was buried in the little family plot at Old Blair, beside Bardie. I failed to find her grave and was leaving in disappointment, but suddenly noticed the simple lettering which recorded her burial, round the foot of the tall column which commemorates Bardie. Grass and moss had almost obscured the inscription: perhaps a reflection of the way in which her life and activities have also been forgotten.

I think she would not have minded. Life, for her, was 'not the wick, nor the candle, it was the burning.'

Bibliography

Atholl, K, *Women and Politics* (Allen and Unwin, 1932)
Atholl, K, *Searchlight on Spain* (Penguin, 1938)
Atholl, K M, *Working Partnership* (Arthur Barker, 1958)
Beever, Anthony, *The Spanish Civil War* (Orbis publishing, 1982)
Berridge, Trevor, *Attlee* (Cape, 1985)
Berry, Paul, and Bishop, Alan, *Testament of a generation* (Virago, 1985)
Blake, Robert, *The Decline of Power, 1915–1964* (Paladin Books, 1986)
Boothby, R, *Recollections of a Rebel* (Hutchinson, 1978)
Branson, Noreen, *Britain in the 1920s* (Weidenfeld and Nicolson, 1975)
Brenan, Gerard, *Personal Record* (Cambridge University Press, 1974)
Bullock, Allan, *The Life and Times of Ernest Bevin* (Heinmann, 1967)
Butler, David, and Slaman, Anne, *British Political Facts 1900–1979* (Macmillan, 1979)
Butler, Lord, *The Art of the Possible* (Hamilton, 1971)
Carlton, David, *Anthony Eden* (Allen Lane, 1981)
Chelwood, Viscount Cecil of, *All the Way*
Cockett, Richard, *Twilight of Truth,* (Weidenfeld and Nicolson, 1989)
Colvin, Ian, *The Chamberlain Cabinet* (Gollanz, 1971)
Cooper, Duff, *Old Men Forget: Lives and Letters* (Century Classics)
Cross, J A, *Sir Samuel Hoare* (Cape, 1977)
Documents on British Foreign Policy
Donner, Sir Patrick, *Crusade* (Sherwood Press Ltd, 1984)
Duff, Shiela Grant, *Europe and the Czechs* (Penguin Books, 1938)
Duff, Shiela Grant, *The Parting of Ways* (Peter Owen, 1982)
Eden, Anthony, *Memoirs* (Cassell, 1962)
Feiling, Keith, *The Life of Neville Chamberlain* (Macmillan, 1970)
Fisher, Nigel, *Harold Macmillan* (Weidenfeld and Nicolson, 1982)
Gilbert, Martin and Gott, Richard, *The Appeasers* (Weidenfeld and Nicolson, 1967)
Gilbert, Martin, *Winston Churchill: The Wilderness Years* (Macmillan, 1981)
Griffiths, Richard, *Fellow Travellers of the Right* (Constable, 1980)
Grigg, John, *Lloyd George: The People's Champion 1902–1911* (Eyre Methuen, 1978)
Grigg, John, *Nancy Astor: portrait of a pioneer* (Sidgwick and Jackson 1980)
Grigg, John, *Lloyd George: From Peace to War 1912–1916* (Methuen, 1985)
Hamilton, Sir Ian, *Gallipoli Diary* (Edward Arnold, 1920)

Hansard, 1924–38

Hardy, P *The Muslims of British India* (Cambridge University Press, 1972)

Harris, Kenneth, *Attlee* (Weidenfeld and Nicolson, 1982)

Harrison, Brian, 'Women in a man's House', *The Historical Journal* Vol 29 (1986) pp 623–54

Henderson, Sir Neville, *Failure of a mission*

Hodson, H V, *The Great Divide* (Oxford University Press, 1985)

Hodgson, Stuart, *The Man Who Made Peace* (Christophers, 1938)

Hyde, H Montgomery, *Baldwin* (Weidenfeld and Nicolson, 1976)

James, Robert Rhodes, *Memoirs of a Conservative* (Weidenfeld and Nicolson, 1969)

James, Robert Rhodes, *Anthony Eden* (Weidenfeld and Nicolson, 1986)

Jenkins, Roy, *Baldwin* (Collins, 1987)

Jones, Thomas, *A Diary with Letters* (Oxford University Press, 1954)

Koss, Stephen, *The Rise and Fall of the Political Press in Britain* (Hamish Hamilton, 1984)

Low, D A (ed), *Congress and the Raj* (Faber and Faber, 1949)

Macleod, Iain, *Neville Chamberlain* (Muller, 1961)

MacMillan, Harold, *Winds of Change* (Macmillan, 1966)

MacMunn, Sir George, *The Indian Mutiny in Perspective* (Bell, 1931)

McBeath, Innes (ed), *Daughters of the Glen* (Leura Press, 1979)

Manchester, William, *The Lost Lion* (Sphere Books Ltd, 1984)

Marquand, David, *Ramsay MacDonald* (Cape, 1977)

Mitchell, David, *The Fighting Pankhursts* (Paddington Press, 1979)

Moore, R J, *The Crisis of Indian Unity* (Clarendon Press, 1974)

Mowat, Charles, *Britain Between the Wars* (Methuen, 1956)

Muir, Sir William, *Intelligence Records Indian Mutiny 1857* (T T Clarke, 1902)

Naylor, John F, *Labour's International Policy* (Collins, 1938)

Nicolson, Harold, *Diaries and Letters* (Fontana, 1969)

Orwell, George, *Homage to Catalonia* (Penguin Books, 1953)

Pakenham, Thomas, *The Boer War* (MacDonald and Co, 1982)

Pandey, P N (ed), *The Indian Nationalist Movement 1885–1947* (Macmillan, 1979)

Pankhurst, Richard, *Sylvia Pankhurst: Artist and Crusader: an intimate portrait* (Paddington Press, 1979)

Philips and Wainwright (eds) *The partition of India—Policies and Perspectives* (George Allen and Unwin Ltd, 1970)

Pimlott, Ben, *Hugh Dalton* (Capel, 1965)

Preston, Paul, *The Spanish Civil War, 1936–39* (Weidenfeld and Nicolson, 1986)

Pugh, Martin, *Electoral Reform in War and Peace, 1906–1918* (Routledge and Kegan Paul, 1978)

Pugh, Martin, *The making of modern British Politics* (Blackwell, 1982)

Raymond, John (ed), *The Baldwin Era*

Roberts, Brian, *Randolph* (Hamish Hamilton, 1984)

Rose, Norman, *Vansittart: Study of a Diplomat* (Heinemann, 1978)

Roskill, Stephen, *Hankey—man of secrets* (Collins, 1974)

Royle, Trevor, *Kitchener Enigma* (Michael Joseph, 1985)

Sadie, Stanley (ed), *New Grove Dictionary of Music and Musicians* (Macmillan, 1981)

Seal, Anil, *The Emergence of Indian Nationalism* (Cambridge University Press, 1972)

Seton-Watson, Hugh *The East European Revolution* (Methuen, 1950)

Seton-Watson, Hugh *The Pattern of Communist Revolution* (Methuen, 1952)

Simon, Brian, *Studies in the History of Education. The Politics of Educational Reform, 1920–1940* (Lawrence Wishart, 1974)

Simon, Rt Hon Viscount, *Retrospect* (Hutchison, 1952)

Skidelsky, Robert, *Oswald Mosley* (Macmillan, 1975)

Stocks, Mary, *Eleanor Rathbone* (Gollancz, 1950)

Symonds, Richard, *The Making of Pakistan*

Taylor, A J P, *The Origins of the Second World War* (Penguin Books, 1964)

Templewood, Viscount, *Nine Troubled Years* (Collins, 1954)

Trevelyan, Sir George, *Cawnpore* (Macmillan, 1900)

Vansittart, Lord, *Lessons of my Life* (Hutchison, 1943)

Wheeler-Bennet, John, *Munich—Prologue to Tragedy*

Wrench, John Evelyn, *Alfred Lord Milner* (Eyre and Spottiswoode)

Who Financed Hitler? (Raven Books, 1979)

Index: The Families

BAMFF HOUSE, ALYTH (EAST PERTHSHIRE)

ARDVORLICH HOUSE, LOCHEARNHEAD (WEST PERTHSHIRE)

Index: General